WaterMark, Inc.

2250 Highland Avenue South #101

Birmingham, AL 35205

In this book, the names and incidents in the stories (apart from the author's accounts of herself and her spiritual journey), do not refer to specific people or situations but are an amalgamation of many characteristics and events. Any resemblance to actual people or specific incidents is coincidental.

In this publication, the author shares her spiritual journey to becoming a medium. The book is sold with the understanding that the author and publisher are not engaged in rendering professional services, and disclaim any responsibility for any liability, loss, or risk, personal or otherwise, which is incurred as a consequence, directly or indirectly, of the use and application of any contents of this book.

Book design and layout by Pilar Taylor, TaylorDesign

Cover design is by Linda de Jesus, Wing & Prayer Design

To contact the author, please vist wmibooks.com

TO TOUCH THE SOUL

How to Become a Medium

by Rev. Judith Rochester, PhD

To my children, Drummond and Susan, who have supported me on my journey.

To my students and clients who have taught me so much.

To touch the soul ... is the whole object behind every phase of what is called mediumship.

Silver Birch, the Spirit Guide of Maurice Barbanell

Acknowledgements

While I am credited as the sole author of this book, many people have created it, and I would like to honor their contribution.

The early Spiritualists, through their pioneering spirit of exploration into the unseen, have been an inspiration for the book. Also, their recognition of God and Spirit as the sole agency for their service as mediums, has encouraged me during the writing of this course on mediumship.

I want to thank several Lily Dale teachers who have influenced my work: Patricia Price, whose teachings captured the joy of Spirit, infused all of us in her circle with a love of service; Neal Rzepkowski, who selflessly shared his vast knowledge of spiritual subjects with light hearted humor; and Betty Shultz, now in spirit, whose affection for her 'Boys', moved me to be true to my soul in communication with my spirit guides and teachers.

This book grew out of the Tuesday night circle that I offered with the Church of the Living Spirit for ten years. I appreciate the generosity of the church, and give thanks for the blessings of the students during our learning experiences together. A special thank you to the co-presenters from the circle – Steve Cybart, Craig Duke-Thomson, Tommy Hammerbeck (in spirit), Carol Hanson, Brenda Hawkins, Jim Leonard, Mary Ockuly, Dan O'Rourke, Beth Runkel, Carolyn Sampson, Bonnie White, Willa White, and Shirley Yusczyk—and to the guest presenters —Sherry Lee Calkins, Kitty Osbourne, John White and Bonnie Woods.

I want to express my appreciation to the students in my summer workshops who inspired me by their earnest search for higher ground through their unfolding mediumship and who are now healers, mediums and teachers in their own right. To mention a few – Anita Barreca, Richard Betts, Cindy Brown, Pamela Carrington, Leonard George, Gail Heil, Cinnamon Mancini, Dorothea Polite and Sue Stush.

I am especially grateful to Amy Gary, my editor and publisher, who has guided me every step of the way with loving kindness, practical know-how and a brilliant mind. Without her generous help, the book would not have been produced. I want to express my heartfelt thanks to Pilar Taylor for her tireless work in creating the beautiful design and layout for the text. I am indebted to Linda de Jesus for her uplifting cover design, her understanding of scientific research in the field of mediumship and her interest in my work. I thank Lucinda Wilson who gave me valuable insight, feedback and support through her review of the book. Many thanks go to Judy Ault who has opened new doors through her generous contribution of media and technical advice.

To Addariah Waugh, I express my gratitude for sharing her understanding of the workings of Spirit in our discussions of Spiritualism and mediumship that have enriched my thought. I want to say how much I appreciate Brenda Reading whose love of God's healing ways has contributed to my ministry.

Ultimately, I owe everything to my spirit guides and teachers who are the guiding light for the teachings presented in the book.

Finally, to my community of like minded souls, I give thanks for the opportunity to serve Spirit.

Preface

I have always loved learning. When students tell me the circle is the highlight of their week, I know how they feel. To me the class, circle or workshop – whatever the format – is a sanctuary, a hallowed place where I can let go of worldly concerns and open to God and Spirit. Here there is loving acceptance of who I am, no matter what I say or do. With other like minded souls in the group, I am free to seek whatever feeds my soul and ffulfills my inner longings.

In this book, I encourage you to create your own sacred place so that you can explore the teachings in your own sanctuary with the same feeling of freedom from the world of care. Here you can embrace the unseen world of the spirit and enjoy the benefits of mediumship in an atmosphere of loving acceptance of who *you* are, no matter what *you* say or do.

My hope is that you will more fully realize the nature of life itself, through the knowledge that the change called 'death' is but a passing from the earthly plane to the next; and also, through awareness that as a soul, you are always at-one with a world of love, harmony, wisdom, beauty and goodness. My intent is to help you become a medium and unfold your spiritual gifts, where you will experience this divine unseen dimension of life and share it with others in loving service to Spirit.

First, in Part I, you glimpse it through the guidance from Spirit for your daily life. Next, in Part II, through communication with your spirit loved ones in the spirit world, you become more aware of it. As you begin to perceive the spirit loved ones of others with the influence of your spirit guides and teachers, you can give messages to help others open to a new understanding about life – that it's not limited, but eternal; that it's loving and full of wonder.

In Part III, you realize the truth about life in ways beyond your ordinary understanding. You learn to become an instrument of your spirit guide or teacher and perceive the world in its unseen dimension through the eyes of Spirit. You become aware of the higher planes of life.

You learn to serve by giving and receiving a reading and public message in Part IV. In this way, your soul is awakened in deeper ways to the infinite unseen as you reach out with love as an instrument of Spirit to help another.

You will discover another aspect of the magnificence of the unseen world of life as you understand the plight of the lost soul in Part V and help them towards the light of the beyond. In the course of this, you experience the wondrous nature of absent healing. Here you share your compassion for another in need, as an instrument of your spirit healers.

Another phase of your mediumship unfolds in Part VI as you open to receive inspiration from your spirit inspirers through the written word. You communicate soul-to-soul with a spirit intelligence who conveys a higher truth from a sphere of life far beyond this one. Inspirational speaking too is a way to receive and express your soul's understanding that comes from the unseen dimensions beyond your normal grasp.

Finally, in Part VII, you will gain a perspective from an ancient spirit teacher of a divine order of life as you explore your gift of prophecy.

In all this, you are supported in your soul through spiritual laws that move you forward on your path and help you to develop your skills of mediumship.

The love, light and life of the unseen world is ever present as you seek with an open heart and mind, and as you trust the worth of your own experience. Trust in the infinite nature of life.

I hope you enjoy your journey and learn to rely on the wise and loving intelligences who come to guide and teach you. Seek them in your ups and downs; ask them to keep you on your path of loving service.

Blessings to you as you open the door to your new world.

TO TOUCH THE SOUL
How to Become a Medium

by Rev. Judith Rochester, PhD

Table of Contents

Part I: Attune to Spirit for Daily Guidance 9

Chapter 1: Open to the Unseen 11
The Unseen World 11
Spiritual Unfoldment 13
Your Daily Practice 15

Chapter 2: Discover Your Gifts 21
Your Soul Senses 21
Use Your Gifts to Unveil the Unseen 22
What is a Medium? 26

Chapter 3: Learn the Language of Spirit 29
What Does It Mean? 29
Strengthen Your Gifts 34
Gain a Deeper Understanding of the Language of Spirit 36

Chapter 4: Let Spirit Guide You in Your Daily Life 45
Guidance and Your Life 45
Attune to Spirit for Guidance in Your Life 50
A Guided Meditation: Meet Your Spirit Guide in Your Sanctuary 54

Part II Communicate with Spirit Loved Ones 59

Chapter 5: Connect to the Life in All Things 61
Law of Vibration 62
Psychometry 65

Chapter 6: Visit with Your Loved Ones 71
How Our Spirit Family Communicates 71
Visitations 73
Communicate with a Spirit Loved One 75

Chapter 7: Identify a Sitter's Spirit Loved One with Evidence 79
Evidence 79
Explore Evidence 82
Receive Evidence That Identifies Another's Spirit Love One 86

Chapter 8: Give a Medium's Message 91
A Medium's Message 91
The Language of Space and Time 93
Give and Receive a Medium's Message 95
Guided Meditation: Your Spirit Family Reunion 98

Part III Be an Instrument of Your Spirit Guides and Teachers 103

Chapter 9: Free Your Soul To Contact Spirit 105

The Law of Attraction *105*

Awaken Your Soul's Desire in Your Seven Centers *106*

Stir the Active and Receptive Modes of Your Soul's Desire *110*

Chapter 10: Get to Know Your Spirit Guides and Teachers 113

Why Do They Come? *113*

Who They Are *114*

Communicate With a Member of Your Spirit Band *117*

Chapter 11: Be an Instrument of Your Spirit Control 121

Three Ways to Be with Spirit *121*

Give a Medium's Message as an Instrument of Spirit (Partners) *124*

Chapter 12: Help Others Know Their Spirit Guides and Teachers 129

Draw the Spirit Guide or Teacher of Another *129*

Perceive Another's Spirit Guide or Teacher *132*

Guided Meditation: Teachers on the Higher Planes *138*

Part IV Give A Reading and A Public Message 143

Chapter 13: Be Of Service 145

The Law of Loving Service: *146*

Use the Law to Uplift Another with Prayer *148*

Chapter 14: Give and Receive a Mini-Reading 151

Evidence: Review and Enhance Your Skills *151*

Guidance: Review and Enhance Your Skills *156*

A Mini Reading *159*

Chapter 15: Give and Receive a Full Reading 165

What Makes You a Good Medium? *165*

Refine Your Readings *167*

A Regular Reading *172*

Chapter 16: Thank You for the Opportunity to Serve Spirit 179

Commitment to Serve Spirit *180*

Public Demonstration of the Continuity of Life *183*

Guided Meditation: Your Garden of Love *187*

Part V Rescue A Lost Soul 191

Chapter 17: I Once Was Lost, but Now Am Found 193

Law of Creative Responsibility *194*

Chapter 18: Souls in Transition 197

The Natural Transition from This World to the Next *197*

Who Needs to Be Rescued? *198*

    Absent Healing 200

  Chapter 19: Rescue a Lost Soul 205

    In What Sense Do We Rescue? 205

    Psychic Self Defense 206

    A Rescue Circle 207

  Chapter 20: A Journey Beyond 213

    Guided Meditation: Visit the Astral Plane 213

Part VI Write and Speak Inspirationally 217

  Chapter 21: Seek the Truth Through Inspirational Writing 219

    The Law of Truth 220

    Inspirational Writing: A Phase of Mental Mediumship 220

    Soul Knowledge 222

  Chapter 22: Receive Inspiration from Your Spirit Inspirers 223

    Who is Your Spirit Inspirer? 223

    Receive Daily Guidance Through Inspirational Writing 226

    Gain Insight from Spirit through Your Word 229

  Chapter 23: Be Inspired 233

    Spirit Teachers and Their Writings 233

    To Touch The Soul 235

    Commune with Your Spirit Teacher in Your Place of Inspiration 238

  Chapter 24: Speak Your Mind 241

    Inspirational Speaking – A Phase of Mental Mediumship 241

    Create A Talk 244

    Guided Meditation: Receive Inspiration in Your Temple of Wisdom 247

Part VII Explore Your Gift of Prophecy 251

  Chapter 25: What is Prophecy? 253

    Prophecy: A Phase of Mental Mediumship 253

    Prophecy is a Fact 254

    Meet Your Spirit Prophet 256

  Chapter 26: Strengthen Your Gift of Prediction 261

    Predictions and Their Soul Benefits 261

    We Create Our Own Destiny 266

    Sharpen Your Predictions for Yourself 269

  Chapter 27: Predict and Prophesy 273

    Predict the Future 273

    Predict the Future for Another 275

Prophesy as an Instrument of Your Spirit Prophet *279*

Explore Your Gift of Prophecy in a Cave of Crystal *284*

Chapter 28: Receive A Vision of Humanity from the Ancient Ones 289

A Guided Meditation: The Ancient Ones *289*

Chapter 29: In Closing 295

Your Unfolding Path *295*

Chapter 30: Bibliography 297

PART I: ATTUNE TO SPIRIT FOR DAILY GUIDANCE

What is important is that you should become aware of your true self and of the access you can have to the source of all being. You should know that the Great Spirit is not inaccessible, remote, far off, unreachable, but is within yourself and that you have a spiritual armoury, a strength, a reserve, a potency, on which you can call in times of difficulty and crisis.

Moreover, in addition to this tremendous potential within yourself, you can also reach out to the infinite power of the spirit … . You can climb a ladder, on which, rung after rung, there are beings waiting to help you as you are ready to reach them.

Silver Birch, the Spirit Guide of Maurice Barbanell,
The Philosophy of Silver Birch, edited by Stella Storm, 64, 65.

Open to the Unseen

Forty years ago, in a period of emotional and mental upheaval, I prayed for help. I began to meditate and begged for release from my inner turmoil. One day, much to my surprise and delight, a magnificent light came to me, drew my mind up out of the darkness and dissolved the heaviness in my heart. Gazing into this light, I felt its love, intelligence and life all at once, and I realized that I had attuned to a dimension beyond my normal awareness. I was astounded and puzzled by this experience. It was surreal - too good to be true it seemed. Yet I felt at home in its shining presence as I had never felt before. Here was serenity, and a sweet reassuring sense that all was well, that I was fine, and whole and right with the world.

In the days and weeks that followed, the light continued to shine. Its ethereal nature touched me deep within – in my soul – healing and nurturing a new life in me that I had somehow lost along the way. Gradually the light took on different forms as spirit guides who exuded the same life-giving vibration. In my need for support on a day-to-day basis, I called on them for guidance. They came with messages of hope and comfort, of information, direction and insight that spoke to my heart and my spirit. I sensed their divine goodness and compassion, and I was grateful. Their communications expressed a gentle wisdom superior to anything I had ever known, and while I sometimes doubted the truth of what I received, I knew in my soul, that these beings in this higher realm held the key to my spiritual unfoldment. Over the years, as I learned to attune to them, they guided me in my daily life and eventually helped me to become a medium. And as my mediumship unfolded, I began to see a basic teaching in their communications – that we are spirit in nature, and we are here to unfold our souls.

The Unseen World

Through no unusual talent, I had awakened to a dimension of life called the *unseen world*. The unseen world isn't seen by the physical senses; it's not known to the ordinary mind. When I 'saw' the light and later communed with my spirit guides and teachers, my eyes were closed in meditation – I perceived them with my *inner senses*. In this same way, the medium attunes to the unseen and receives information from Spirit that is beyond the normal capacity of the mind. The unseen is of the spirit; it is a dimension of goodness, truth, love and intelligence. As I opened to my spirit guides and teachers for guidance, I became aware of these forces in my daily affairs – my life improved and I became a better person.

This spiritual realm is also a natural state of our soul as I came to realize when Spirit ignited the spark of life in me – I felt completely whole there. I knew that the world that had suddenly opened to me was real: I wasn't making it up or hallucinating. I knew, with an inner conviction, that the communications I received from these higher beings were true. At the same time, I reaffirmed my intuitive sense by testing the accuracy of the guidance I received.

Yet as I went about my day, influenced by my physical surroundings, I wondered 'How can I make sense of these experiences as a person living in a material world? How can I explain these events and the unseen dimension? Is there a bigger view – a philosophy – to help me understand this new world so that I can find my way in it?' As I continued to communicate with my spirit guides and teachers, studied with teachers who were experienced mediums, and read books on the subject, I discovered encouraging answers to these questions.

The Spiritual Laws

The Need for Reassurance

When we open to the unseen, we are in a different *kind* of world. While we like it there, we need to be able to trust it in order to fully embrace it. And like most of us, I wanted reassurance that attuning to the unseen world always be right for my soul.

Spiritual Laws Order the Unseen

It is a great comfort to realize that there are positive forces – *spiritual laws* – that order the unseen world, just as physical laws order the material one. For example, the law of gravity ensures that we are grounded on earth, and things have a spatial place and predictability. Our physical laws help us to make sense of our surroundings and ensure that we know how to find our way. In fact, we depend on them without thinking because they never change. Similarly, through spiritual laws, we can make sense of the unseen. With the ever-present support of these beneficial energies, we can attune to the unseen and communicate with our spirit guides and teachers with confidence. As mediums, we learn to rely on these laws to achieve each stage of development.

The Laws and Our Soul

In my first encounter with spiritual laws, I understood them to be outside myself: To benefit from them, I thought I needed to change my behavior in accordance with them. But as I gained insight, I realized these forces were an innate part of my very being. Functioning from within, the laws are an *expression of the soul*. Through them, we grow spiritually and fulfill our higher purpose. (For more information on the spiritual laws, see *River of Life: How to Live in the Flow* by Marilyn J. Awtry.)

Seven Laws and Mediumship

In this book, I will identify seven spiritual laws. Although many spiritual laws are at work all the time, I focus on a specific law in each part that is central to your progress at that stage.

The Law of Life

The most basic spiritual law is the *law of life*. It describes our essence – our soul. This life force is so much a part of us that we hardly pay attention to it. Yet we rely on its presence. It's what stirs us with love, moves us to overcome hardship, through it we find hope in the face of loss, and optimism in the face of failure. We can dream, create and uplift others because of it.

Like all spiritual laws, the law of life operates within us all the time, whether we are conscious of it or not. For example, though I had lost touch with myself and my world those many years ago, the spark of life remained alive within me. It could not be snuffed out even though I was unaware of it. The law of life makes it possible to attune to the unseen and commune with Spirit. (I use Spirit with a capital 'S' to refer to the higher powers including spirit guides and teachers.)

As I became aware of the life within me, I opened to the invisible realm by reaching up with my soul. Spirit was able to bring guidance by communicating with me soul-to-soul – on the inner plane. As a developing medium, you too will become aware of this law and how to awaken the spark of life within you so that you can attune to Spirit and receive guidance on a daily basis.

Spiritual Unfoldment

The way to become a medium is often called *spiritual unfoldment*: you simply allow your soul to emerge in order to develop your mediumship. This approach to learning and growth is the way the law of life expresses itself. Think of the soul like the seed of a flower planted in the earth. It naturally grows from its own source; and given the right conditions, it blossoms to maturity. The soul too grows from within. And with the right conditions, it will flower. As a soul, we have a natural longing for oneness, for spiritual fulfillment, and mediumship is one path towards it.

Part I is the first step to unfolding your soul to become a medium. You will learn how to receive daily guidance from a spirit guide. In this chapter you learn how to attune to the unseen and awaken your soul; in Chapter Two, you discover your soul's gifts; Chapter Three teaches you how to use your gifts to receive symbolic messages from Spirit; and in Chapter Four you're able to receive guidance from a spirit guide to help you in your daily life. At the end of Part I, a guided meditation will take you to your Sanctuary where you meet and converse with your spirit guide about your spiritual progress.

Your Path

Listen to Spirit
As I look back over the years since my experience, I realize that I was guided in my unfoldment though it wasn't always obvious to my conscious mind. It wasn't always easy either. But the more I listened to Spirit's messages from deep within, even in the face of conflicting events, the closer I felt to my true self and journey. You too will discover that the awareness of your life within – nurtured by Spirit's guiding presence – will sustain you on your path despite your ups and downs.

Your True Teachers
In working with my spirit guides and teachers, I came to realize that they are our true teachers. They are able to connect to our soul with a wisdom and compassion that no earth teacher can. My aim is to facilitate your relationship with them, to do everything I can to help you gain understanding from within.

Ask Spirit
Ask your spirit workers for anything you need and they will show you how to accomplish it. It may take time, persistence and a lot of growth, but you will achieve what you want as long as it benefits your spiritual progression. Any time you're confused or you question something, including what I have said, ask them. Let them be your source of knowledge and enjoy this wonderful way of seeking with your soul.

Embrace Your Unique Way
I will show you how to access your natural ability to be a medium and use it. Your spirit guides and teachers will ensure that you express your talent in your own unique way, one that suits you, one that is fulfilling. From them, you will learn to be true to your highest self.

Your Long Term Purpose
People want to be mediums for many different reasons. It's important to determine your own genuine heart's desire because it will show you your own approach to mediumship. For example, my approach is based on the initial awak-

ening of my soul to my spirit guides and teachers: my motive in becoming a medium was to find my spiritual path and purpose through communication with them in the spirit world. For this reason, I offer a comprehensive approach to mediumship – seven areas of development – to help you explore your spiritual purpose as you progress through each of these phases of service to Spirit. Some reasons people want to become mediums include:

To serve God and Spirit	To bring people comfort by communicating with their spirit loved ones
To help people	To understand the spirit world, to find my spiritual way
To heal people	To learn from my spirit guides and teachers
To do rescue work	To gain meaning and spiritual understanding
To counsel and uplift	To write and speak inspirationally
To find answers first hand	I always wanted to be a medium (I'm not sure why)
To understand the unseen dimensions	To make sense of my own childhood

I don't know – I'm curious …

Reflect on your own life and path, and ask yourself the reasons you want to be a medium.

Why I want to be a medium: _____

_____

_____

Your Immediate Purpose

In addition to your long term goal, pay attention to your immediate one: What do you want to learn from this course? What do you want from this teaching? This helps you to know where you're starting from, and even if you don't know or you change your mind as you go along, still you've clarified your initial purpose. It also helps to be aware of what you want. This may overlap with your long term goal. Some of the things that students say they want from this course include:

To focus better	To learn how to develop	To fine-tune my skills
I'm curious	To give readings	To discover my gifts
I'm searching	I want to give clearer messages	To be able to relax
To know my spirit guides	To find my spiritual way	I've always wanted to do this
I need to find answers	To communicate with my child who passed	To find peace
To learn it all	To understand my premonitions	I need to start from the basics
To help people	To serve as an instrument of Spirit	To understand the spirit world

What I want from this course: _____

_____

_____

Guidelines for Learning

Study on Your Own or with a Group
When people who came to me for readings began to ask 'How can I become a medium?' I decided to teach them, and after fifteen years of classes, I wrote this book using those materials. It is a course that you can study on your own, with a few friends and/or with a teacher. This also suits those of you who don't have access to a teacher or who may not feel ready to join a formal group. As well, the book may be used by teachers as an instructional guide. Suitable for beginners, it is also enlightening for the more experienced.

Exercises
You become a medium by doing the exercises. Through your inner awareness, you learn to unfold your gifts, open to the unseen and receive messages from your spirit guides and teachers. Here are some suggestions to help you.

- Read each exercise beforehand so you are prepared for it.

- You may want to read a prayer, relaxation or meditation aloud to record it, and then play it back to do it. Or you can ask someone else to read it as you go through it, or you may simply do it from the written word. When you see three dots (…) in the text, pause to give yourself time to do what you need.

- Keep a record of your experiences, insights, communications and feedback. This reinforces your learning because it brings your inner events into the physical world, and affirms your belief in their worth. It also helps to map out your spiritual unfoldment. When you reread them later, you will often be amazed at the workings of the spirit in your growth.

- The journey is ongoing. Enjoy the process as you proceed step-by-step in your learning, and trust in the exercises to show you the way.

Attitudes
As you become sensitive to the unseen dimension, you will learn the importance of positive attitudes in the development of your mediumship. Here are a few pointers to prepare you for this kind of growth.

- Many of the exercises and teachings will help you to cleanse your old thoughts and feelings that are no longer beneficial to you on this path.

- Your daily communications with Spirit will help you to link with their happy, loving thoughts and elevated ideas. Nurture an optimistic attitude.

- Suspend your critical thoughts during your practice. These will undermine your need for receptivity to God and Spirit. Then set aside a specific time to discuss them with Spirit to ensure that you meet your mental needs and interests.

- Be kind to yourself as you make your way. Accept yourself and realize that your perceived weaknesses are the gems of new insights that may otherwise not have been discovered.

- Develop physical habits that create balance between your body and mind, such as regular exercise, healthy food and normal sleep patterns. Excessive drinking, smoking and eating may interfere with your progress.

Your Daily Practice

One of the most valuable ways to help yourself unfold your spiritual gifts is through your *daily practice*. Set aside a regular time to spend alone in **prayer, relaxation, meditation, communication with Spirit** and **absent healing**. Here your soul comes to life and opens to the unseen. As you become stronger within, you will attune to your spirit guides and teachers, maintain a strong connection to them and receive their messages.

Through your daily practice, your soul will grow naturally and steadily. Think of yourself as a gardener who knows that with loving care, the delicate life of a flower grows in its own time. It can't be forced. This is the wonder of life. Similarly, we can't force our soul's unfoldment for it grows from its own source. We flower as developing mediums when we pay attention to our soul's needs – to our pace, our interests, what feeds our spirit, what moves us to higher ground.

Your Sacred Place

Find a space where you can be free from outside distractions to focus your mind for daily practice. You want to create a place of harmony where you sit with God and commune with your spirit guides and teachers. You want to quiet yourself in order to sense their loving presence, and be aware of their communications. Consider enhancing the serenity and beauty of your space with your favorite things, such as music, a candle, flowers and plants, religious and spiritual items, natural objects like stones, shells or pine cones, water to drink, aromatic essences or incense, colors that suit you, a comfortable chair or pillows, meditation cds, books and study materials. Above all, make your sacred space a sanctuary for your daily practice that entices your spirit. What inspires you to reach for higher ground? What soothes and comforts you? What helps you to find your inner calm? Ask God and Spirit for answers and let them be with you.

To stimulate your interest, you may want to read inspirational books, contemplate spiritual or religious ideas, record your insights or discoveries, journal or study. As you develop, use this spiritual haven to prepare talks or give readings. As you persist, you will begin to feel the power of God as soon as you enter your sacred space. Also, the uplifting vibrations created by your devotional practice will trigger the presence of your spirit guides and teachers who will be ready to commune with you. You will have created a truly *sacred place*.

→ Exercises for Daily Practice

These are some ways to get started in your daily practice. Select only a few to do in one sitting.

Prayer

Prayer awakens your soul to the unseen: You come to life through contact with God. The uplifting vibrations of the infinite spirit flow into you, and transform you and those you pray for. Begin and end every spiritual activity with a prayer. Mediums understand God in many different ways – Divine Spirit, Infinite Intelligence, God the Father, Goddess, Father-Mother-God, Earth Mother, Being, Universal Mind and Great Spirit, for example. Explore your own concept of God. Be as true as you can to your soul's longing.

Who or what is the God of your own understanding? _____

_____

_____

_____

These prayers are simple, yet they have a subtle power to touch your spirit. Be still and aware as you open to God. Following each prayer, record what you felt, thought or sensed. Trust your own way of coming to God and your own experience of your soul.

Pray: Give Thanks

Sit quietly in your sacred place. Close your eyes and let yourself reach up towards God from within. Think of your blessings, and give thanks for each one. Your life may seem lacking, but note the many things you're grateful for that perhaps you take for granted; such as, your day, a friend, your breath, your ability to love, the tree outside your window, the laughter of children, your spiritual search, your pet. Notice how you feel. In giving thanks, you move out beyond yourself that is absorbed in the affairs of the day, and experience yourself that appreciates the good in your life and knows gratitude – your soul. Give thanks and open your eyes.

My experience of giving thanks to God: _____

_____

_____

_____

Pray: Ask for Help

Relax in your sacred place and close your eyes. Reach up with your heart and mind to whomever or whatever you conceive God to be. Ask for help with anything that troubles you. For example, if you feel lost or discouraged, call on God to draw near. Keep asking; then wait for aid to come. It may come immediately or in the next few days at unexpected times. Notice that your vulnerable self, when you open in this prayer, allows God to reach you within. When you receive help such as insight, comfort, relief or healing, you are released from your troubled self to a more enlightened one – to your soul. Give thanks and open your eyes.

My experience of asking God for help: _____

_____

_____

_____

Pray: Sense the Presence of God

Sit in your sacred place with your eyes closed and take a few deep breaths as you relax. Open your heart and reach up beyond yourself to seek God's presence. Focus your mind on a divine quality such as love or goodness. As you keep your focus, repeat the word to yourself; for example, love … love. … Then relax your reaching and open to receive. In this passive state, sense God's love flowing into you. As you allow the divine quality of God to infuse in you, notice that you feel more of your higher nature, more godlike in your love – more fully your soul. Give thanks and open your eyes.

My experience of the sense of the presence of God: _____

_____

_____

_____

_____

Relaxation through Meditation

When you *relax*, your busy mind recedes, emotional stress releases, muscle tension dissolves, and your soul can emerge.

Relax: Be Aware of Your Breath

In your sacred place, sit comfortably with your spine upright. Close your eyes. Become aware of your breathing and relax. As you inhale, notice how soothing your breath feels. As you exhale, release all your worries and concerns. Relax. Continue to breathe in and out. Relax. … Feel your lungs relax as you fill them with your gentle breath. Now focus on this relaxing energy and let it flow like a liquid light into your lower body filling every cell and organ with peace. Relax. See the flowing light move gently into your legs and feet. Sense this energy as it releases any tension, and feel your renewed life streaming throughout your lower body. … Draw this current up your body and back to your lungs. Relax… Now, let your breath flow into your upper body and feel its vital energy. See it as a liquid light, and feel it soothe your neck, throat, arms and hands as it flows into your muscles. Relax. Continue to inhale and exhale; feel your breath like a relaxing wave of new life flowing up into your face, head, and brain cells. Be aware of the streaming energy throughout your upper body. …Let it gently return to your lungs. Relax. Notice how you feel in your relaxed self, more fully your soul. … Open your eyes when you are ready.

My experience of relaxing through awareness of my breath: _____

_____

_____

_____

Relax: Heal Yourself with Your Flame of Life

Sit quietly in your sacred place and take a few deep breaths to relax. Close your eyes. Focus deep within to a sense of life, to a feeling of being alive. Relax. Notice where it is in your body – perhaps your gut, heart, throat, head – or it may be nowhere in particular. Feel this life as a soft flame and let its gentle vibration spread throughout your system. Feel its healing comfort. … Now scan your body and focus on your physical needs. Perhaps you need energy, or relief from muscle tension. Let this flame of life seep into these states and refresh you. Relax in your physical body. … Focus on your emotional system and notice any disharmony here. Let this flame gently flow into it and dissolve the tension. Let it ignite your heart with love and your spirit with happiness. Relax. … Be aware of your mental states and notice any troubling thoughts. Let the flame of life shine into them and bring relief. Feel your peace of mind. … Relax in your renewed sense of life. You are more fully yourself. This is your soul, your spirit nature. When you are ready, open your eyes.

My experience of relaxing by healing myself with my flame of life: _____

_____

_____

_____

Guided Meditation

In mediumship development, a *meditation* is often a *guided* journey within that helps you to embrace your soul, and learn from your spirit guides and teachers as you explore the unseen.

Meditate: Be at Peace in Nature

Sit quietly in your sacred place and close your eyes. Imagine yourself in a peaceful place in nature. Go where your mind takes you, perhaps by a lake, a clearing in the woods, a desert or a mountain. It may or may not be familiar to you. … Be aware of your feet on the ground and notice how quiet it is. How peaceful! Breathe in the fresh air and sense how these natural surroundings feed your soul. How good you feel!

Look around you now. What do you see? Notice the beauty everywhere and fill your being with it. Be at peace. … What do you hear? Listen to the sounds of nature and let them reach deep within you. … Feel at peace with yourself and with nature. What do you sense here in this pristine place? Perhaps the sky opens your mind to an expansiveness, or the water soothes your heart or the earth brings you closer to your own inner stability. Stay in this place of tranquility and replenish your soul. Let the peace of nature infuse your being. … When you feel ready to leave, look around one last time, and then imagine yourself back in your sacred place. Slowly open your eyes and be aware of your physical body and world.

My experience of meditating on being at peace in nature: _____
_____
_____
_____

Communication with a Spirit Guide

The following meditation is an introduction to *communication with a spirit guide* by opening to the light of spirit without contacting a guide as a spirit entity. It was the way I was introduced to my spirit guides and teachers: I learned to connect with them by attuning to their vibrations of light and developing a sense of their presence. This will enhance your sensitivity to the fine energies of the higher realms, and lay a strong foundation for receiving messages from them. Some of you may sense, and a few of you may even hear the light of spirit, instead of seeing it. These ways are equally good.

Meditate: Open to the Light of Spirit

Take a few deep breaths to relax in your sacred place. Close your eyes. Call on God and Spirit to help you with your spiritual unfoldment. … Look up from within and see a shining light far above your head. You feel drawn to it and you reach up to be closer. Let yourself move towards it. … Become lighter and lighter as you release your earthly body, and float up beyond your normal consciousness. … Notice how free you are in your spirit as you let yourself go and enjoy your higher state in the glow of the ethereal light. … Gaze around you and see a sky-like space that glistens with the reflection of the light. Sense the harmony everywhere. Feel the peace of your soul. … Move closer to the light and notice that it too comes near. As you feel its gentle vibration, sense its spiritual nature. It shines into you and clears your mind. It surrounds you with tender care and fills you with love. You feel whole and connected with the universe. … Remaining close, become aware that the light is the emanation of a higher intelligence that comes to help you. Feel at-one with this heavenly presence … uplifted by its purity and goodness … buoyed up by its life. Stay now with the light of Spirit. … Gradually, the light recedes. Your soul is strengthened with new light and life that will never leave. Give thanks for all you have received and slowly return. Feel yourself floating down. … Be aware of your soul merging with your physical state in your sacred place. Gently open your eyes.

My experience of opening to the light of spirit: _____
_____
_____
_____

Absent Healing

The following is a combination of prayer and meditation to introduce you to *absent healing* – a way to heal others at a distance. Here you are helped by God and Spirit who send their life energy through you to those in need. This is a powerful way to begin to serve as a medium because you learn to be a conduit for the higher powers.

Absent Healing: Be a Channel of Infinite Love

Begin with the prayer *Sense the Presence of God* and open to God's love. … Keep your eyes closed and continue to be aware of your soul and the loving vibrations flowing in you. Stay open to God's presence and ask for the light of spirit to draw near to help you send healing love to others. … As you open to the influence of Spirit, you are elevated in your spirit. Now let the divine love fill your heart to overflowing. Feel it expanding beyond your body like the rays of the sun. … Sense the warmth of your love and a strong desire to reach out to others with loving kindness. … Think of those who are suffering, and as they come to mind, let your love go out to them. … As God and Spirit pour infinite love into you, be a channel of compassion and loving kindness: Reach out to anyone in need through your loving heart. Sense and see them in healing love. … When you feel the healing power begin to recede, give thanks to God and Spirit for the opportunity to connect to others with love. Gently open your eyes and become aware of yourself sitting in your sacred place.

My experience of absent healing through my prayer-meditation: _____

_____

_____

_____

As you continue to do absent healing, let God and Spirit guide you to express the power of love in different ways; for example, in addition to your loving heart, through life affirming words, uplifting thoughts and comforting prayers. Your hands too can be a conduit as you open them to allow healing energy to go out to others. Trust in how you're guided: one method will sometimes work better than another.

You may also be impressed to send love to those you have slighted or hurt, or been angry with. When you are a channel of God and Spirit's loving presence, you feel a soul connection to others even in the face of painful conflicts and differences. Feel the loving force flow out from you and touch another's soul. … With infinite love, all is forgiven, all is made right. And in your caring for others with a genuine loving heart, you too are healed. You are released from the suffering of your old ways. You are more fully yourself, your soul.

Discover Your Gifts

Your Soul Senses

You Have the 'Gift'

You may have received a message from a medium and wondered 'How does she do that? She seems to pull information out of the air!' or 'How did he know this? I never told him anything!' It seems miraculous. Surely this is a *gift!* And while mediumship is awe inspiring, and Spirit's ways are full of wonder, everyone has this special gift. It is often referred to as a *sixth sense* because the information is gained through an ability other than the five physical senses. Actually, we have *five* gifts: Just as we perceive the material world with five physical senses, we perceive the unseen with five *inner* or *soul senses*.

Our spirit guides and teachers use these senses to communicate from the unseen world with information that isn't known through normal means. In this way, Spirit was able to help me on my path. The spirit light, in its non-physical nature, influenced my *soul eye* and I was moved out of the darkness as I looked into its ethereal brightness. When I heard spirit's voice I was guided by the messages I received with my *soul ear*. The higher vibrations of spirit's presence touched my *soul sense* so that the heaviness of my heart lifted and I came to life.

These are often called *psychic gifts* because the word 'psyche' in Greek means 'soul'; they are also referred to as *spiritual gifts*. They were named by French practitioners of mesmerism who discovered that under hypnosis, their patients could perceive things beyond the normal capacity of the human eye, ear, and sense. They called these supernormal senses *clairvoyance, clairaudience* and *clairsentience* meaning *clear vision, clear hearing* and *clear sensing* respectively. (*How to Read the Aura, Practice Psychometry, Telepathy and Clairvoyance,* by W.E. Butler,15, 16.) Two less frequently used soul senses are *clairscent* and *clairgustance* meaning *clear smell* and *clear taste.*

In mediumship, we receive information with our soul senses through the uplifting influence of our spirit guides and teachers. Working on the unseen level, spirit intelligences impress our inner senses so we can See, Hear, Sense, Smell and Taste what is not physically present. These inner perceptions are the content of our messages. (I capitalize these senses to distinguish them from our physical ones, but once you are accustomed to thinking of them as inner or soul senses in Part I, I will no longer continue to do so.)

Clairvoyance: Clear Inner or Soul Seeing

As you open your soul eye to the elevated influence of Spirit, you gain visual messages from the unseen. Some of the things you can See include people, things and events; energies, thoughts and feelings; animals and natural phenomena; and spirits, spiritual influences and higher planes. Clairvoyant images may be moving or still; in color or black and white; clear or hazy; and fully or partially visible. For a discussion of other forms of clairvoyance such as *objective* (where you See the phenomenon as if it were in the world of matter, but others do not), and *X-Ray* (where you See through matter), read *Definition* by Cora L.V. Richmond, *NSAC Spiritualist Manual*, 2004 Revision, 26, 27.

Clairaudience: Clear Inner or Soul Hearing

Spirit impresses your soul ear with sounds from the unseen to bring information you can Hear. Such sounds include – noises of people, things and events; music and laughter; natural phenomena, birds, and animals; and voices of spirits. Clairaudience may be experienced as a mental hearing or a thought conveyed directly to your mind from Spirit.

Clairsentience: Clear Inner or Soul Sensing

Your inner ability to sense the unseen is open to the influence of Spirit who conveys messages with information you can Sense, such as feelings, thoughts and physical conditions of people; vibrations of things, animals, and nature; events and places; and the presence of spirits. Clairsentience may sometimes be experienced as intuition, 'gut feel' or a 'just knowing'.

Clairscent: Clear Inner or Soul Smell

Spirit influences your inner sense of Smell with messages from the unseen world that convey information through such things as the fragrance of flowers, perfumes, cooking, tobacco, and the scent of nature.

Clairgustance: Clear Inner or Soul Taste

Your soul's ability to Taste what isn't physically present is used by Spirit to bring messages in the form of taste. Through Clairgustance such tastes as chocolate, sauces, baked goods, fresh fruits and vegetables can be received from the unseen.

Use Your Gifts to Unveil the Unseen

The following exercise shows you how to open your gifts to perceive a rose in the unseen world with Spirit's guidance. As you move through it, let yourself be spiritually uplifted. Enjoy what you See, Sense, Hear, Smell and Taste with your soul's awareness. Open to the beauty of the unseen!

The perception of a rose is a standard way for developing mediums to discover their gifts. For those of you who are experienced mediums, and are familiar with the exercise, remind yourself that the unseen is always fresh with life and yields new understanding. No matter how often I do this exercise, I'm grateful for its insight. I hope that you too will be uplifted whether you are a beginning or a more advanced learner. The method used is a form of *creative visualization* that opens your soul senses to the unseen through Spirit's influence: You are asked to look up at a clear white sky, screen or space to perceive a rose as you rely on the vibration of the spirit light. This is in contrast to the use of creative visualization to develop the power of the mind without the influence of Spirit.

I will walk you through a meditation and ask you to call on your spirit light to help you perceive a rose in the unseen dimension of life. The aim of the exercise:

- To use your gifts to perceive the beauty of the unseen world, and to trust in what you See, Hear, Sense, Smell and Taste.

- To sense the presence of your spirit light and receive a brief message of guidance.

⇾ Exercise: Perceive a Rose in the Unseen World

Prepare
Sit quietly in your sacred place and close your eyes. Pray with a prayer of your own choice. … Take a few deep breaths and relax. Focus on your breath and be aware of its soothing energy as you inhale and exhale. Let it flow throughout your body and relax. Be at peace.

Open to the Unseen
Look up to your spirit light shining above your head. Call on it to come close and draw you up into the unseen dimension. … Reach up with your heart and mind, and move closer to the light. Notice that you begin to feel lighter and lighter. … You are releasing your material body. Be aware of your soul self … you feel free … happy … loving. You shed old thoughts and cares. Be at peace in your spirit.

Be Aware of Your Spirit Light
Open to the presence of the spirit light and the vibrations that emanate from it. … Notice how you feel. … Trust that Spirit is with you to guide and direct your learning.

Use Your Gifts
Focus in front of you to an expanse of sky, a space or a screen with a clear white background. Look up into this area and ask your spirit light to help you open your soul senses. Stay focused and prepare to perceive a rose before you with Spirit's guidance. Now **See** a magnificent rose appear before you. What do you See? … Notice its shape. What color is it? … Look at its petals. Does it have a stem, leaves, thorns? Take your time and enjoy the beauty of this flower. … How is it situated – outside in a garden? … inside in a vase? … Is it single, part of a bush, or a bouquet? …

What do you **Sense** with this rose? … Love? Joy? … Notice your first impression of your rose. … How do you feel as you perceive this rose? … Perhaps you Sense the warmth of the sun with this rose …

Open your inner **Smell** to the rose and notice its fragrance. … You may Smell its perfume, its sweetness or some other scent. …

What do you **Hear** with your rose? … Its leaves rustling? A trickling stream near it? A water fountain in a garden? … A bird chirping? … Are there any other sounds? Listen. …

Open your inner **Taste** and notice a dew drop on the petal of your flower. Taste it with your tongue. What's your first sensation? … Is it cold or lukewarm? … How does it taste? …

Receive Messages
Stay with your rose and enjoy your experience. … As you sit quietly, be aware of the presence of your spirit light surrounding you and your rose. Ask for guidance: What message is your rose bringing you from the unseen? You may receive it directly from your rose, from your spirit light or you may be aware of it coming from within yourself. Open with your inner or soul senses and communicate with the unseen world. You may **Hear** something such as words or music, or you may receive a thought as a mental hearing; you may **Sense** a message, such as a comforting feeling; or you may **See** something, such as a smile or a sign of encouragement. … What is your message? …

Give Thanks
When you are ready, give thanks to your rose and your spirit light for what you have received. Hold this experience close to your heart and mind. Let your awareness of the ethereal world strengthen and support you, guide and teach you as you move forward in your learning.

Return
Now the rose fades; the sky, space and screen recede. You retain your uplifted state as you gently return. Notice your regular breathing. Open your eyes and be aware of your sacred place.

▸ *My Experience:*

What I Saw _____

_____

_____

What I Heard _____

_____

_____

What I Sensed _____

_____

_____

What I Smelled _____

_____

What I Tasted _____

_____

My Message of Guidance from My Rose and My Spirit Light _____

_____

_____

Other Highlights _____

_____

_____

Feedback on Your Experience
You have just used your gifts to perceive a rose in the unseen. Some of you may have felt an elevated state of consciousness. For others, your experience may have seemed quite ordinary. The images may have seemed other-worldly, or they may be what you're used to perceiving in your imagination. Whatever your experience, become aware of the subtle changes in and around you as you continue in your spiritual unfoldment.

One Soul Sense Dominates

You may have found that one or two soul senses were clearer or easier to use. For example, your ability to Sense was strong, but you didn't See as well, or at all. Or, you Saw clearly, but didn't Hear. This is normal. On the other hand, you may use your Sense to See, strange as it may seem. For example, you may Sense colors, people or shapes. Or you may pick up 'sounds' visually from the unseen by Seeing words. However you perceive the unseen, know that your spirit guide is using your unique nature to help you. At the same time, ask Spirit to show you how to develop *all* your gifts since you will benefit from the freedom to discover a greater range of the unseen. Exercises will be provided to unfold your gifts as we progress. When you become a practicing medium, you may settle into one preferred way.

Awareness of Your Spirit Guide

When you perceived a rose, you became more familiar with your spirit light, and sensed its presence *like a spirit guide*. It takes time to have a close connection to your spirit guides and teachers. As you awaken your soul, you help to create a stronger link. And one of the best ways to do this is through your daily practice. Also, each exercise brings you closer to Spirit.

It's important to realize that you need not perceive your spirit guides and teachers face-to-face in order to benefit from their guidance and support. For example, you received a message from Spirit, in the above exercise, without perceiving the form of an entity. (However, you will have the opportunity to meet and talk with your spirit guide in the guided meditation, *Meet Your Spirit Guide in Your Sanctuary*, at the end of Part I, and Part III is devoted entirely to your spirit guides and teachers.)

At this stage, you are learning to become aware of your spirit guide. Here are some ways to tell that Spirit is with you during your daily practice and the exercises as you move forward.

- As you open to your spirit light or guide, you have a heightened awareness of your soul: This is also due to your own efforts.

- When you invoke the presence of Spirit, you See or Sense a fine vibration in and around you or Hear an ethereal sound that is uplifting, loving and healing.

- Due to the vibration of your spirit light or guide, your soul senses become clear and bright.

- When you open your gifts to Spirit, you experience elevated states, such as peace, love, happiness, freedom and higher understanding.

- When you sit with Spirit, you feel a spiritual comfort in your heart and mind.

If you are aware of any of these states, record your individual experience of them. And as you progress, notice your increasing familiarity with the presence of your spirit light or guide.

Are there other ways that you can tell that Spirit is with you? Record your experiences _____

_____

_____

_____

What is a Medium?

So far you know that a *medium* uses her gifts to communicate with her spirit guides and teachers to gain information from the unseen that is not known by normal means. But what *kind of information* is this? Let's look at two messages I received from mediums. (I have revised and added to the spoken messages that contained 'ums', half sentences and vague words.)

1. 'There is a man here from the other side of life who is wearing a hat as he steers a ship through a narrows. With a chuckle, he says he would never hit the sides, and cautions you to stay on track as you move ahead.'

2. 'A teacher comes to you with love from the world of spirit. She's in a long skirt and limps. A thin woman with long hair, she holds up a piece of art. She helps you with your classes.'

Here are some details about my life to help you understand the meaning of the messages and their importance for me.

> Message 1. My deceased grandfather had been a captain of a ship and maneuvered it through a canal system. I had a picture of him wearing his captain's hat and looking very confident. He had a sense of humor. I knew this was him. I was moving to a new part of the country and I needed to be attentive to many details. His message helped me to be mindful. I was comforted by his visitation from the spirit realm.

> Message 2. I had a teacher who had passed to spirit and who fit the description given by the medium. She had polio as a child and walked with a limp. She taught me art and was a strong influence when I was young. I was proud of a big colored fish I painted in her class. For me, a fish means manna: Her message confirmed that my new workshops would be spiritually helpful. I was grateful for her guidance from the other side of life.

Two Kinds of Information

When we examine these messages, we can decipher two kinds of information. The *first kind* **identifies** a spirit loved one. In Message 1, facts about my grandfather were provided – that he was a man, wore a captain's hat, drove a ship, was confident and had a sense of humor. With this information, I knew that my grandfather was bringing a message to me. In Message 2, facts about my former teacher were given – that she was female, had long hair, walked with difficulty, was thin, wore a long skirt and taught me art in her class. With this information, I knew that my childhood teacher was communicating with me.

The *second kind* **guides** us in our lives. In Message 1, I was guided with the advice to stay focused with a move I was about to make. In Message 2, I was guided with reassurance that the classes I was preparing would be spiritually uplifting.

Definition of Mediumship

The first kind of information provides the *essential ingredient of mediumship*. (This applies to messages and readings which are the most familiar ways in which a medium brings information from the spirit world.) Here is a standard definition:

> A *medium* communicates with the spirit world in order to prove that life continues beyond our earthly existence. This is called *proof of the continuity of life*. This is done by bringing factual information or *evidence* that accurately identifies a spirit loved one for a sitter. A *sitter* is the person who receives the message or reading.

The second kind of information is the *psychic* component of a medium's message. Not all mediums include this element in their messages and readings. Their focus is entirely on evidence. In this course, you learn to give messages and readings that include both *evidence* and *guidance*. (In Part II, you will learn how to give such a message – a medium's message – for another person.)

For the remainder of Part I, you will use your gifts to receive guidance from Spirit to help you in your daily lives. These are psychic messages. Spirit helped me to become a medium by starting with this method of 'spiritual self-help' and I share it with you. Its benefits include:

- It is a form of self-help where you develop your gifts and grow spiritually in your personal life as you strengthen your relationship with your spirit guides and teachers.

- When you are able to improve your daily life through Spirit guidance, you can better help others do the same as a practicing medium.

- As you learn from your own experience, you will become familiar with the kinds of problems that can impact a person's life, and will have more tolerance and compassion for others.

Mental Mediumship

We are doing *mental mediumship* here. It is most commonly practiced today. The word 'mental' does not mean that we receive information from our own minds. It refers to the way our spirit guides and teachers work with us, and the nature of the results. They influence our soul senses through our conscious mind or voluntary nervous system, and produce messages perceived by us alone, by our five inner or soul senses. The information, then, is *subjective*. We are in a light trance, an elevated state, yet in control of ourselves. The two messages cited above are examples of mental mediumship.

Physical Mediumship

By contrast, in *physical mediumship* Spirit bypasses the conscious mind to influence the automatic nervous system and produce phenomena that are perceivable by others – they are *objective*. Here the medium is in a deep trance. An example of physical mediumship is *materialization* where the figure of a spirit loved one can be seen by others as an opaque or misty material form. This kind of mediumship is less commonly practiced today.

Learn the Language of Spirit

What Does It Mean?

Beginning students and experienced mediums alike can be confused about the meaning of a message because we try to grasp it in our normal way – with our conscious mind. But Spirit speaks to our soul in order to lift us out of our earthbound state and free our minds to the wonders of the unseen world.

Symbolic Meaning

The language of Spirit is like the messages of the dream – *symbols* convey their meanings that move us deeply. Think of the impact of a dream image that stayed with you during the day or even longer. Movies, too, rely on symbols to move us to tears or laughter, stir us to noble thoughts or evoke our most vulnerable longings. A *symbol* is an object, word, image or sign used to represent or mean something else. For example,

1. A dove is a symbol of peace.
2. The cross symbolizes the Christian faith.
3. Money is a symbol of success.
4. An image of a blue sky is a symbol of a new opportunity for one person; for another, happiness.

In each case, what the symbol represents is its meaning: a message with a dove *means* peace. Symbols get their meanings in different ways. Some symbols have a *universal* meaning (like #1). They come down to us through the centuries in stories and myths. Others may have a *religious* meaning (#2). *Cultural* values give other symbols their meaning (#3): In some indigenous cultures, for example, money is not a symbol of success. Symbols also can have *individual* meanings (#4): Our personal history, interests, experience and talents determine their meaning along with varying degrees of influence from the other categories. As mediums, we want to grasp this kind of meaning. Similar to understanding a symbol in a dream, we get the meaning by asking *What does it mean to me?*

Literal Meaning

Spirit also communicates from the unseen with language that expresses a *literal* meaning: It refers to actual things, people, events, living creatures and energies from this and higher planes. For example, if I Saw a lake that accurately described a place from my childhood, it would be a literal meaning. Or I may See a watch my spouse bought for my birthday that I hadn't yet been given. Literal meanings are critical in mediumship: You will learn to bring accurate evidence to identify a spirit loved one for a sitter in Part II Chapter Seven.

They are also important for you and your sitter to receive daily guidance from Spirit that refers to the actual conditions in your lives in directly descriptive ways. For example, you ask 'Is the house I want to buy in good condition?' and Spirit shows you the corner of the cement foundation that is cracked. Anything that can be perceived in this world with the physical senses can also be perceived with your soul senses and used to inform us through its literal meaning. You may hone into the personality of a pet, a workplace environment, the contents of a document, the fine details of a piece of jewelry, a child's room, a farm, a conversation or the chorus of a musical, to gain insight for yourself or another.

Develop Your Code with Spirit
Often the same message could be gained through a symbolic or literal meaning. For example, you may See two gold bands entwined in a circle of silver light and you know that this is a *symbolic* message from Spirit that means that a wedding is to take place. Someone else may receive a *literal* message that conveys the same information by Seeing the details of an actual wedding. Why are there differences? One way may be more efficient for Spirit to get the meaning across; your mind may be more at ease with one form or the other; or your sitter may be better helped in a particular way. You may not always know whether a message refers to an actual situation or not, but with practice you will grasp the difference. Ask as you go along. Trust Spirit to help you develop your mutual code of understanding that works best and is most enlightening for you.

→ Exercise: Learn the Meaning of Colors

A color in a message can easily and quickly show you its meaning. Its many shades (pale, bright, dark) reflect a wide range of precise meanings. Further a color can come in many shapes (a bird, a chair or a piece of clothing) and locations (on a road, in a room or in one's hands) to capture the subtle meaning of a message. For example, if you See a red boat speeding on a lake, and if its shade of red for you means 'too much excitement' or 'danger', then your message will include a recommendation to slow down, be more attentive and careful. On the other hand, if you See a speeding boat that is green where its particular shade of green for you means 'balance' or 'well-being', then your message will confirm the stable and beneficial nature of a fast route ahead. In the following exercise, you will

- focus on each color,
- notice what you See, Sense, Hear, Smell or Taste,
- grasp the meaning of the color, and
- record what you receive.

For example, in the two samples in the chart below, first I focus on the color 'white ': I open with my soul senses, and I See and Sense a soft white color, and I record this. I become aware of a sense of purity and goodness with this color and I record this as its meaning. Second, I focus on the color 'orange': I open with my soul senses, and I See and Sense a bright, clear orange color and I record this. My first impression with this color is optimism and energy, and I record this as its meaning. I will walk you through this exercise step-by-step. As always, read the instructions before you begin. Have a pen ready to record your findings on the chart below.

Prepare
Sit in your sacred place. Close your eyes and pray. Take a few deep breaths and relax. Call on your spirit light or guide to draw you up to an elevated state. Relax. Be at peace. ... Focus within and look up in your mind and notice a clearing – like a sky or a screen – in or above your head. Let the light of spirit illumine the white space before you. ... Let your

own shining life brighten your soul senses and open your Eye, Ear, Sense, Smell and Taste. ... Prepare to be shown each color by Spirit in a clear and positive way that nurtures your soul.

Focus on Each Color
Begin with the first color, Red. It emerges now before you on the screen of your mind. Be aware of how alive it is, how vital its energy as it comes to you from the unseen. What do you See? ... Sense? ... Do you Hear, Smell or Taste it? ... You may use one or several senses. What shade of the color do you perceive? ... How would you describe it? ... Are you picking up anything else?

Grasp the Meaning of the Color
What is your first impression as you perceive your color? ... That is your meaning. If you don't get a first impression, notice what you feel or Sense as you view your color. ... That is your meaning. Or perhaps you have a strong reaction to it deep within. What is it? ... That's your meaning. Some of you will have a thought with it. ... That may be your meaning. Or if nothing is clear, ask Spirit for a word, thought, feeling or sensation to get its meaning.

Record What You Receive
Open your eyes and retain your inner focus. Write down what you perceived and its meaning in the spaces provided. Be brief and move from one color to the next without doubting yourself. A color has many shades and meanings. Whatever you receive is just right for you at this time. Throughout the exercise, maintain your heightened state of connection to the unseen to the best of your ability.

You may find it easier to limit the exercise to four or five colors for your first sitting. Then return to it another day and select another group. Feel free to do this with other exercises.

The Meaning of Color		
Color	What I See, Sense, Hear, Smell, Taste	Meaning
Sample white	I See and Sense a soft white	purity, goodness
Sample orange	I See and Sense a bright, clear orange	optimism, energy
Red		
Orange		
Yellow		
Green		
Pink		
Blue		
Purple		
Violet		
White		
Gray		
Gold		
Silver		
Add More Colors:		

> *My Experience:*

_____

_____

_____

You may have begun to notice the vibrant nature of color when you perceive them in the unseen. They exert a strong impact on our subtle nature, and for this reason, are used in meditations for healing and other benefits. (If you wish to further your understanding of the nature of color, see *The Power of Rays: The Science of Colour Healing* and *Colour Meditations: With Guide to Colour Healing* by S.G.J. Ouseley.)

→ Exercise: Explore the Meaning of Animals

Our spirit guides and teachers bring us messages through the vibrations of animals (including birds and other living creatures). As you discover the meaning they bring to you, you will realize their power to help you. Attuning to animals in the unseen dimension of life is sometimes called 'animal medicine' (See *Animal – Speak: The Spiritual and Magical Powers of Creatures Great and Small* by Ted Andrews) because their healing energies touch us deep within. Some of you may even have an animal as one of your spirit guides! (See Part III.)

Since animals are more complex than colors, the meanings you receive from them will likely be more detailed. You may perceive them in lively ways; they may talk or bring guidance with their words or behavior. Or you may commune with them silently with your heart, thought or instinct, as well as your inner soul senses. For example, you may See a beaver building a damn and Hear the words 'get busy'. A wolf may call to you to run through the woods, and teach you how to shed old ways and be free. Or a deer stands in the midst of young saplings, and as it chews their new green leaves, you Taste the fresh nourishment of the leafy greens and realize your own system's needs. These are symbolic messages, but you may also be given literal messages; for example, you Sense a familiar pet that passed away a few years ago, who comes through with love that lifts your sagging spirit, or a baby blackbird you rescued appears squawking assertively, just as it did in real life, and you're reminded to speak your own mind too. Follow the same procedure as you did in the prior exercise. Before you begin, fill out the left hand column with some animals of your choice.

The Meaning of Animals		
Animal	What I See, Sense, Hear, Smell, Taste	Meaning
Deer		
Raccoon		
Blue Jay		
Bear		

Wolf		
Cat		
Add More Animals:		

My Experience:

_____

_____

_____

➔ Exercise: Explore Your Own Interests (Optional)

In addition to understanding the meaning of colors and animals, you can explore many categories of things. Consider the random list of things below. Choose one that interests you. For example, if gems appeal to you, make a list of different kinds of gems and repeat the exercise above. You can derive whole systems of knowledge from this simple method. For example, if you make a list of numbers, and attune to them with your soul senses through Spirit guidance, you can develop an understanding of numerology. An exploration of shapes can begin your study of sacred geometry. If you focus on parts of the body with your soul senses, you can use your natural ability to be a medical intuitive. Attune to flowers and plants and you gain knowledge of their healing properties such as, their use as herbs and essences. Meditation on sacred symbols is a way to grow spiritually.

Let yourself be guided by Spirit as you probe the unseen dimension for its treasures. You never know what wonders you will uncover to help you grow and flourish.

Birds • Numbers • Gems • Planets • Shapes • Parts of the Body • Flowers • Sacred Symbols • Whales

Add More Items: _____

_____

_____

The Meaning of _____ (My Choice)		
List	What I See, Hear, Sense, Smell or Taste	Meaning

An Ongoing Learning

Each of you is creating your own inner vocabulary that appeals to you and your spirit guides and teachers. Be guided from within. You may be tempted to look for the meanings of things in books, or on the Internet, in the belief that you don't have the knowledge within yourselves. And while there is a great deal of expertise out there, you can find out what you seek by opening your soul senses and attuning to Spirit for guidance. Further you *need* to do this: It builds your mediumship 'muscles' because you learn to rely on your gifts and Spirit's guidance. You learn to trust in the value of what you receive. Always seek your answers *first* by using your own natural abilities. *Then*, when you want to get more information, look elsewhere. You will gain confidence when you find confirmation of your own meaning in a book or on the Internet. And if you don't, realize that your own messages are right for you, that you perceived something the author didn't. For a reference book on symbols and their meanings, see *The Secret Language of Symbols* by David Fontana

Strengthen Your Gifts

This is a change of pace. You may want to focus on only one gift at a sitting and return to it periodically in your daily practice.

➔ Exercise: Open Your Gifts to the Unseen World and Enhance Them

We are all born with the gifts of our soul, yet most of us haven't used them in our lives. Here you will learn how to bring them to life. Your spirit light or guide (whatever works best for you at the moment) will help you to:

- clear and cleanse to make room for each soul sense to emerge, and
- nurture it with the manna it needs to grow and become strong.

Prepare

Sit in your sacred place. Close your eyes and pray. Relax and be comfortable as you call on your spirit light or guide to lift you up into an awareness of your soul self. Enjoy this time to explore your soul senses and relax. … Feel free and light in your elevated state. … Be at peace. …

Clairvoyance: Clear Soul Seeing

Cleanse and Clear: Look into your mind and notice any mental clutter that might interfere with your inner clarity. Is your mind busy with concerns of the day? Do thoughts fly in and out, or conflict with each other? Is it dark or light? Happy, calm, confused? Be aware of your mental state without trying to change it. Now ask your spirit light or guide to shine into your mind as you open it for cleansing and clearing. Watch what happens. … How do you feel with this difference? … Perhaps Spirit has some guidance for you.

Nurture: As you look up, let Spirit open your soul Eye to the unseen sky and its loving light. Allow your inner Eye to be touched and nurtured by the soothing light vibration. Sense your inner Vision seeking the light and moving up to embrace it. Now your Vision expands as everything around you fills with sparkling light. Notice a new clarity in your expanded Vision. Stay with your new Vision.

▸ *My Experience:*

_____

_____

Clairaudience: Clear Soul Hearing

Cleanse and clear: Look into your mind and become aware of any noise that interferes with your inner quiet. Are you talking to yourself? Are there other voices or sounds coming and going? Is your mind chaotic or calm? Relaxed, open or overwhelmed? Be aware of your inner state without trying to change it. Now ask your spirit light or guide to pour quiet vibrations into your mind as you open it for cleansing and clearing. Listen to what happens. … How do you feel with this difference? Perhaps Spirit has some guidance for you.

Nurture

As you direct your inner Ear upwards, let Spirit open it to the unseen sky and its heavenly silence. Allow your inner Ear to be touched and nourished by the healing vibration of pure silence. Sense your inner Ear seeking the silence and reaching up to be filled with it. … Now your inner Hearing blends with the silence as the vast reaches of space are filled with its infinite quiet. Notice how your Ear is acutely aware of the sound of silence. Stay with your new state of inner Hearing.

▸ *My Experience:*

_____

_____

Clairsentience: Clear Soul Sensing

Cleanse and clear: Look into your system and be aware of any stress that interferes with your sensitivity to your soul Sense. Are you letting old hurts or resentments disturb your calm? Are you prone to aches or physical tension? Is your general state unsettled or stable? Loving, peaceful or heavy? Be aware of your inner system without trying to change it. Now ask your spirit light or guide to infuse your system with life as you open it for cleansing and clearing. Sense what happens. … How do you feel with this difference? Perhaps Spirit has some guidance for you.

Nurture: As you direct your inner Sense upwards, let Spirit open it to the unseen sky and its life. Allow your soul Sense to be awakened and soothed by the energy of vital life. … Be aware of your inner Sense, reaching up to infinite life to be filled with its nourishment. Now your soul Sense blends with it and everything in the vast expanse of space is alive with joyful life. Notice a new sensitivity and openness with your expanded soul Sense. Stay in this state.

▸ *My Experience:*
_____
_____

Clairscent and Clairgustance

Cleanse and clear: We will deal briefly with Clairscent and Clairgustance since they are less commonly used. Notice the smells and tastes that linger in your system that interfere with your ability to Smell and Taste the ones that come from the unseen. Let your spirit light or guide bring vibrations of freshness and purity to your inner states, and notice how old stale smells and tastes disappear.

Nurture: Open these soul senses to Spirit and become aware of the vibrations of purity and freshness from the unseen. … Take them in and notice your newly awakened states of inner Smell and Taste. Stay in them. …

▸ *My Experience:*
_____
_____

Return
Give thanks and return to your awareness in your sacred space.

Gain a Deeper Understanding of the Language of Spirit

➔ Exercise: Use Your Soul Senses to Deepen Your Understanding of Spirit Messages

As usual, read over the worksheet below. Have a pen ready to record what you receive. Using the worksheet, you will open your gifts to Spirit to receive messages as you focus on each item. I will guide you step-by-step to use all your soul senses to get as much detail and clarity as you can. Don't force anything. At the same time, you want to seek upwards with your soul senses and stretch yourself. As you reach into the unseen towards Spirit, open your soul senses and allow whatever you perceive to come to you. Open to the life of each thing, event or creature and let it reveal itself to you. This is its meaning. This is the message being given to you.

For example, consider the first item –**Bird**. As you call on Spirit and open with your soul senses, suppose you Hear the whirring of sparrows' wings. You Sense the gentle lightness of their flight, and See several at a bird feeder, flitting about with excitement. You feel lighthearted and free in your spirit. You continue to watch and the whole scene seems bathed in spiritual energy that revitalizes you. The meaning or message you receive: Be lighthearted and free in your spirit. Let your spiritual energies revitalize you.

Prepare
(Try this shortened form of relaxation and readiness.) Sit in your sacred place and close your eyes. Begin with a simple prayer: ask for positive messages to help you. … Take a few deep breaths and relax. Relax. …

Attune to Spirit's Presence
Call on your spirit light or guide to help you. Reach up to the higher planes with your heart and mind. Relax and let yourself be lifted up in your soul, free from your earthly self. Be at home in this lighter self. Float up and release all concerns. … Look up with your inner senses now, and open them to a space in front and above you. You may be aware of it as the sky, your mind or a screen that is clear and bright. Open to your Sense of spirit's presence nearby. Be at peace and let your mind be open to receive. … Ask Spirit to communicate with uplifting, clear images, bright light and sweet soothing sounds, where you are moved in your soul senses in positive ways.

Perceive a Bird
When you're ready, open your eyes and glance at the first word **Bird**. Close them and ask Spirit 'Please show me a bird.' As you wait with your soul senses open to the sky, notice that a bird appears before you. What is your first impression? What do you See? What is it doing? What color is it? Are there more than one? What do you Sense? Do you Hear anything? What do you Smell? Do you have any sense of Taste with it? Stay for a while with this bird that has come to you in the unseen world. From this bird's presence, what message do you pick up? … Can you Sense its life? What is it showing or telling you? …   Does it have a symbolic or a literal meaning? Or both? …

Now as you open your eyes to record what you perceived, stay up in your elevated mind; that is, stay in a kind of light trance so you can return inwardly again to your soul senses and move to your next item. Use the worksheet to describe your bird and record your message. (You may want to open and close your eyes as you receive information.)

Perceive Music
Glance now at the next word **Music.** Close your eyes, relax again and feel yourself in an elevated state. Take your time and enjoy your explorations. Quietly open with your soul Ear. Ask Spirit to bring you sounds of music in an uplifting way and wait. … Now begin to Hear music. What is your first impression? What kind of music is it? Listen and notice if there are other things involved here, such as instruments or people's voices. … Do you See anything with this music? Many kinds of sounds can be music such as the sound of water or a gentle breeze. Notice all the details of your music message. … Do you Sense the life of the musical sounds brought to you from the unseen? Do you Taste or Smell anything? What message is the music bringing to you? … Does it have a symbolic or literal meaning, or both? When you are ready, open your eyes and record what you have perceived while you maintain your higher state of consciousness. Remember to ask Spirit when you need help.

Perceive a House
Move to the next word **House** and close your eyes. Open your inner senses and look up to the space above. Be uplifted as you ask Spirit to bring a house to you to perceive with your soul senses. Now a house emerges on the screen. What is your first impression? Do you See, Sense, Hear, Smell or Taste the presence of a house? What does it look like? Does it have a yard or garden? What do you Sense as you view this house? Are there any people with your house? You may want to go inside or perhaps you're already in one of the rooms. Attune to your surroundings with your inner senses and become aware of the message your house brings you from the unseen. You may Hear it in words or Sense it. Let it speak to you. Does it have a symbolic or literal meaning? Or both? When you are ready, open your eyes and record your perception.

Perceive a Star
The next word is **Star**. Close your eyes and open to the space before you. Make sure you are in an uplifted state. If not, take time to relax with a few deep breaths and revisit your meditation. Watch now as a star appears before you. What is your first impression? Notice it with all your soul senses. I leave you to do this on your own now. … Attune to the life of your star and be aware of the message it brings to you. When you are ready, open your eyes and record your experience.

Perceive a Vehicle

Now see the word **Vehicle** and close your eyes. Reach up with your inner senses and ask Spirit to show you a vehicle. Keep your mind up and allow a vehicle to be shown to you on your screen. What kind is it? What is your first impression? What do you See? Sense? Hear? Smell? Taste? … Notice all the details given to you and continue on your own. … Take your time to open to the message your vehicle brings to you from the unseen dimension. Open your eyes when you're ready and record your experience.

Perceive an Item of Your Choice

See the item that you have selected and close your eyes. Look up within and focus on the sky before you as your selection emerges. What is your first impression? Open your soul senses to it and become aware of all the details presented to you. … Continue on your own and enjoy your exploration of your chosen item as you perceive it in the unseen. … Does it have a symbolic or literal meaning or both? Let your item speak to you. Awaken to its life and let its meaning come. When you're ready, open your eyes and record your experience.

Return

Give thanks to Spirit and gradually return to your sacred place. Take a few deep breaths and be aware of your physical body. Look around and notice your surroundings.

A Deeper Understanding of the Language of Spirit		
Item	What I See, Hear, Sense, Smell and Taste	Meaning/Message
Bird		
Music		
House		
Star		
Vehicle		
My Choice		

▸ *My Experience:*

Which soul sense(s) were you especially pleased with? What do you like about your gift(s)? _____

_____

_____

Which soul sense(s) are more challenging for you? What would you like to be able to do? _____

What message(s) was (were) most significant for you? What made it (them) so? _____

Take time with God in prayer and Spirit in quiet reflection and ask for help with your development. With an open heart and mind, you will receive what you need to enhance your strengths and overcome your challenges. Your answers may come in messages perceived with your soul senses, or you may receive an insight in a dream or any time of the day when you least expect it. Ask and trust in the guidance of the higher powers.

→ Exercise: Receive a Message by Asking

You should do only one or two of these exercises in one sitting. Later on, as you give messages and readings, you may want to return to these questions to gain guidance for yourself or others.

We begin now to link the messages we receive from Spirit to our specific interests and concerns. For example, you may have received a message that was uplifting and moving, but you wondered what it meant in the context of your life. Was it a message of optimism about the job interview coming up next week? Did it refer to positive results you were praying for regarding a family situation? Or was it a message about your life in general?

Here are some simple ways to gain answers from Spirit about your life. Read over the exercise. After you ask your question, sit in a receptive attitude and allow Spirit's answer to be shown to you as you open your soul senses to receive. Be confident in your natural gift to perceive the unseen, and trust in Spirit's loving guidance. Record what you perceive (#1). Then open to the meaning or message that you pick up from what you perceive, just as you did above and record (#2). Prepare and meditate as you did in the prior exercise.

→ Exercise

Ask Spirit: How am I doing at this time in my life?

1. What I See, Hear, Sense, Smell and Taste: _____
_____
_____
_____

2. My Message _____
_____
_____

Ask Spirit for a question of your choice. _____

1. What I See, Hear, Sense, Smell and Taste: _____
_____
_____
_____

2. My Message _____
_____
_____

Ask Spirit for help with a situation. _____

1. What I See, Hear, Sense, Smell and Taste: _____
_____
_____
_____

2. My Message _____
_____
_____

Ask Spirit for a gift. Let spirit put a gift in your hands as you hold them out. Sensing it through touch may make it clearer to you.

1. What I See, Hear, Sense, Smell and Taste: _____
_____

2. My Message _____

Yes or No

You will ask a question where the answer is either *yes* or *no* (or *'true'* or *'false'* respectively), but first you need to determine how to perceive a *yes* and a *no*. To do this ask a question where you know that the answer is *yes*, such as (for me), Is my name Judith? and another where you know the answer is *no*, such as, Is my name Matilda? In each case, notice what you perceive and record it. For example, for a *yes* answer, you may hear a harmonious melody, sense a warm feeling or see a sunset; for a *no* answer, you may sense a grating of metal, hear a harsh horn or see a gray sky. Or you may simply Hear or See the words.

Ask Spirit your known yes question. _____

What I See, Hear, Sense, Smell and Taste: _____

You now know that what you perceived **means** *yes.*

Ask Spirit your known no question. _____

What I See, Hear, Sense, Smell and Taste: _____

You now know that what you perceived **means** *no.*

Now you are ready to ask a question where you don't know whether it has a *yes* or *no* answer, but you want to be able to find out in order to check the accuracy of your answer, such as Does the book on my desk have over 200 pages? or Will it rain tonight?

Ask Spirit your yes/no question where the answer is unknown to you. _____

What I See, Hear, Sense, Smell and Taste: _____

From what you perceived, you know whether your answer is yes or no. You can use this method for questions where you may not be able to verify the answer but you will know that what you have received is accurate.

→ Exercise: Ask for Messages to Help My Partner

Another way to understand messages in the context of your lives is to work with a partner. You give and get messages. Do the exercise at the same time as your partner, then share what you have received and give feedback, each taking your turn. In the course of your sharing, you will become aware of how each message applies to your life. If you are studying alone, partner with someone at a distance with whom you feel comfortable. Know that whether your partner can *take* (accept) your message or not, what you receive from Spirit has merit. At this stage, your primary aim is to learn to work with Spirit. Read the exercise together. Fill in Step 2. *Your Partner's Choice* for each other. Also consider a question you would like answered by Spirit and record it in Step 3 before you begin.

Prepare with a relaxation and meditation of your own choice.

Step 1. With love in your heart, pray for your partner's happiness and ask Spirit that your messages contribute to it.

Step 2. Receive messages from Spirit for your partner using the chart below. Do this silently at the same time as your partner.

	Messages for My Partner	
	What I See, Hear, Sense, Smell and Taste	*My Message*
Tree		
Scene		
Animal		
A Piece of Jewelry		
Your Partner's Choice		

Step 3. You and your partner will silently write down a question you would like answered.

My Question _____

Step 4: Without knowing your partner's question, ask Spirit for an answer and record your perception and the message in the chart below.

What I See, Sense, Hear, Smell and Taste: _____

_____

The Message: _____

_____

_____

Step 5. Take turns to share the messages you have received, and record them in the spaces below. As you do this, stay in your elevated states of contact with Spirit, and ask for insight into the area in your lives to which each message is directed. Notice how Spirit helps you. Discuss with your partner and explore this together.

Be open to your partner. If a message has meaning for you, share your response. If it doesn't, there is a protocol to follow: Say something like ' I can't place it now but I will take it, thank you.,' 'I will think about it, thank you', or simply 'Thank you'. Be gracious and kind. Help each other in gentle and supportive ways.

Messages Received from My Partner for Me		
	What I See, Hear, Sense, Smell and Taste	*My Messages*
Tree		
Scene		
Animal		
A Piece of Jewelry		
My Choice		
Answer to My Question:		

Later in the quiet of your sacred place, ask Spirit for guidance regarding the messages you got from your partner. Also, do this with the feedback from your partner about the messages you gave. This helps you to ground yourself in your own understanding and not become overly influenced by another's feedback – whether it is 'negative' or 'positive'.

Let Spirit Guide You in Your Daily Life

Guidance and Your Life

The Law of Life
When my spirit guides came to me many years ago and touched my soul, they also awakened me to my world. They showed me that the law of life worked in all things, in all my conditions. When I connected to that life through my daily challenges, I perceived the truth from Spirit's eye and began to grow as a soul. For example, some of my earliest messages were about travel. Spirit showed me the way through difficult driving conditions. With their guidance, my attitudes changed over the years, from my sense of travel as an inconvenience, to a respect for all of us sojourners, from all walks of life, traveling together. With this appreciation of my situation, my travels went smoothly; things would work out well. I was more connected to my world and its life.

In the area of work, Spirit helped me on a day-to-day basis: from showing me how to change my anxiety about teaching, to a love of helping others learn, and to a trust in my soul's longing to find my way to spiritual service. As a single parent, I was shown how to release my judgments of how my children should be, to See the beauty and power of their souls, and to realize that I was the guardian of their own magnificent journeys, guided by God and Spirit with loving appreciation.

Kinds of Guidance
Through Spirit guidance, we may seek comfort, information, or inspiration. Sometimes we need healing. We may want confirmation that we're on track. Or we may seek insight or direction about a situation that is troubling. Sometimes we need reassurance that things will work out, even if it's not quite the way we hoped. At others times, we are faced with difficulties that are so overwhelming, we don't know where to turn, what to do.

Nothing is Too Difficult for Spirit
It is a great comfort to know that our spirit guides and teachers can draw near and guide us no matter what our difficulty. All we need to do is open and ask – as long as we want answers, as long as we genuinely seek. Trust Spirit on a daily basis and you will be amazed by Spirit's ability to know your deep inner states, and from their enlightened perspective, to draw you into your higher self where you are at-one with the unseen and can overcome the obstacles on your path.

A Special Kind of Help

We are moved by Spirit's guidance in ways that other kinds of help don't do because the messages come to us from within: Spirit communicates soul-to-soul where we are brought to life by this contact. As a result, it is always beneficial. It opens us to a greater awareness of our true nature, our higher self. Through spirit guidance in our daily life, we are opened to the unseen, to a sense of its goodness, reality, its love and intelligence operating in our lives.

A Higher Perspective

Guidance brings a fresh perspective to a situation. It comes through a glimpse of the truth, a melting heart, a renewed strength, a clear vision and in a thousand unexpected ways. We realize that all is well after all, that we are human and that feels good. Another piece of our self comes to life and we can step forward on our path. Further, their help comes to us with a compassion beyond our heart's experience, an intelligence that surpasses our normal mind, and a goodness that only our soul knows within its depths. In their presence, we can seek without fear of judgment or rejection. And as we receive guidance from Spirit, we become the person we know in our hearts we truly are, and we can be at home in this world.

↠ Exercise: Reflect on the Guidance You Have Received from Spirit

Think of a particular message of guidance you received from Spirit that you especially liked.

Describe it: _____

_____

_____

What did you like about it? _____

_____

_____

_____

↠ Exercise: Your Life and Your Conditions

Is there any specific kind of guidance you are you seeking at this time? For example, you may feel a strong need for healing, or perhaps reassurance. Or you may need direction right now in your life. The following diagram depicts the major kinds of conditions in most people's lives. Read it and notice if it reflects the situations in your life. Cross off any that don't apply and add ones that do. In the blank diagram provided for you on the next page, rearrange them to portray your life. Include every condition that is relevant to you.

Your Life: Your Conditions

HOW TO BECOME A MEDIUM

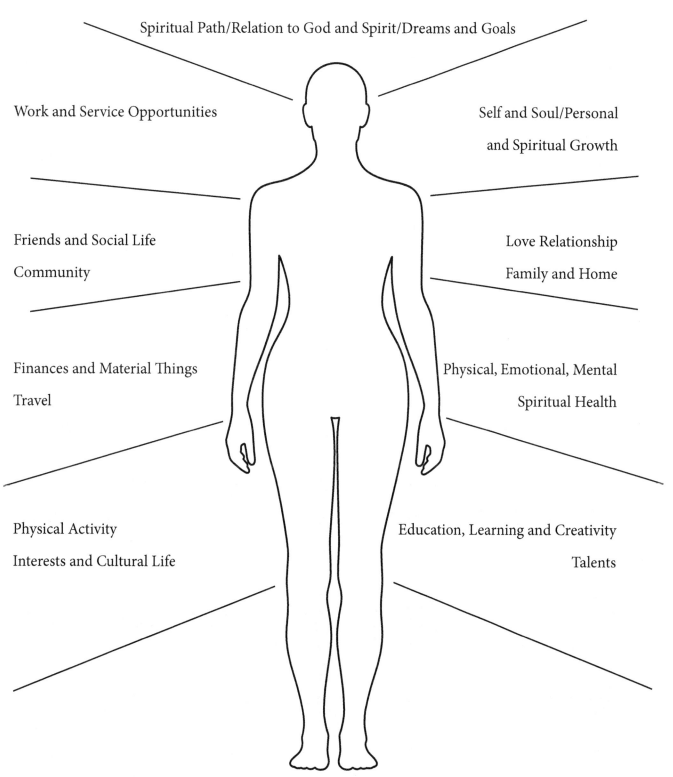

Note: Diagrams similar to this can be found in many books on spiritual and self development. There is no specific relevance to the placement of each category beside the diagram.

My Life: My Conditions

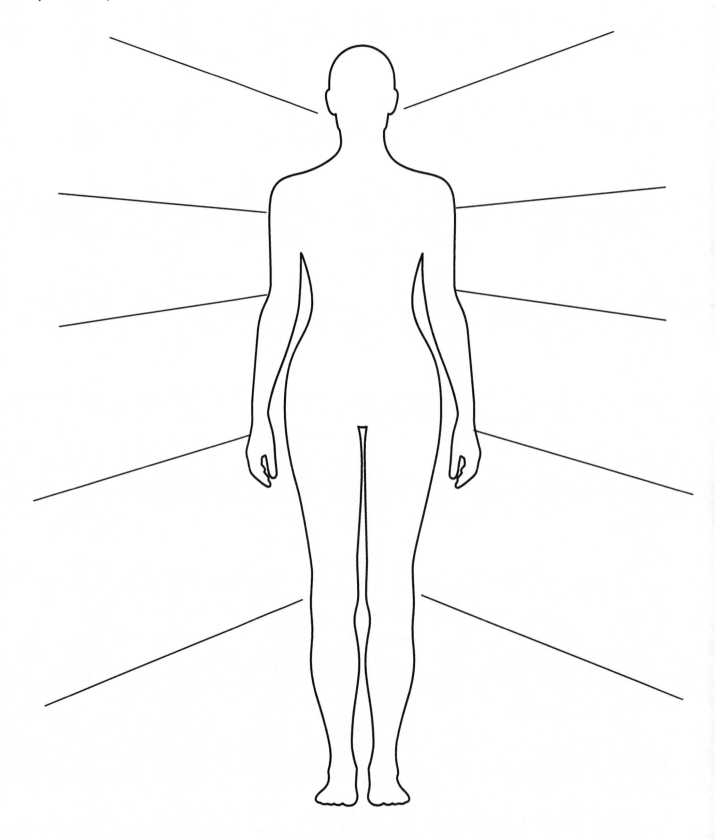

My Situation

What are the conditions in your life for which you might want to receive guidance from Spirit? Look over your diagram of *My Life: My Conditions*. Pay special attention to your areas of greatest need or interest and select *one situation* for which you would like to receive guidance from Spirit. It may be Family and Home, or your main focus right now may be on developing your Talents. Or perhaps Finances may be most pressing. *Star it.* Describe your situation and your feelings connected with it.

My Situation: _____

_____

_____

How I Feel About it: _____

_____

_____

Find Strength in Your Soul to Face Challenges: What to Do with a Disappointing Message

We all face difficulties in our lives. A strong sense of our inner life can buoy us up and help us to handle them with optimism. Sometimes a message of guidance from Spirit will reveal a condition in a 'negative' light. Often our first reaction is fear. We may get upset or angry. These are reactions to what we perceive as a threat to our stability. Even the smallest sign of something wrong in our lives can challenge our trust in the goodness of the world and our self-worth. What are we to do with a disappointing message?

First, remind yourself that you are a soul and stay rooted in this strong sense of yourself. Know that nothing can harm your shining life within, and that you live in a world of goodness and loving light. You may want to sit quietly in your sacred place, and pray, relax and meditate to reconnect with your divine self.

Second, realize that as a soul you are learning to grow through your earthly challenges. Also, your soul provides the strength to make the changes needed to progress on your spiritual path. Then call on Spirit and discuss your situation to gain understanding. Let your spirit guide show you how to change the situation in the unseen dimension. Trust in the guidance of Spirit and the presence of God to help you unfold, and notice the difference in your life.

Some further insights:

- An unsettling message may be the result of too much stress and too little time to relax and be quiet within. Slow down. Sit in your sacred place and prepare yourself for Spirit communication before you ask for guidance. If you are worried, fearful, and angry, for example, spend time in your daily practice to get help from God and Spirit to deal with these states.

- A negative message may be the projection of your own anxiety: Spirit's message comes to you through your mental filter. At the same time, recognize that your mental states, no matter how troubled, are valuable ways to learn.

- Sometimes we are given a message that helps us to prepare for a difficult situation, and Spirit is ready to help us to meet the challenge ahead. And as many of us know, it's often through trying times that we are transformed in magnificent ways we could never have foreseen.

- Ultimately, as we gain Spirit's perspective, we have a greater sense of our soul nature and the unseen operating in our life. Our problems don't disappear, but we learn to handle them with greater mastery and understanding of our divine purpose.

→ Exercise: Let God and Spirit Shine in Your Life

This is a simplified version of the prayer exercises in Chapter One. Here you learn to be a strong channel for God and Spirit, and send love, life and light to help yourself and others.

Prepare
Sit quietly in your sacred place and look at the diagram of your life and your conditions. Close your eyes and pray: Call on God to draw near as you sit in a receptive state. Open to God's presence and focus on divine love. Reach up and let God's love come to you. Sit and allow God's outpouring of love to flow into you. Embrace the divine love in you. Filled with infinite love, See yourself in the diagram surrounded by your life's conditions and Sense God's love pouring out to you and your situations in life. Notice how you feel in this world of love.

Let the Light Shine into Your Life
Call on your spirit light or guide and notice how close you are to Spirit's uplifting vibration. Be aware of how easily you breathe. Sense Spirit's light as it pours into you and brightens your entire being. Your soul shines with new life. As the inner light overflows in you, it expands into all the conditions of your life. It shines into them with the luster and beauty of the unseen. See and Sense them in the light of Spirit. Enjoy your higher state.

Let the Loving Light Shine into the World
Sense yourself now as a channel of God and Spirit: Let the loving light and life flow from you and through your conditions into the world. Ask that the situations of those in need be healed. Let any who come to mind receive healing, as you sit in the power of the Infinite and shine. Remind yourself often that with God's presence and Spirit's guidance, you can help yourself and others. When we attune to the nourishing love, light and life of the unseen, we are all transformed.

Return
When you are ready, give thanks to God and Spirit and gently return to your sacred place. Open your eyes and be aware of how you feel.

My Experience: _____

_____

_____

Attune to Spirit for Guidance in Your Life

In this exercise, you will receive guidance from Spirit for the condition that you starred above on your diagram. You will learn how to:

- attune more closely to your spirit light or guide

- ask Spirit for guidance with your situation

- open to the unseen and receive guidance from Spirit with your soul senses

- discuss your message with Spirit and gain insight into its meaning

- if necessary, let Spirit change your message to help with your situation

HOW TO BECOME A MEDIUM

➤ Exercise: Receive Guidance for a Situation in My Life

When you read over the exercise, notice that in your preparation, you are invited to relax with a method of your choice. Please feel free to do this for any exercise or meditation. I use *Be Aware of Your Breath* throughout the book because it's a powerful way to reach deep states of relaxation with ease.

Prepare
Sit quietly in your sacred place, close your eyes and pray. … Relax with an exercise of your choice. …

Attune to Spirit
Call on your spirit light or guide to draw near and help you with your situation. Relax and be aware of your breath. … Reach up with your heart and mind. Ask Spirit to come close. … Relax. Continue to focus upwards and ask Spirit to be with you. … Begin to notice a fine, uplifting vibration around you. Attune to it and let it become stronger. … How at home you feel in its presence! This is the influence of your spirit light or guide who draws near and helps you now to sense your soul within you. You feel lighter as you release yourself from your earthly world. … As a spirit, float upward. Let go. … Embrace your feeling of freedom and joy as you experience the unseen dimension of life.

Reach Up to Receive a Message
Next notice a clearing before you. Here you will receive a message from Spirit with your soul senses which brings guidance for the condition you starred in your diagram. Ask that help be given in an uplifting way. … Now notice that you are more aware of Spirit's presence than ever before. Sense the higher vibrations of light and love around you. … Feel an elevated state of your soul brought on by Spirit's positive influence. You may begin to See or Sense your spirit guide as a being who stands beside you.

Ask for Guidance from Spirit
Recognize this presence in whatever form you perceive, and give thanks. Request guidance for the situation you've identified above, and continue to keep your soul senses open. You may do it by making a general request, such as 'Please help me with ….' or 'I need guidance with ….' or 'Please show me the truth about ….' as you bring to mind the condition. Or you may want to ask a specific question about your condition, and include a time frame, like, 'Will my work improve in the next six months?' or a calendar date, such as, 'When is the best time to travel this winter?'. Or use any of the methods from above, such as using an item, or asking for a symbolic or literal message.

Open Your Soul Senses to Receive Guidance
Focus your soul senses ahead, and notice that the clearing before you is illuminated with a soft loving light. … Your perception is clearer than ever before. Now open your gifts to receive your message of guidance from Spirit. … What is your first impression? What do you See in the clearing or ethereal sky above you. … What do you Sense? … Hear? … Perhaps you even experience a Smell or Taste. …

Perhaps you See your situation or a scene unfold before your inner Eye. Or Spirit may talk to you with words that you can Hear: your message comes in a conversation. … You may See a symbol that represents the meaning that Spirit wants to convey. … Perhaps you are a part of what you perceive. Notice every detail of the message that is given you by Spirit from the unseen. … How do you feel as you witness this portrayal of your life? …

Discuss and Fine Tune Your Message
To grasp the meaning of your message with greater clarity, ask Spirit to write a word or sentence in the upper portion of the clearing. … Or listen to Spirit's spoken word. … See how this helps you. To gain a fuller understanding of your situation, you may want to See a symbol that captures Spirit's message. Ask to be shown one beside your original message. … Also, ask for greater details if you want them, and Listen to Spirit's reply, or See or Sense your answer. …

Change Your Message

here may be changes you would like to make to the message you receive to improve your situation and bring more harmony and happiness to your life. Ask Spirit for help and discuss it as Spirit makes the adjustments right before you. … Finally, let your spirit light or guide talk with you about your situation. Open your inner Ear and Listen for further guidance. Take this opportunity to share your heart with this loving intelligence who comes to help you in your daily life. … If you have received a clear, short, satisfactory message, you may want to ask for guidance with another condition at this time.

Prepare to Leave

It's time to take your leave. But before you do, make a special mental note of your message, and resolve to keep it close to your heart and mind to reinforce your connection to God, Spirit and the unseen in your daily life. …

Return

Your message fades in the clearing ahead and you prepare to leave. Thank your spirit light or guide for the guidance you have received. … When you are ready, come gently down from your elevated state to your normal consciousness. … Be aware that you are sitting in your sacred place. Take a few deep breaths and open your eyes. Give thanks to God for all you have received.

▸ *My Experience:*

How did I feel with my spirit light or guide? _____

_____

What guidance did I receive for my situation(s)? _____

_____

What words and/or symbol did I receive? _____

_____

What soul senses did I use to receive Spirit's message? _____

_____

What was the content of my discussion with Spirit? _____

_____

What changes did I make, if any? _____

_____

How was I helped? _____

_____

_____

Know the Truth

You want to be able to rely on the *truth* of the messages you receive from your spirit guide; you want to *know* that the information you gain from the unseen is accurate. For example, I'm anxious about an eye appointment tomorrow, and I want to know how it will go. During my daily practice, I ask Spirit for guidance about it. I'm pleased when I Sense a comforting 'no need to worry' message from Spirit. Yet I wonder if I'm deluding myself. So I ask again. And I get the same soothing message. Now, I'm no longer anxious and enjoy a productive day. At the doctor's office the next day, I learn that my vision is fine. Spirit showed me the truth, the message I received was accurate.

→ Exercise: Test the Accuracy of Spirit's Guidance

In the following exercise, you learn to test the accuracy of the guidance you receive as Spirit helps you to develop your gifts. Just as I did with my eye appointment, compare your messages of guidance from Spirit to the facts as they occur at a future time. In this way, through trial and error, Spirit will teach you to unfold your gifts. With practice, you *will know* when a message is true.

Don't be discouraged if messages that are very clear turn out to be inaccurate Know that at this stage of your learning, Spirit is like an athlete who sometimes forfeits a game in order to strengthen a set of muscles, and is not as concerned with accuracy, but with honing your gifts and creating a working relationship.

1. Sit for your daily practice in your sacred place. Close your eyes, pray, relax and ask Spirit for a message of guidance with a situation in your life that will happen in the future such as, later in the day, tomorrow, next week, month or year.

2. Record the message you receive from Spirit in the chart below. When the situation takes place, describe it and compare it to your guidance from Spirit to determine its accuracy. Do this in a natural way, as situations arise where it's beneficial to know the outcome. Don't force it or focus on trivial issues. Also, question Spirit about the details of upcoming events, such as the kinds of things you can do to handle situations effectively.

3. In each case, listen to Spirit's guidance to learn from your experience, and fine tune your gifts for greater precision and accuracy.

Guidance from Spirit About a Future Event		
My Message About a Future Event	The Actual Future Event	Spirit's Guidance
Later Today		
Tomorrow		

Next Week		
Next Month		
In the Summer		
Next Year		
Your Choice:.		

▸ *My Experience:*

_____

_____

A Guided Meditation: Meet Your Spirit Guide in Your Sanctuary

In this meditation, I will lead you to your Sanctuary in the unseen world where you meet your spirit guide who brings you guidance about your spiritual unfoldment as a medium.

Prayer
Let us begin with a prayer.

> *Divine Spirit! We give thanks for the opportunity to meet our spirit guide and receive guidance about our spiritual enfoldment and mediumship. Protect us onn our journey and keep us in your loving light, now and always, Amen.*

Prepare
Sit quietly in your sacred place. Close your eyes. … Notice your breath and relax. Relax. … Imagine your self surrounded by an infinite loving energy. As you breathe in, feel its life flowing into your lungs and relax. … As you breathe out, release the concerns of the day. Be at peace. … Breathe in this soothing vibration and let it move into all parts of your body down to the tips of your toes and up to the top of your head. Relax. … Feel it like a calming stream moving into every cell of your system. Your muscles relax; your entire body is at peace. Relax. Your mind is clear, your thoughts are still. Relax. …

My Path
In this relaxed state, feel yourself becoming lighter and released from your earthly world. Move up gently into the inner sky. Float up and notice that you feel more and more your spirit self. ... How light you are! Let go. Let yourself float up and be free ... be at peace. ... Feel the harmony in this loving energy that surrounds you in the unseen. ...

Now, look ahead to a winding path leading upward. What does it look like? ... Step onto it and walk along. How does it feel? ... It may be just like earth, or it may be entirely different. Look on either side of the path and notice what you See. ... Do you Hear anything? ... How uplifted you feel!

You round a bend and up ahead is your Sanctuary. What do you Sense as you approach this spiritual site? ... What do you See? ...

Stand before your Sanctuary and notice its entrance. ... How do you feel? ... Is there a door to open? Step across the threshold and look around. What a wondrous place! Is it a natural setting? ... Or enclosed? ... A temple? ... A room? ... Is it familiar or new? ... Open and embrace your special place. Here you are your true nature – your soul. Let yourself just be in this divine space. ...

My Spirit Guide
Now prepare to meet your spirit guide. Be aware of a presence approaching you as the light in your Sanctuary brightens with an ethereal sheen. What is your first impression of your spirit guide? ... What do you See? ... Hear? ... Sense? ... Take your time and notice every detail about the spirit presence who stands before you. ... You greet each other. How do you feel with this magnificent being? ...

Your spirit guide talks with you. Listen and notice how you feel as you Hear the voice of your spirit guide and what is said. Perhaps you Hear Spirit with your thought and communicate mind-to-mind. ...   How amazing to have this conversation! ... Feel free now to ask questions such as, 'Who are you?' ... 'Where are you from?' ... 'How are you helping me with my mediumship?' or anything that's on your mind. ...

My Sanctuary and My Soul Self
Together, you stroll around your Sanctuary. ... Your guide points out different areas in this place and explains how they reflect who you are – your divine self. ... At the same time, you realize that you are shedding old parts of yourself that are no longer beneficial to your growth – thoughts, feelings, attitudes and ideas – as you explore your space. ... What do you Sense in each area? ... See? ... Hear? ... Smell? ... Taste? ... What do you do in it, if anything? Let Spirit show you. ...

My Message
Now you sit down together. Your spirit guide prepares to bring a message to guide you at this time with your spiritual unfoldment as a medium. Perhaps you know how you want Spirit to help you. Open to Spirit's love and See a space before and above you that shines with the life and light of the unseen. ... Notice now as a magnificent message is illuminated for you. What is revealed to you? ... Notice how you feel with it. ... Is the guidance given to you in a literal message? ... A symbolic one? ...

Open with your soul senses and let your spirit guide help you to understand your message and bring you the guidance you seek. Take your time and absorb everything deep into your being. ... Thank Spirit for the teachings that support your spiritual progress. ...

My Gift
Your spirit guide has a gift for you to remind you of this experience. It may be anything – a key, an inner light, a sense of being loved, a pen, lots of time, a color, an animal or a word. Receive your gift, now, from Spirit and notice what it is.

... Open to its meaning and how it can help you on your path. ... Consult Spirit for clarity. What is this special reminder that will bring you back to the awareness of the teachings that have taken place here? ...

It's time to prepare to leave. ... You get up and walk to the entrance with your guide. ... Know that this presence is there for you as you ask and seek spiritual unfoldment to become a medium. Know too that you can return for fresh insight whenever you wish. Look around once more and give thanks to Spirit for what you have received. ...

My Journey Back

You say your goodbyes, step back over the threshold and begin your return along the path. ... Now, floating in the ethereal sky, you come down gently and slowly. ... You move closer and closer to your earthly self. ... Yet your soul is alert and shining, full of the fine vibrations of the higher spheres. Slowly you come back to your sacred place. ... When you are ready, open your eyes, look around you and notice how alive the world is!

▸ *My Experience:*

My Path _____

_____

_____

_____

My Spirit Guide _____

_____

_____

_____

My Sanctuary and My Soul Self _____

_____

_____

_____

My Message _____

_____

_____

_____

My Gift _____

_____

_____

_____

My Journey Back

Reflections on My Experience

PART II COMMUNICATE WITH SPIRIT LOVED ONES

We would speak to you all of the afterlife – not merely that life immediately following death, but the life of the spirit which is eternal, and which grows in beauty and power as it stretches into infinity. You have nothing to fear … .What is death but a sleeping and awakening to a life more radiant and more harmonious than life on earth can be?

White Eagle, Spirit Guide of Grace Cooke, "Life After Death" in Arthur Conan Doyle's *Book of the Beyond*, edited by Ivan Cooke, 244.

Connect to the Life in All Things

I sit on the edge of my mother's bed. She's dying and I can do nothing to alleviate her misery. I feel a sense of hopelessness. As she lies speechless and suffering, I feel the darkness of death and I am filled with gloom. So this is the end, I think. In my mind, death is one thing, the afterlife is another. My beliefs are vague on these things. I am taking a course on meditation, but I am not familiar with mediumship.

Perhaps Spirit empathizes with me or my mother reaches out in a final gesture of love, for without warning, a vibrant golden ball of energy appears a few feet above her head. As I stare into it, I recognize the shining vibration as my mother. It beams with her vitality, joy and even humor, and I know that without a doubt I am seeing my mother's soul. The intensity of the light that is her presence expresses a higher state of being, one untouched by suffering. She communicates to me with a rejoicing spirit and freedom beyond her normal capacity.

The golden force dissolves. I look at my mother: she is more relaxed. I feel an immense comfort for I know that her suffering will pass and that in some aspect of her consciousness even now, her soul is vibrant with joy. A week after her death, she appeared in the same way, a shining golden energy, exuding her vivacious personality and humor. Then she became her old self in her favorite soft blue dress and wavy gray hair. She talked with a lightheartedness I hadn't seen in her for some years and I felt relief that my mother was happy and free from pain.

The fact that she is actually alive in the afterlife fills me with a pervading calm – my mother has simply passed from this life to the next. Her soul has moved to a higher existence. Through contact with the spirit of my mother, I know that life is eternal.

I realize that now I can live in this world without fear, for nothing can destroy my spirit. In my new awareness of eternal life, I feel a buoyancy and release from a burden that has shadowed me through life – a heavy dread of death. I am filled with light and optimism. The world is full of life right to its end and beyond. I feel a power from my communication with the spirit of my mother, a joy that stays with me and creates a sense of the triumph of the spirit over suffering. I know the truth of the continuity of life from my soul-to-soul connection with my spirit loved one. I have been touched in my soul and this has changed me forever.

My mother demonstrated the corner-stone of mediumship – she showed me that without a doubt, she was still alive in the beyond. In a message or a reading, a medium brings information that proves that a spirit loved one of the sitter exists on another plane of life. The sitter *knows* that her loved one is still alive. She no longer relies on belief or faith as I too had tried to do. This *knowing* brings the sitter to an awareness of the truth of eternal life – death is not an end but a transition from one state of existence to another. The joy and freedom the soul realizes with this affirmation of life is indescribable. But how does a medium identify *unfamiliar spirit loved ones*; that is, family and friends of someone else in spirit? The answer lies with the law of vibration – and one's gifts.

Law of Vibration

The *law of vibration*, operating in the unseen world, states that everything – people, natural objects, things, events, and all living creatures on this plane and the next – express what they are through their emanations or life force. In this way, a soul gives off information about itself, its history and present state. A person who perceives its vibrations can know all about it.

In Part I, you used the law of vibration without realizing it. For example, when you opened your soul senses to perceive a rose in the unseen world, you identified it as a rose with a particular color, shape and smell through the **kind** of vibrations it expressed. The law was also at work when you became aware of the presence of Spirit in and around you. Perhaps the air around you looked brighter, or it felt finer and purer, or your mind seemed clearer and free from distracting thoughts, or you felt more relaxed. You attuned to the **rate** of Spirit's vibration.

As you unfold as a medium in Part II, you will apply the same principle of vibration to connect with spirit loved ones in the spirit world. For example, a male and female express different *kinds* of vibrations that can be distinguished in the unseen dimension through one's gifts. Their appearance, behavior, work, relationships, the events in their lives and everything about them reflect particular *kinds* of vibrations that you can pick up with your soul senses. The *rate* of vibration is a very important factor in your development as a medium too. A spirit guide or teacher expresses a faster *rate* of vibration that reflects its elevated state of existence. A medium needs to attune to this higher vibration in order to be a channel for spirit communication.

You can see, then, how a medium can identify the spirit loved one of another without prior knowledge of the spirit entity or the sitter. With the help of one's spirit guides and teachers a medium uses her gifts to perceive their vibrations. Also, as you become sensitive to the nature of vibrations, you will discover that your soul naturally uses the law to seek higher understanding from the unseen dimension of life.

Raise Your Vibrations and Elevate Your Soul

We live on the earth plane yet we want to communicate with spirit entities on a higher plane of existence. To do this, we *raise our vibrations,* and in turn, our spirit guides and teachers lower theirs to commune with us. When we raise our vibrations, we increase their rate and elevate our soul. For example, you raise your vibrations in daily practice through prayer, relaxation and meditation. You increase your rate of vibration not by speeding up your conscious mind but by relaxing it and letting your soul emerge. In deeper states of consciousness, you are closer to Spirit.

In raising your vibrations, you improve the quality of your messages: your soul senses are more attuned to the influences of your spirit guides and teachers. Also, as you elevate your soul, you clear away the stress of the day and make room for inner states of peace, love and clarity of mind – qualities that are beneficial to you and make you a better instrument for spirit communication.

→ Exercise: Be Aware of the Vibrations In and Around You

- Sit in your sacred place. Notice how you feel and how the room looks. Close your eyes and begin with your simple prayer of thanks: Think of all the things you are grateful for, no matter how small, and give thanks to the God of your own understanding for all your blessings. Take your time and reflect on all the good in your life. Be as sincere as possible in your gratitude.

- End your prayer and notice, before you open your eyes, the quality of your inner state compared to when you began. Did you release an old attitude, embrace a new one?

- Open your eyes and be aware of the difference in the room, if any. Perhaps it is lighter or clearer, the colors more vivid.

▸ *My Experience:*

_____

_____

→ Exercise: Raise Your Vibrations From Within

In addition to your daily practice, here are some other ways to raise your vibrations from within through Spirit's help.

- Scan your inner states for any lower vibrations such as tense muscles, racing thoughts, upset feelings or fatigue. Notice them without judging or trying to change them. Select one area and let yourself feel it without fear, anger or shame.

- Close your eyes, relax and call on your spirit guide or light to help you release it. Listen with your inner ear to Spirit's insight.

Now open this area to the loving vibrations of your spirit guide or light. You may want to use your inner senses: See and sense spirit's love, light and life in you as the old condition releases and welcome your new state of higher vibration. Sit quietly for a moment and let your soul be fed by spirit's presence.

▸ *My Experience:*

_____

_____

_____

Still other ways to do this:

1. Scan your inner system for a pain, headache, worry or concern. In your imagination, take it out of your body and hold it in your hands. Use your inner senses to see, sense and even hear it. As you become aware of it, what do you learn about yourself? Attune to the uplifting presence of Spirit, and ask for greater clarity about your condition. Now be aware as the elevated spirit being lifts away the pain or discomfort with its soothing fine vibrations. How does your inner state change? How do you feel?

2. Be aware of any tension within. With the help of Spirit, sense your heart as a flame of gentle love. Let it expand and flow into your tense state. Relax and notice what happens. Continue to sense your loving vibration as it fills your entire body. How do you feel?

3. Give yourself a general cleansing with light: With Spirit's help, use your inner eye to see a shimmering white light above your head that showers you with its pure vibrations. Let this divine light infuse every part of your being. Relax in it. Now the white light changes to a beautiful color. As you look into it, your soul is nourished. How do you feel?

1. _____

2. _____

3. _____

Do you have your own ways of raising your vibrations within? Describe them. _____

_____

_____

↳ Exercise: Raise Your Vibrations from Without

There are many ways to raise your vibrations in this way. For example, when you set up your sacred place, you created a peaceful and uplifting space with flowers, music, candle, incense, soothing colors, inspirational books, comfortable clothes and suitable chair because they helped to raise your vibrations.

Extend this to your life: Open your soul to natural surroundings and let their pure vibrations uplift you. Become aware of what nurtures your soul in the places, people and activities around you. Pay attention to what energizes you in your daily habits to do with food, exercise and sleep, and what kinds of work and special interests renew your spirit. Notice how laughter, children, animals, loving friends and family can raise your vibrations.

▸ *My Experience:*

_____

_____

What are some of the other ways to raise your vibrations that work well for you? Describe them.

_____

_____

Psychometry

Psychometry is the ability to gain information about an object, its owner and its history by touching it and attuning to its vibrations. The word "psychometry" comes from two Greek words – "psyche" which means "soul", as you know, and "metron" that signifies "measure". Psychometry is the power to measure or understand the story of a soul and its conditions through touch. Think of the impressions you've felt when you held an heirloom piece of jewelry, worn someone else's jacket or sweater, sat in a spot that was someone's favorite, used a neighbor's tool or borrowed a pen. You may have experienced the owner's personality, taken on another's physical size, picked up unfamiliar scenes and images or sensed an unusual mood. Through contact with something that belonged to them, you attuned to their vibrations and had a taste of psychometry.

→ Exercise: Do Psychometry with a Natural Object

Sometimes I collect a bunch of rocks, leaves, sticks, bark and pine cones on my nature walks, and bring them to class. I invite students to pick a natural object from the pile in the middle of the room to do psychometry. This is a wonderful way to wind down from a busy day. As the group does the exercise, I sense the uplifting atmosphere in the room and feel an inner calm.

- Find a natural object that appeals to you.
- Sit quietly, close your eyes and relax.
- Open your soul senses as you ask Spirit to draw near and uplift you.
- Pick up the object and hold it in your hand. Open to its vibrations: Notice your first impression with it. You may pick up feelings, sensations, images, thoughts, sounds or smells. Relax and let it express itself to you.
- In a few minutes, open your eyes.

▸ *My Experience:*

_____

_____

_____

The most common experience – a feeling of peace. Some other experiences include a feeling of lightness or freedom from a leaf; sensations of heat, cold, or energy from a piece of bark; an image of water, of stability or a sense of the earth from a stone; and a smell of grass or a rustling sound of wind from a pine cone. You can also practice psychometry as you raise your vibrations during nature walks. Reach out and touch anything you're drawn to, and explore nature's unseen world with psychometry. When you are relaxed, open and feel its spirit close to you, you can pick up a message from it. Just ask.

Guidelines: Psychometry for a Person

- As soon as you hold an item in your hand that belongs to the person you are about to read, you will receive impressions. Pray, relax and open to Spirit *before* you pick it up.
- To gain information about a person, use something he or she owns. A piece of jewelry, a watch, keys, or glasses work well. An item that has not belonged to anyone else will ensure that you won't be confused by the vibra-

tions of several owners. This isn't always possible and you will learn to hone in on the vibrations for the person you have in mind.

- You may get only one or two pieces of information. Trust whatever you receive. Know that it is significant. For example, Sally held a ring that belonged to Suzie seated in front of her and suddenly she saw a bright blue color that seemed to be everywhere. That's all she got for as long as she held the ring. Finally she gave the ring back apologetically and said "All I got was a beautiful color blue that surrounded me on all sides."

- At first Suzie couldn't identify it, then said, " Of course! I'd forgotten. I bought the ring when I spent the summer on a tiny Greek island as a student. Everything around me was a clear bright blue – the huge open sky and the expanse of sea – and I was very happy there. Thank you for bringing that back to me at this time when I especially need it."

- You may see scenes, people or events and have no idea if they have meaning for your sitter. But again, trust what you receive. Emily had never done psychometry before and as soon as she held Jane's bracelet, she saw a flagstone path in a garden, and realized she was privy to the details of someone's beloved yard where they had loved to walk. It turned out to be a garden that Jane had fond memories of when she was young.

- Sometimes you can't determine the source of the information you receive, such as the person who made the article. Tim held a turquoise stone in an unusual shape that was Jake's key chain. He saw a man at a table with a visor and some tools. Then he heard laughter of people at a party. Jake recognized the second part – he just returned from a fun packed holiday. He puzzled over the first part. Perhaps it's the craftsman who made it since he bought it at an artisan's shop?

- Don't be afraid to be wrong – there is a sense in which you can't be. You receive what you do for a reason. Treat this exercise as an exploration to enhance your sensitivity to vibrations.

- You may question whether you are making it up, especially if your partner can't identify anything. The best way to overcome any doubt is through practice. Ask spirit to teach you to do psychometry to help others, and in time you will develop beautifully.

→ Exercise: Do Psychometry for a Partner

Have a personal item ready to give to your partner. Also have paper and pen ready so that you can write down what you receive as soon as you touch the item. You will hold each other's object and record your information at the same time.

Prepare
Sit facing each other. Begin with a silent prayer and relaxation. Reach up within, open your soul senses and ask for your spirit guide or light to draw near. When you feel elevated and attuned to Spirit and the unseen world to the best of your ability, open your eyes.

Receive Information from the Vibrations of the Object
Exchange your items and immediately begin to record what you receive from the vibrations of the object in the space below under *My Psychometry Reading for____(Name of Partner)*. Stay open to receive whatever comes to you. Whenever you feel that nothing more is coming, ask your spirit guide or light for more. You may want to close your eyes and open inwardly to do this. Feel the flow of receiving and then giving out as you record your impressions. Remember to record everything you receive, such as what you see, think, feel, sense, smell, hear or taste.

My Psychometry Reading for_____(Name of Partner)

Share

 When you are both completely finished (5-10 minutes), read the message you received, one partner at a time. Offer feedback for your partner about the information that you can identify. Stay as open as you can to understanding the message and jot down your notes under *Feedback from My Partner*. If you don't recognize the information, reassure your partner that you will take the information and reflect on it. Often, you will realize the truth of what was said later. When you have finished, silently give thanks to God and Spirit for what you received.

Feedback from My Partner: _____
_____
_____
_____
_____
_____
_____
_____
_____

➔ More Psychometry Exercises

1. Do Psychometry without a Partner

Select an item that belongs to a family member or friend with whom you can check out your results after you have done your reading. You can also select things in your home to explore psychometry on your own. You may find that you pick up new ways of understanding old situations, or information you forgot or that brings back memories. Or you may be stirred to research your family, past events or relationships to confirm your results.

In this exercise, you work on your own in your sacred place. Record what you receive and follow the same procedure above where it applies.

A Special Note: The ability to gain information from the unseen dimension comes with a responsibility to use it to benefit others in ways that respect their right to privacy. Ask your family member or friend if you can read them and verify your results with them. Be sensitive and treat them as you would like to be treated. Also, select someone who is supportive of your desire to become a medium. If you can't find anyone, search your home for items to practice on.

2. Do Psychometry with or without a Partner

Follow the same procedures above, using envelopes with items in them rather than things themselves. For example, you (and your partner) can put photographs, letters, names, questions and drawings in their own numbered envelopes so their contents are unknown to you (and your partner), but you have a record of them. Hold an envelope in your hand, pick up the vibrations of its contents and record what you receive.

If you are working on your own, use several envelopes and shuffle them around or turn them over so you are unfamiliar with what you are about to read. Identify each 'reading' by number. Open each envelope to assess your results.

Psychometry Readings

Reading 1 _____
_____

Reading 2

Final Thoughts about Psychometry

Can you pick up information about the future from an object? There are two different views. Some argue that since a physical object exists in time and space, it can't contain vibrational information about the future. Others hold that it can contain information about the past, present and future since the vibrations are expressions of the soul.

Is psychometry a psychic or mediumistic method? The most common view: Psychometry itself (the use of touch to pick up information from the vibrations of an object) is purely a psychic ability through which one attunes to vibrations from the unseen dimension of this plane alone and not the spirit world. If one picks up the vibrations of a spirit loved one, one is using one's gifts, in addition to the use of touch, to attune to the realm of Spirit.

Ask your spirit guides and teachers about these positions. My aim here is to use psychometry to help you develop your sensitivity to vibrations. And since I want you to work closely with Spirit and to develop your gifts to become mediums, I've influenced the process. Explore psychometry as you are guided – perhaps you discern the future and spirit loved ones, and perhaps you don't. Open your mind to whatever comes and let it flow without restraint. (For more information on how to continue to develop your psychometry, see *How to Develop and Use Psychic Touch*, by Ted Andrews. For a discussion of psychometry, see *Mediumship and Its Laws*, by Hudson Tuttle, 83-88.)

My Thoughts:

Visit with Your Loved Ones

How Our Spirit Family Communicates

Many of you have connected with your spirit loved ones on your own or through a medium, and you felt the joy of knowing that death was not an end for them, but a new stage of life on a higher plane. Spirit communication touches us deeply – even a faint sound of a loved one's voice, a trace of scent of an old familiar perfume or a glimpse of the face of a beloved in spirit can transport us to new states of love and harmony. In this contact, we are uplifted from our earthly minds to an awareness of ourselves as souls. And no matter how often we visit with them, or how experienced we become, our spirit is renewed, more vital and complete in this contact with their more perfect world and existence.

Everyone can communicate with their spirit loved ones through their gifts. When my mother appeared to me, I wasn't a medium – I used my gifts naturally without questioning them. And many of you have had similar experiences.

As you open to members of your spirit family, you will find that they make themselves known in ways that are familiar and that reflect their earthly life, such as their interests, personality, appearance, health and habits. For example, your brother who loved music will likely come through with musical sounds; a neighbor who enjoyed good food, may show you this activity; a dog lover will appear with dogs; a teacher will be in a classroom. Your spirit family includes all the spirits in the beyond who know you, such as, members of your earth family, friends, co-workers, teachers and pets.

The following accounts show how contact can be made with spirit loved ones through one's gifts. Some experiences may be familiar to you. You may have dismissed others as unreal or 'just your imagination'. You may realize that you've been in touch with your spirit family all along!

Clairscent: Inner or Soul Scent

This is one of the easiest ways to know that a spirit is close because smell moves us without the interference of our questioning mind.

- I smell my mother's perfume that is distinctive. I don't know its name. She comes that way when I need reassurance and I always feel calmed by that smell and with it a sense of her closeness.

- When I drive out to the country, I often smell my grandmother's lilac blossoms. It can be the middle of winter, but the scent of lilacs fills my car. I'm uplifted by this smell and I'm overcome with a feeling of love.

- My father used to smoke a pipe as he sat engrossed in a book. Sometimes when I'm immersed in a book, I smell his pipe. I get a feeling that he's looking over my shoulder and giving me permission to spend my time in a book.

- Our neighbor used to mow our lawn when I was small. Now and then I'll smell the scent of fresh cut grass and go to the window to see who is cutting mine and I realize he's here from the beyond to remind me in a humorous way that it's time to do it!

Clairvoyance: Inner or Soul Sight

Spirit communicates through our inner vision in many ways. Often spirit loved ones will appear visually several times before they speak.

- As I was falling asleep, I saw my mother and father in spirit standing at a distance, arm in arm, in a beautiful light. They were smiling and expressed a feeling of 'all is well'. The conflicts I was having in my marriage seemed to fade with this message of love and well-being.

- When I am crafting, I sometimes see my father's face, with his mustache and full head of hair, bent over in concentration. We used to do the work together and this inspires me to focus more intently on detail.

- My favorite aunt loved to laugh and wear bright clothes. Once she appeared when I was a bit down and showed me every detail of an outfit she had worn including jewelry and a hat. I was energized and amused by her. And she was so real!

- I sat relaxed with my eyes closed and saw my brother's army boots. Nothing else, just his boots. I realized that this was his way to say that he was doing fine in his new home.

Clairaudience: Inner or Soul Hearing

We can hear our spirit loved ones in a variety of ways as these illustrations show.

- I was driving on a busy highway and as I was about to change lanes, I heard my name called. I was so startled, I kept to my lane just as a car sped past me that I would have hit had I moved. I turned to see who had called me to warn me away from danger and realized that no one else was around. I believe it was my grandfather from the other side of life who was always very protective, but I'm not sure.

- When I prepare something from my mother's recipe book, I sometimes hear her words from spirit to remind and guide me. It turns out much better when I listen. She brings a know-how to the process that I don't have.

- All my relatives played the piano and sometimes I hear piano music from those who have passed, and I am transported to a higher state that seems to be closer to what they experience over there than we do here. I don't see who is bringing it, I just hear it and it comes often when I need inspiration.

- My friend and I spent hours sharing our ideas. He was an especially deep thinker. When he passed, I expected him to communicate. I thought about him all the time, but I never saw or heard from him. Then I realized that some of what I took to be my thoughts were his! This was his way of communicating: I needed to open my inner ear to hear his thoughts mentally, and to send mine in the same way. As I did this, we enjoyed sharing our ideas once again, only now we talked about spiritual things.

Clairsentience: Clear or Inner Sensing
Sensing our spirit loved ones is often a very real and vivid way to experience the unseen dimension.

- Right after my husband died, I felt his arm around me throughout the day. I sensed him as if he were close physically and almost expected to see him in the room. Then a month or two later, I no longer sensed him like that but instead, he seemed further away as if he had left. I asked him what was happening, and he showed me that he was now more fully in his spirit and that if I lifted myself up a little, I could communicate with him as a spirit. And so we attune to each other this way: I sense his spirit and I feel a happiness and love that grows each day.

- When I'm walking around my house in my bare feet on a hot summer day, I sense the house my grandparents lived in, where I spent many carefree holidays. I'm aware of their presence close by and I sense an old feeling of being pampered by them.

- One day, I worried about my cat who hadn't returned home. Then I sensed my spirit cat close by who came with a loving light and a sense that everything was being taken care of from that side. Sure enough, it was. My cat returned shortly!

- On holidays when our family is together, I sense the warm and generous personalities of my aunt and uncle and I know they are with us. Both were outgoing and beloved. I think they come around to enjoy the company and social fun.

- Sometimes I sense an ache in my hip bone and I'm aware of my old friend in spirit who I cared for when she broke her hip. It's an easy way for her to get my attention in order to convey a message. Once I acknowledge her, the ache disappears.

Clairgustance: Inner or Soul Taste
Tasting is a way to connect with spirit loved ones. However, we may find it difficult to describe.

- Now and then, when I'm sitting down to eat, I will suddenly have a taste of the bitterness of beer when there is none in sight and I'm taken back to childhood when my father gave me a sip from his mug. I can feel the froth on top that I didn't like and I hear him laugh at me.

- Once when I had an urge for something sweet, I could taste my grandmother's peach pie. I saw flashes of our old fruit farm and smelled a peach fresh from the tree. I had a sense that I was being encouraged to counteract my cravings with fresh fruit!

- I think about my grandmother in spirit when I taste the salad dressing on crisp lettuce that I used to make to help her with dinner. I sense her standing beside me as I make it and how she would shift from one foot to the other to relieve the pain of her varicose veins.

- When my child was sick recently, I was questioning whether to give him medicine. Out of the blue, I felt my mother from spirit who comes when we have issues with her grandkids. At the same time, I tasted the medicine she used to give us – the kind that we liked as kids. With this, I had a strong sense that she was encouraging me to go ahead. I did and my son improved.

Visitations
Your spirit loved ones come to visit you from the spirit realm they inhabit and they return to their home following communication with you. The bond that you established on earth helps you to make contact quite easily once you

know how to raise your vibrations and use your gifts to perceive them. Though they appear in ways that are familiar to you from your earthly relationship with them, they are not living in the past. Just as we do here on earth, they continue to live their lives on a higher plane as they fulfill their purpose as part of their soul's progression.

They visit for a multitude of reasons – for celebrations such as birthdays, weddings, family reunions and holidays, and for passings and memorial services. They come to comfort and uplift in times of change, stress and ill health. Often they visit to let us know that they are alive and happy in the beyond. They bring loving support, guidance, and reassurance for us, our families and friends. As you unfold your mediumship, you will be able to discover, in communion with them, what their lives are like, and why and how they visit.

The notion of a 'higher plane' or 'spirit realm' or 'the beyond' may conjure up a faraway place that takes great effort to traverse in order to connect with your spirit loved ones. However, since we too are of the spirit, we contact the spirit world simply by altering our inner states to let our soul emerge. Only a veil separates us from our spirit loved ones. Once you are in an elevated state, it lifts as you open your soul senses and perceive the unseen.

↛ Exercise: Visitations from My Spirit Loved Ones

This is an opportunity to examine your experiences of connecting with your spirit loved ones. The examples above that describe how contact was made with spirit loved ones by using one's gifts, may refresh your memory about their details.

- (a) Select several instances of visitations from spirit loved ones that occurred on your own without a medium and/or those that happened through a medium in a message or a reading.

    or

- (b) If you have neither experience to draw on, quietly reflect on several loved ones in spirit, and as they come to mind, recall your memories about them and let the scenes play out in your mind's eye.

- Sit in your sacred place and take a few moments to be still with God in prayer, to relax and to open to your spirit or guide or light. You want to record your experiences in an elevated state, so you are fully aware of the details of your contacts with your spirit family or your memories of them.

- Record your experiences in a freely flowing natural way that is comfortable for you.

- Let the following questions guide you in your accounts. How did your spirit loved ones appear? Who were they? What did they do or say? What gifts did you use to communicate during their visitation or what physical senses were reactivated in your memory of them? How did you feel and respond? What else was relevant to you?

▸ *My Experiences of My Spirits' Visitations or Memories:*

1. _____

_____

_____

_____

_____

2. _____

_____

_____

_____

_____

3. _____

_____

_____

_____

_____

How Did You Identify Your Spirit Loved Ones?

When I saw my mother's spirit after she passed away, I knew who she was because she appeared the way she had been here, except that she was more youthful and bright. I recognized her the same way I would if she had walked into the room. Yet she was a spirit visiting me from the beyond who wanted me to know that she was alive and happy. When I saw and sensed her, I connected to her through her vibrations. I was attuned to the unseen world and the law of vibration was the vehicle for me to use my gifts to perceive my mother.

Let's look at how the law of vibration supports your gifts to help you to identify a spirit loved one.

Examine your own experiences of communication above and notice the *kinds* of vibrations that helped you to know with your soul senses that a specific person was with you. In other words, how did you perceive this loved one? For example, was it his or her appearance, voice, behavior, words, personality or surroundings? Looking over your visitations or memories, what particular aspects of your spirit loved one helped you to identify him or her?

Now examine the *rate* of vibration you sensed with each spirit; that is, did you feel yourself connected to the spirit world with less of an earthly vibration and more uplifted in your soul? Reflect on your visitations and memories and notice the effects on your soul senses in your link with each spirit loved one.

In order to communicate more fully with your spirit loved ones and to bring clear, accurate and uplifting messages from the spirit world, you will learn to focus and strengthen your inner or soul senses so that you can decipher the kinds of vibrations that are presented to you from the spirit world. In this way, you gain the kind of information that identifies a spirit loved one beyond a reasonable doubt for others, as well as yourself. You also want to continue to raise your vibrations, to learn to reach beyond yourself and open your soul senses to the higher powers in order to attune to finer frequencies of vibrations and capture the sense of the presence of spirit for others and yourself.

Communicate with a Spirit Loved One

Hints to Help Your Connection

Take time to think about your spirit loved ones before you sit down to communicate. Talk to those you would like to come; recollect memories. Your thoughts and loving feelings can draw them to you. Also, your quiet reflections build your readiness to receive them and help them to prepare as well. You may also want to have a question ready for your spirit loved ones.

- Sit in your sacred place and ask them to come to visit with you. Ask with your genuine heart's desire. Then allow the energies to build in you and to strengthen your soul. If you are too demanding, you may block the flow of communication.

- If a spirit comes to you and not to other family members, it doesn't mean you're closer to God, more spiritual or lovable. Perhaps their focus is on the concerns of the world at the moment, or they may doubt the possibility of communication, or they don't realize how easy it is to do.

- You may want a particular loved one to come and another one shows up instead. We are not privy to the broader picture of what's going on in those realms: We rely on our spirit guides and teachers to show us the way. We often don't realize the inner workings of our own selves either. For example, we may be too anxious about communicating with a particular family member and another one comes to help us feel more comfortable with the process and prepare the way for the connection we want.

- Although spirit loved ones are on a higher plane and we sense their elevated state, they aren't gods. We don't pray *to* them. They are evolving, just as we are, and our prayers *for* them are as helpful as their prayers are for us.

- Your spirit loved ones have the same identity as they did on earth – they are the same people in this sense. But in their world, unlimited by matter, a realm of love and harmony, the spirit is free to be more fully itself. Much of the physical, emotional and mental suffering of this world is released in such an environment. We communicate, then, with our familiar loved ones, but they are happier, brighter, more loving and understanding as a rule.

Working with Your Spirit Guides and Teachers

Continue to call on your spirit guides and teachers to help you even if you aren't sure to what extent they are with you. As you call on them and open to their presence, you strengthen your soul and can sustain the higher states of awareness that are necessary to work closely with them. It's important to work with them in *all* you do as a developing medium in order to make your experiences as beneficial as possible.

For example, when you communicate with your spirit loved ones, ask Spirit to draw near as you raise yourself up to meet them. Their presences create an elevated atmosphere of a fine, pure vibration that surrounds you and your spirit loved ones. This helps your family and friends to come through to you more easily and express themselves more fully. Also, the influences of your spirit guides and teachers enhance your growth. Uplifted and protected in this shower of loving light and life, you can use your gifts beautifully. Listen to them; let them teach you every step of your way.

➤ Exercise: Communicate with a Spirit Loved One

You have attuned to your spirit light or guide to receive messages for yourself in Part I. Here, I will walk you through a similar procedure. You will attune to Spirit, open your soul senses to perceive the vibrations of a spirit loved one and receive a message.

Prepare

Sit in your sacred place and relax. … Pray. … Ask God and Spirit to help you communicate with a spirit loved one. Trust that whoever comes to visit is exactly right for you at this time. Relax. Be at peace. …

Open your soul senses

Reach up with your hear and mind and call on your spirit light or guide to draw near. Let yourself open to the pure uplifting vibrations of the spirit realm. Ask to be taken up ... and up ... and begin to feel more fully in your spirit. Let go ... release the hold of earthly forces and reach up with your soul. Raise your vibrations.

Next, open to the higher realms with your inner senses, direct them upwards and let them too draw you up with their focus. You are in an elevated state of your soul. Around and above you, the vibration is pure and perhaps a white or soft color. How peaceful, how free, how happy you feel! ...

Attune to Your Spirit Guide

Become aware of yourself as your spirit. Feel the love around you and notice that your mind and soul senses are clear. Now sense your spirit guides uplifting presence near you. Take a moment to enjoy your guide who has come to help you to commune with a spirit loved one. You may sense and hear this spirit with your soul senses or you may simply sense their uplifting and loving vibration. ...

Visit with a Spirit Loved One

With your spirit guide at your side, you become aware of a spirit loved one approaching you. What is your first impression as this presence comes closer? What do you See? ... Sense? ... Hear? ... Smell? ... Taste? ... Stay open as you and your loved one communicate. ...

I leave you to be together. Enjoy the wonder of this visitation with your spirit loved one. ...

Do you have a question for your loved one? Open with your soul senses to the message from your spirit loved one. ...

It's time to prepare to leave. Enjoy a few more minutes together. ... Say goodbye and know that you will meet again when the time is right for you both.

Return

Guided by your spirit light or guide, you find yourself coming back. Down, down where you feel a little heavier and more in touch with the earth. ... Sitting now in your sacred place, you still feel the glow of communication with your loved one. Give thanks for all that you have received and for the blessings of spirit communication. Invite your spirit light or guide to help you in your learning as you record your experience.

▸ *My Experience:*

Who came to visit me? _____

_____

_____

_____

How did my spirit loved one appear to me? In what ways did they identify who they were? _____

_____

_____

_____

What gifts did I use to perceive my spirit loved one?

What information or guidance did I receive? Was it helpful?

How did I feel with my spirit loved one's visitation?

How did I feel with my spirit guide at my side?

What else do I want to remember about my experience?

Identify a Sitter's Spirit Loved One with Evidence

Evidence

Just as you felt uplifted by your contact with your own spirit loved one, you will realize the great joy, as you develop as a medium, when you contact the spirit loved one of someone else and help them experience the same elation of their soul when they realize their dear one is alive in the beyond.

When you communicated with your own spirit loved one in the last chapter, you could identify them without much information since you already know them: Sensing their presence alone may have been enough to convince you. But as a medium, the situation is quite different since you will contact a spirit loved one of your sitter whom you haven't known in this life (as we discussed at the beginning of Part II). In this chapter, you will learn to bring the kind of information by which your sitter can know that their spirit loved one is present and alive. This is *evidence*. You will allow your spirit guide to use your gifts to see, sense, hear, smell and taste as you have done before, only now your focus will be on those who passed on.

Many Kinds of Evidence

Think of the variety of ways we distinguish people on this plane; for example, their physical appearance, the sound of their voice, their home and the material things they like, their personalities, ailments, interests and work. The next plane is no different in this regard: Spirit loved ones present themselves in ways that are familiar to the sitter.

Here is a fact sheet of the many kinds of evidence that you will encounter as a medium. Open your mind to the different ways that spirits show us who they are. Notice those kinds of evidence that are familiar to you and those you would like to explore. Also, be aware of what gifts you may use to perceive the evidence. (The examples suggest the most common methods, but if Spirit uses your gifts differently, trust what works.)

Fact Sheet: Evidence

Physical Appearance:
- Male or female; human, animal or other creature

- Body size and shape, face, hair, clothes; distinguishing feature; age

- Behavior

Often a spirit loved one will present themselves in their physical appearance at the beginning of a message or reading. The information is usually perceived with the soul sight. Less frequently, the soul sense or ear may be used. For example, you may see *a female wearing a straw hat, old clothes* and *digging in the garden*. She is *smiling*. Or you may sense *a large muscular man with a thick beard*. Or you may hear that *a child is skipping in her new pink party dress*.

Personality

Many personality traits can be cited that provide evidence of a spirit loved one, such as:

- Outgoing, quiet, optimistic, compassionate, angry, kind, happy, nervous, religious, powerful, hard working, a worrier, supportive, intelligent, talkative.

When you identify the personality of a spirit, you bring a human quality to their presence that adds a reassuring familiarity for the sitter. Often these are picked up with your soul sense, but your other gifts can also be used here. For example, you may sense a man's *angry* or *quiet* personality; or see and sense the *hard working* nature of a person; or hear the *talkative* chatter of another.

Relationship of the Spirit Loved One to the Sitter

- Family members and in-laws, friends, co-workers, colleagues, teachers, mentors, neighbors, pets

It's very helpful to identify the relationship of the communicating spirit to the sitter because it places the spirit in the context of a sitter's life. It isn't always easy to do this – what distinguishes father from grandfather, mother from mother-in-law or aunt, cousin from friend? There are ways to identify the distinctive vibrations of each which we will do later.

Meanwhile, ask Spirit. All the soul senses may be used here, although the most common is to sense the spirit's relationship. For example, I sense *your father* with you who … Or, I hear a woman from the spirit world who says 'I am *your sister* that you have been dreaming about recently.' Also, pets can come through with a relative and help to identify them, or they come directly for the sitter. They can have a big emotional impact on the sitter and evidence is just as important with them. For example, I see *a large black dog with a white star on its forehead standing beside a man*.

Objects Linked to Spirit Loved Ones

- Rings, watches, china, furniture, books, tools, linens, computer, flowers, clothes, boat, money, other things

Objects are often significant pieces of evidence because when a spirit loved one passes, the things they leave behind retain their vibrations and we hold them close to our hearts. All soul senses come into play here, including smell and taste. For example, I see your grandmother who holds up *a silver ring with a small diamond* that I sense *she left to you*. Or I smell *mustiness* as I sense *a piece of linen embroidered by hand*.

Scenes Connected to Spirit Loved Ones

- Particular rooms in a home, special pieces of furniture or equipment, garden

- Places in nature such as a lake, farm, a wooded trail

- Sports and entertainment events, cultural and community spaces, scenes of celebration

Spaces that a person spent their time in when they were on the earth plane provide evidence and conjure up powerful memories that help the sitter feel close to their loved one. They may or may not include the spirit loved one. They can be picked up with any of the soul senses. For example, I see *the afternoon sun streaming in as a woman sits writing a letter at her desk, and glances at the photo of a young man in uniform*.

Words
- Name of the spirit or others he or she knew
- Words or phrases used by him or her
- Distinctive voice or accent

A name, like a familiar phrase or accent, is a convincing piece of evidence. It is most commonly heard, but you can also see or even sense it. Sometimes a name is given through the name of an object. Phrases and distinctive accents are often sensed. For example, I hear the name *Paul* and a young man appears. Or, I see a *violet* (*Violet*) and …

Health and Well Being
- Health conditions from serious illnesses like cancer, diabetes, emphysema or heart attack to less serious ones such as high blood pressure, arthritis or varicose veins
- States of wellness like enjoying walking, running, swimming; eating nutritional foods and supplements

The state of health of a spirit loved one often has played a big role in their life and death, especially in their older years, and has affected those around them. With the soul sense, the condition can be picked up quickly and clearly. For example, I sense someone's *hands* –I feel them – they're *large and stiff like I have arthritis*. Or, I sense *a feeling of vitality as I begin my brisk daily walk*.

Death
- How a loved one passed including accident, natural death, suicide, illness
- Concerns of the sitter about the death including grief, regrets, family conflicts, funeral
- Information about the loved one's transition to 'the other side' and existence there

Since the death of a spirit loved one is often the last time the sitter saw him or her, the subject is a welcome one: Any evidence that confirms the sitter's care giving or intentions, or that helps the sitter to understand death as a liberation of the spirit is a blessing. All soul senses come into play here since the evidence can vary so widely. For example, I hear your mother who says *she heard your soothing words and felt your hand on hers as she lay there unable to move, and she was comforted by your loving care*. Or, he shows me *the flashy tie you put on him for the funeral and he was happy with it*.

Work
- Kind of work such as nurse, miner, stay at home mom, sales rep, hairdresser, teacher, mechanic, X-ray technician, artist, computer analyst, student or accountant

Work provides evidence that often defines a person in his or her earth life. For example, I see a man who *inspects the engine of a car and wipes some oil from his hands with a cloth. He's a mechanic*. …

Special Interests, Talents and Dreams
- Interests, such as, travel, collecting stamps, a favorite sports team, quilting or playing golf
- Talents like cooking, woodworking, inspirational speaking, gardening, or playing the violin
- Dreams ranging from sailing around the world, or buying a new house, to mountain climbing, or writing a book

This kind of evidence often gets to the core of a spirit loved one's heart's desire on the earth plane, and may open an inspirational link between the spirit and sitter. All soul senses can be used in this broad topic. For example, I hear your aunt's *inspirational words from the podium* and sense *the uplifted audience*.

History of Spirit Loved One
Information about a spirit loved one's past includes such events as

- Overcame a childhood illness, lived through a war, fought in a war, crossed the ocean as a child, was very poor or very wealthy, and excelled as an athlete.

A spirit loved one's past can be relevant evidence that confirms known facts and at the same time sheds light on the behavior of a family member. For example, I sense a grandfather *who wore a military uniform* is here.

Religion or Spiritual Practice of a Spirit Loved One
Included here, for example,

- Specific religious denominations, spiritual beliefs and practices
- Opinions and beliefs about God and the afterlife, heaven and hell, suicide and other controversial subjects

Information about a loved one's beliefs can bring evidence and also encouragement for the sitter to seek honestly in their own way. For example, your mother was *a devout Catholic and always believed in spirit communication*.

Other Kinds of Evidence That You Would Like to Add:
_____
_____
_____

Explore Evidence

This is an opportunity to use your gifts to explore different kinds of evidence without any pressure to identify a spirit loved one. I will walk you through this exercise where you will follow the same procedure as you did in Chapter Three for *Exercise: Use Your Soul Senses to Receive a Message* when you asked Spirit to show you an item in the unseen world, and you opened your soul senses to perceived it and determine its meaning. Here you may perceive a spirit loved one who is familiar, someone you don't know or a spirit presence. Your aim is to become familiar with evidence, and your spirit guide will help to do this.

As always, read over the exercise and notice the worksheet where, instead of items listed, several kinds of evidence have been selected for you to perceive. And here there is no column to record the meaning of the message since what you perceive is the literal meaning. There is space for a category of your choice. Review the list *Fact Sheet: Evidence,* above and record your pick now.

Your spirit guide will work with you in this learning process. Spirits may be brought in to help you – some familiar or unfamiliar – or the evidence alone may be given without any identifiable spirit presence. Your aim is to perceive the evidential details to the best of your ability whether you sense any presence or not.

Don't demand from Spirit: Reach up with your heart's desire, open your soul senses, and allow your spirit guide to draw you into the higher realms and show you what you seek. If at any time, you feel yourself getting tired and unable to maintain your uplifted state and focus, return to your normal state in your sacred place. You may want to do only one piece of the exercise during one sitting. Ask Spirit for guidance.

⇾ Exercise: Use Your Soul Senses to Explore Evidence

Have a pen ready to record what you receive. I will guide you step-by-step to focus on each piece of evidence in your worksheet, and to use your soul senses to get as much detail and clarity as you can.

Prepare
Try this shortened form of relaxation and readiness. Sit in your sacred place and close your eyes. Begin with a simple prayer giving thanks for all that you will soon receive. Ask that your gifts be awakened more fully, and that you perceive positive and uplifting evidence. Give thanks.

Relax by focusing on your breath and as you inhale, let the life energy flow into your entire body from the tips of your toes to the top of your head. As you exhale, release all concerns of the day. Stay with the streaming energy within and sense its loving light and life revitalizing you throughout your body and mind. Relax. Be at peace. …

Your Spirit Guide
Call on your spirit guide to help you. Reach up to the higher planes with your heart and mind. Relax and let yourself be lifted up in your soul, free from your earthly self. Be at home in this lighter state. Float up… and up. … Be at peace in your soul. …

Become aware of the presence of your spirit guide near you and let the uplifting vibration infuse you: Feel the love in your heart and the light in your mind. Open your soul senses and notice how full of life they are with Spirit's influence. …

Look up with them to a space in front and above you. You may be aware of it as the etheric sky, a screen that is clear and bright, or a clearing ahead. Ask Spirit to guide and teach you now as you begin.

Physical Appearance
When you are ready, open your soul's eye and glance at the first kind of evidence **Physical Appearance**. Read the examples listed. Now close your eyes and ask to be shown the physical appearance of a spirit. … Open to whatever appears before you now. Notice all the details. What do you see? … sense? … hear? … Take in fully this first view … and be aware if it changes. … When nothing else is given to you, return to the category of *Physical Appearance,* and ask for more evidence: Is this a male or female, or other creature? … Ask to be given more details about their appearance such as body build, face, hair and clothing. … Are there any distinguishing features? … What gifts are you using to pick up these details? If something is fuzzy or blank, ask Spirit to help you. Finally, is this person or creature doing anything? What is their behavior? … Before you open your eyes to record what you've received, ask Spirit to talk to you about this kind of evidence. … Open your soul ear and listen to any brief guidance. …

When you are ready, open your eyes and record the evidence you received on the worksheet below. Stay in your elevated mind; that is, stay in a light trance state, so you can return inwardly again to your soul senses and move into your next kind of evidence. Feel free to open and close your eyes as you are perceiving your evidence.

Objects Linked to Loved Ones
Glance now at the next kind of evidence **Objects Linked to Loved Ones** and read the examples listed. Close your eyes again and feel yourself in an elevated state. Take your time and enjoy your explorations. Sit quietly and open with your soul senses. Ask Spirit to show you an object linked to a spirit. … Become aware now of an object before you that is linked to a spirit presence. What is your first impression? … Let it unfold before you. … What do you see? … Notice

all the details before you. … What do you sense? … hear? … Perhaps you smell something or taste it. … You may or may not have an awareness of the spirit linked to this object. Stay with your experience and notice if anything else unfolds. Some of you may have perceived something clearly and quickly, and want to ask Spirit for another object linked to another spirit. Repeat the process and enjoy your connection to the unseen. …

When you are ready, open your eyes and record the evidence that you perceived while you maintain your higher state of consciousness.

Health and Well Being
Move to the next kind of evidence **Health and Well Being** and read the examples listed. Close your eyes and open your soul senses to the space above and before you. Ask Spirit to infuse and uplift you as you attune to the health condition or state of well-being of a spirit. ….. It is important here to experience this condition with your soul and not your finite self: You want to sense or see it, hear, smell or even taste it and then be able to release it – you don't want to take it on as part of your own self. Spirit will help you with this. Open now to receive and notice your first impression. … What do you perceive? …

Do you sense a health condition … or a state of well-being? … How does it feel? What is it? Do you see the health or well-being of a spirit? … Or do you hear someone talking about their condition? … Let whatever is given to you unfold now. … Once you've identified the situation, release it. When you are ready, open your eyes and record your experience.

Your Choice of Evidence
Read the next kind of evidence that you have picked to explore. Close your eyes. Take a few deep breaths and relax. Look up within and focus on the space before you as your choice of evidence emerges. What is your first impression? Open your soul senses to it and become aware of all the details presented to you. … Continue on your own and enjoy your exploration of your chosen evidence as you perceive it in the unseen. … When you feel ready, open your eyes and write down what you perceived.

Return
Give thanks to your spirit guide and to the spirits who helped you with this exercise. Gradually return to your sacred place. Take a few deep breaths and be aware of your physical body. Look around and notice your surroundings. While your experience is still fresh, take a moment to answer the questions at the end of the worksheet.

Receive Evidence from Spirit	
Evidence	What I See, Hear, Sense, Smell and Taste
Physical Appearance	
Male or female/ human, animal or other creature	
Body size and shape, face, hair, clothes/ distinguishing feature/ age	
Behavior	

Objects Linked to a Spirit Loved One Such as, ring, watch, china, furniture, book, tools, linen, computer, flower, clothes, boat, money, or other things	
Health and Well Being Serious illnesses like cancer, emphysema, diabetes, or heart attack, or less serious ones like high blood pressure, arthritis or varicose veins States of wellness like enjoying walking, running, swimming/eating nutritional foods and supplements	
My Choice:	

▸ *My Experience:*

What kind of evidence came to me most easily? Was one kind more difficult to perceive? _____

_____

_____

Which soul sense(s) was I especially pleased with? _____

_____

_____

What part of this exercise was the most significant for me? Why? _____

_____

_____

It is important that you return to this exercise using different kinds of evidence. Select another three or four kinds to explore, and become familiar with the ways your spirit guide shows you how to perceive spirit loved ones. Then at another sitting select three or four more.

Receive Evidence That Identifies Another's Spirit Love One

This exercise is like *Use Your Soul Senses to Explore Evidence*, only here the evidence you perceive will *identify* your partner's spirit loved one(s). Decide who will go first: You are the *medium*. The receiver is the *sitter*. At the end of the exercise, change places. Read the exercise together and be clear about your respective roles.

The aim: For the medium to bring through several kinds of evidence that help to identify a spirit loved one of the sitter. Look over and discuss *Evidence to Identify a Spirit Loved One* that lists the many kinds of evidence that may be received by the medium from the spirit world.

The sitter will use this list:

- to help the medium explore different kinds of evidence with their soul senses, and
- to record evidence the medium brings through, and the spirit loved one(s) identified.

Protocol for Medium and Sitter:

Medium: When your sitter is unable to recognize a spirit loved one by your evidence, trust in what you are receiving as you have learned, and ask your spirit guide for more information that may help. If it doesn't, don't worry and move on. Often your sitter will 'get it' later.

Sitter: Be positive and encouraging. If you can't identify a spirit say something like 'I can't place it right now but I will take it. Thank you.' Think about it later, and ask a family member for insight. Have your pen and *Evidence to Identify a Spirit Loved One* sheet ready. As the medium begins the message, call on your spirit loved one(s). Open to them and ask that they bring evidence for the medium to pick up and clearly identify them. Stay up in your higher state of consciousness to the best of your ability, and record what the medium brings through.

If the medium is stuck and nothing is forthcoming, use your feedback sheet to be a coach and ask questions that help them focus on a specific kind of evidence: What does this person look like? How was her health? Did he have a favorite place? What did she do for a living? In these ways, you can help to direct her inner perception.

Medium and Sitter: You will both prepare and meditate at the same time.

Prepare: Try this shortened form of relaxation and readiness. Sit facing each other in a quiet and secluded area. Begin with a simple prayer giving thanks for all you will receive, and for this opportunity to help each other commune with the spirit world. Ask God to draw near to help you communicate with your spirit guide and your sitter's loved ones.

Relax by focusing on your breath. As you inhale, let the life energy move into your entire body from the tips of your toes to the top of your head. As you exhale, release all stress and concern. Be at peace. … Stay with the streaming flow of energy within and sense its loving light and life revitalizing you throughout your body and mind. Relax. Be at peace. …

Your Spirit Guide

Call on your spirit guide. Reach up to the higher planes with your heart and mind. Relax and let yourself be lifted up in your soul, free from your earthly self. Be at home in this lighter state. Float up… and up… and release all your concerns. Become aware of the presence of your spirit guide near you and let the uplifting vibration infuse you: Feel the love in your heart, the light in your mind. …

Message by the Medium (5-10 minutes): Feel free to open and close your eyes during your message. Open your soul senses and notice how full of life they are with Spirit's influence. How bright and clear is your perception! How sensitive your awareness! Look up with your gifts to a space in front and above you. You may be aware of it as an ethereal sky, a screen of white light or a clearing ahead.

Now ask Spirit to bring in a spirit loved one and notice how the presence appears to you. Allow whatever comes to you to unfold. What is your first impression? … What do you see? … sense? … hear? … or even smell? … or taste? … As soon as you pick up something, give it out to your sitter … Take your time and stay with what you're perceiving. … Notice the details … and share them. … Give out whatever you receive, no matter how small. Everything is important.

You may continue to receive information from Spirit without having to ask for any specific kind of evidence. If so, continue to share what you pick up with your soul senses. When you want greater clarity, ask Spirit to help you. If the flow of information stops, ask your spirit guide to bring you more evidence. You may mention a specific kind, such as, 'Show me his physical appearance'. … or 'Is there an object linked to the spirit?' … 'What was her work?' …

If you are stuck, your sitter is also ready to coach you. Relax and let your sitter direct your focus to other areas of the spirit loved one's life. Don't try too hard; rather let a beautiful scene emerge for you, and enjoy the feelings a spirit loved one had there too; or sense a cozy room where the spirit played when young and spent many happy times; or embrace a family celebration and join in the laughter as you notice the clothes, food and activities of that era and locale. …

Close: You will know that the power is leaving you when you can't sustain your higher state and focus . Signal to your sitter that you are ending the communication with the spirit world. Silently give thanks to God and Spirit for your experience. Gradually bring your awareness back to your body and the chair you sit in. Open your eyes and look around the room. Verbally thank your sitter for the support and guidance.

Feedback by the Sitter(5-10 minutes): This is the time for the sitter to share the evidence received and recorded below, and to explain the ways in which a spirit loved one was fully or partially identified. Then change roles and repeat the exercise.

Evidence to Identify a Spirit Loved One	
Kinds of Evidence	Medium's Evidence and Spirit Identified
Physical Appearance	
Male or female/ human, animal or other creature	
Body size and shape, face, hair, clothes/ distinguishing feature/ age	
Behavior	
Personality	
Examples: outgoing, quiet, optomistic, compassionate, angry, kind, happy, nervous, religious, powerful, a worrier, supportive, hardworking, intelligent, talkative	

Relationship to Sitter Family members and in-laws, friends, co-workers, colleagues, teachers, mentors, neighbors, pets	
Objects Linked to a Spirit Loved One Such as, ring, watch, china, furniture, book, tools, linen, computer, flower, clothes, boat, money, or other things	
Scenes Connected to Spirit Loved One Room in a house, piece of furniture or equipment, sports or entertainment event, cultural or community gathering, celebration, garden or a place in nature like a lake, farm, or trail	
Words Name of the spirit or others he or she knew, words or phrases used by the spirit, distinctive voice or accent	
Health and Wellness Serious illnesses like cancer, emphysema, diabetes, or heart attack. Less serious ones like high blood pressure, arthritis or varicose veins. States of wellness like enjoying walking, running, swimming, eating nutritional foods and supplements	
Death How a loved one passed, like an accident, natural death, suicide, illness/ concerns of the sitter, such as grief, regrets, family conflicts, funeral. The transition to the other side and existence there	
Work Nurse, miner, stay-at-home mom, sales rep, hairdresser, teacher, mechanic, computer analyst, student, X-ray technician, accountant, artist, or other work	

Special Interests, Talents, Dreams Interests like: travel, stamp collecting, a favorite sports team, quilting, golf. Talents such as cooking, woodworking, speaking, playing violin, gardening. Dreams of sailing around the world, buying a new house, writing a book, mountain climbing	
History of Spirit Loved One Overcame a 'terminal' illness, fought in Vietnam, crossed the ocean as a child, was very poor or very wealthy, excelled as an athlete, or other facts	
Religion or Spiritual Practice Specific religious denomination, spiritual belief and practice/ opinion and belief about God and the afterlife, heaven and hell, suicide and other controversial subjects	
Additional Evidence	

Give a Medium's Message

A Medium's Message

You are ready to pull together your learning from Part I and II and give a medium's message. But first, consider these points.

A Message Reviewed

Let's revisit the definition of a medium in Chapter Two where a *medium's message* was introduced. As you reread it, you realize that now you can add the second kind of information to the evidence that you learned to perceive above. In other words, there are two parts to a medium's message.

A medium communicates with the spirit world to receive

- Evidence – information that identifies a spirit loved one; that is, that brings proof of the continued existence of life beyond the change called 'death'.

- Guidance – information that is relevant to the sitter's life.

Guidance

You will be able to bring through guidance for the sitter just as you received it for yourself. It will come symbolically or literally as before, depending on how best to convey the meaning.

Some evidence leads easily into guidance. For example, an object of a spirit loved one that identifies him or her can also have a meaning that is relevant to the sitter's life: A ring that grandmother in spirit holds up, that fits the description of an actual ring she left her granddaughter (the sitter), takes on further significance as she endorses the sitter's recent engagement and confirms the loving happiness she and her fiancé will enjoy.

Or, for example, where a specific kind of work has identified a spirit loved one like the mechanic in the example above (see Chapter Seven *Fact Sheet: Evidence*, under *Work*), the father from spirit may use it to bring advice for his son by indicating that he has the same knack, but 'more schooling would give you an edge'. Family members often inherit the same abilities as their older spirit loved ones and your spirit guide will use this to offer direction for a younger sitter's education and career.

You may notice too how evidence that helps to identify a spirit loved one, may have symbolic meaning for the sitter's life. For example, an aunt walking with a cane, may indicate a slight delay for the sitter as she tries to move forward.

Notice, as you gain practice, how evidence and guidance interact to help the sitter awaken to the higher truths that communication with the spirit world bring, and at the same time illumines their everyday world and journey.

Practice in an Unfoldment (or Development) Circle

The best way for you to move ahead with your mediumship at this stage is to *practice*. To do this, get a small group together to meet once a week and sit in *circle*. Or look for a circle in your area in a metaphysical or healing center, or Spiritualist church. Traditionally, this has been the way for a medium to unfold. Its purpose is to communicate with the spirit world, in a community of like-minded souls, for the development of mediumship. Here, messages are given and received in an environment that is much like what you create in your daily practice. Think of the circle as a sacred place for a group.

As you proceed in your unfoldment, remind yourself that your ability to communicate with the unseen, and the spirit world in particular, is natural – it lies within you. You need to reach and open, as you are learning to do; then you need only *allow*. Just let the influences from the higher planes reveal their messages to you. The circle is a safe place to do this. Trust in the workings of Spirit. Begin and end the circle with a prayer; include a relaxation exercise and/or a meditation.

When you prepare to give a message for someone in the circle, sit silently and call on Spirit to draw near as you open your soul senses. Ask, too, for your own spirit loved ones to be close during the circle. Let your vibrations be uplifted, connect with the presence of your spirit guide and continue as you do when you give a message. Ask your guide to indicate the person for whom you have a message. When you are ready, address the person, 'May I come to you?' or something similar. If the person says 'Yes', proceed to give the message as you have learned to do. When you are finished, close your message with words like 'I leave that with you', 'Blessings' or 'Thank you'. Then another person in the circle is free to give a message. Feedback can be shared following the circle or during a break. Sometimes, brief feedback is given during messages if it doesn't interfere with the flow of the spiritual energy and heightened states of consciousness.

Remember that the circle is a place to learn to grow, so give out whatever you receive no matter how unimportant or strange it seems. You'll be surprised at the wisdom of Spirit and the comfort your message offers. Know that your soul senses perceive the truth – trust them and Spirit. You may not always be able to express a message in ways that a sitter understands. He may not know or has forgotten, but this doesn't mean your message is false or inaccurate. He may come to you later to confirm your message.

(For more information on the development circle, see *The Idiot's Guide to Communicating with Spirits,* by Rita S. Berkowitz and Deborah S. Romaine, p130. The book also offers a broad understanding of mediumship.)

The *Spirit* in Spirit Loved Ones

We have emphasized the ways in which our spirit loved ones appear to us like they were on earth. But their presence is also, in a significant way, different from when they lived here. They are *spirits*. They exist in a non- material world. When we communicate with them, we contact people on a higher plane, living in a finer vibrational atmosphere. The evidence brought through by a spirit from this plane expresses this supernal nature. Many of you have perhaps had an awareness of this.

As you attune more and more to the spirit world and experience your elevated states of consciousness, you'll become aware of the finer more uplifted vibrations of communicating spirits. You will also notice the ethereal quality of the evidence that is brought through to you.

Let's look at some of the ways you may become aware of this. What you perceive *clairvoyantly* may be more translucent than this world: The colors may be more vivid; events and people may seem more real than in this life. Is the light brighter? Perhaps the spirits look more youthful or happy. How do the sounds that you pick up *clairaudiently* differ from earthly ones? More enlivening? Perhaps you have a sense of being stimulated by them? More moved? Notice this vibration.

How do you experience the spirit world *clairsentiently*? Is what you sense vital and real? Do you perhaps feel more energy in your link with Spirit? Freer? More loving? Clearer? Ask for insight into the vibrational aspects of the spirit world and know that there is no right or wrong way to grasp them. You may find that your experiences feel no different from your day-to-day ones, and you are aware of Spirit in other ways. Follow your inner guidance.

The Language of Space and Time

When you locate the information you receive in space and time, your message is specific and helpful. This is true for guidance for yourself and others, as well as for evidence. Also, these methods sharpen your ability to focus with your soul senses. Take your time and explore these tools over several sessions.

Past, Present and Future: You want to determine if and when an event occurs. For example, your sitter has her house up for sale and you see it with a 'Sold' sign in the front yard. But will it happen today? In the future? Or does it refer to a past 'Sold' sign that didn't work out last year?

Close your eyes, relax and call on your spirit guide. Ask to be shown your way to grasp the past, present and future. Your guide may show you the past on your left, the present in front of you, and the future to your right as they have done for many mediums. Ask for a simple way that suits you. Then ask to see the 'Sold' sign in one of these positions.

▸ *My Experience:*

___

___

___

Date, Calendar: Spirit can give you specific dates with numbers and words. Close your eyes, relax and call on Spirit to show you how to receive specific dates. Perhaps you are shown how to scroll up and down a calendar with your soul senses. It stops at the specific date you seek and you see the month, day and year; or you hear the words; or you see your phone light up with the date. Explore this with Spirit.

▸ *My Experience:*

___

___

___

Seasons, Days, Weeks, Months and Years

A sitter may want reassurance about a family reunion taking place in the spring, or you may want to gauge your travel to the weather in the months ahead. Close your eyes, relax and ask Spirit to help you perceive the seasons: You may identify the fall by the sound of crisp leaves underfoot and smell the chilly air; or spring by your sight of a vivid green of new growth. Let Spirit show you your way. How do you perceive days of the week? Do you see the words? Hear them spoken? Sense them? What about weeks? Months? Years? Open your soul senses to Spirit for your insight.

▸ *My Experience:*

_____

_____

_____

Specific Time; Morning, Afternoon and Night

You can develop your internal clock to tell the exact time, and be aware of the times of the day to fine tune a message. Close your eyes, relax and ask your spirit guide to help you to know the time by perceiving your inner clock or watch, and to develop a sensitivity to periods in the day using your soul senses.

▸ *My Experience:*

_____

_____

_____

Amounts

Graphs and charts are quick ways to assess amounts, such as, money and progress. Close your eyes, relax and ask your spirit guide to show you how to perceive a graph or chart to map your growth. Do you see it? Perhaps it's in color. Let it move to indicate its future progress.

▸ *My Experience:*

_____

_____

_____

Numbers, Names of Streets and Places

Discover the detailed information you can be given from your spirit guide to identify a loved one or offer guidance to help a sitter from street addresses to dates of birth, places traveled or lived in and so on. I leave this for you to enjoy on your own with other categories that might come to mind.

▸ *My Experience:*

_____

_____

_____

Give and Receive a Medium's Message

You are now ready to give a medium's message. Know that Spirit is with you to guide you and to shed light within to enhance your soul senses and gain information about a spirit loved one. The loved one who comes through is drawn in accordance with the workings of a higher order in which you play your part. Trust that your spirit guide brings through exactly what is needed by your sitter. Stay strong in your connection to Spirit.

Decide who will be the *medium* and *sitter*. At the end, you will change places. Read the exercise together and be clear about your respective roles.

Aim of the Exercise
The medium communicates with Spirit to receive

- evidence for the sitter that identifies (or helps to identify) a spirit loved one, and
- guidance that is relevant to the sitter's life.

Feedback
Look over and discuss *Give a Medium's Message – Feedback*, below. It's a useful guideline for the medium that summarizes the elements of a message. It highlights the kinds of evidence you've been exploring, and notes the guidance received.

An added feature of the feedback for the purposes of learning – two positive things about the message.

The sitter will use this sheet to

- record the information you receive during the message,
- coach the medium if asked,
- share two positive things about the experience, and
- give feedback at the end.

You will both prepare and meditate at the same time.

Sitter, have your pen and *A Medium's Message – Feedback* sheet ready. As the medium begins the message, call on your spirit loved ones. Open to them and ask that they draw near to help the medium bring evidence that identifies them. Also ask for guidance that is relevant to you. Stay up in your higher state of consciousness to the best of your ability, and record what the medium brings through.

Your attitude is important: Be open to receive. Be encouraging by accepting what is given whether you can identify it at the moment or not. One way to do this is to say 'I can't place it at the moment, but I'll take it. Thank you.' Sometimes you will recognize someone later. Similarly, with the information about your life. A simple smile, a 'Thank you' or a 'Yes' if something is particularly relevant can lend the support your partner needs to trust in what he is receiving.

Medium, if you are stuck and nothing is forthcoming, ask for help from the sitter who will offer coaching with questions that direct your focus on different kinds of evidence; such as, What clothes is he wearing? Can you see his surroundings? How did she pass?

→ Exercise: Give a Medium's Message (Partners)

Prepare
Use this shortened form of relaxation and readiness. Sit facing each other in a quiet and secluded area. Begin with a prayer of thanks for all you will receive, and for this opportunity to commune with Spirit to help each other. Ask God to draw near and bring your spirit guide and loved ones to help you.

Relax by focusing on your breath and as you inhale, let the life energy move into your entire body from the tips of your toes to the top of your head. … As you exhale, release all the concerns of the day. Stay with the streaming flow within and sense its loving light and love revitalizing you throughout your body and mind. Relax. Be at peace. …

Your Spirit Guide
Call on your spirit guide. Reach up to the higher planes with your heart and mind. Relax and let yourself be lifted up in your soul, free from your earthly self. Be at home in this lighter state. Float up… and up. … Become aware of the presence of your spirit guide near you and let the uplifting vibration infuse you: Feel the love in your heart and the light in your mind. Take a few deep breaths and relax. …

The Message by the Medium (5-10 minutes)
Open your soul senses and notice how full of life they are with Spirit's influence. How bright and clear is your perception! How sensitive your awareness! Look up with your gifts to a space in front and above you. You may be aware of it as an ethereal sky, a screen of white light or a clearing ahead.

Now ask your spirit guide to bring in a spirit loved one in a way that will be beneficial for your sitter. Wait now and see who appears before you, or who you hear speaking beside you or whom you sense. You may perceive them as you look within with your eyes closed or as you look at your sitter with your eyes open. Feel the love that comes from the spirit world and notice the kind of evidence given to you. Allow whatever comes to you to unfold. What is your first impression? … What do you See? … Sense? … Hear? … or even smell? … or taste? … As soon as you pick up something, give it out to your sitter. … Take your time and stay with what you're perceiving. … Notice the details … and share them. … Give out whatever you receive, no matter how small. Everything is important. This isn't a time to receive feedback from the sitter about the accuracy of your message. However, you may want confirmation in the form of a 'Yes' or 'Thank you' to keep open a sense of connection and a flow between you and your partner.

You may receive guidance for your sitter as you pick up evidence of the presence of a spirit loved one. Let the kind of evidence direct you to information that helps the sitter in his or her life.

Continue to share what you pick up with your soul senses. When you want greater clarity, ask your spirit guide to help you. If the flow of information stops, close your eyes and ask your spirit guide to bring you more evidence. You may mention a specific kind; such as, 'Show me his physical appearance' … or 'Is there a scene linked to the spirit?' … 'What was her work?' … If you are stuck, ask your sitter to coach you. Relax and direct your focus to other areas of the spirit loved one's life. Let the spirit world open to your soul senses in its own way and enjoy.

If you haven't received guidance that is relevant to your sitter's life, ask for it now from your spirit guide and the spirit loved one. Open your soul senses and let the information flow. What do you see? … Sense? … Hear? … or even smell? … and taste? … Trust what you receive, and ask that you be helped to share it in an uplifting and comforting way. If you are uncertain what condition it's intended for, ask you spirit guide and continue to give out what you're receiving. This is a chance to learn and explore: Don't restrict yourself but offer what you have. If another spirit loved one shows up at any time, follow the same process.

Close

You will know when the power is leaving you – you will find it difficult to sustain your higher state and focus. Signal to your sitter that you are ending the message with something like 'I'd like to stop here and close with a silent prayer.' You want to let the sitter know that you're still in a sacred space until you bring closure.

Silently give thanks to God and your spirit guide in prayer for your experience and this opportunity to help. Send love and appreciation for the spirit loved one(s) who came to visit. Gradually bring your awareness back to your body and the chair you sit in. Open your eyes and look around the room. Verbally thank your sitter for the coaching and support.

Feedback by the Sitter (5 – 10 minutes)

Share the evidence received and recorded, and explain how it fully or partially identified your spirit loved one(s). Also, discuss the guidance that came through and the ways in which it helped you, such as, bringing insight, comfort, direction or confirmation of events or conditions in your life. Finally, offer your partner two positive aspects of your experience. Discuss any other relevant details.

Change roles and repeat the exercise.

Give a Medium's Message – Feedback

I Evidence: Information that Identifies My Loved One(s)
Circle the kinds of evidence the medium gives, and fill in the details below.

Physical Appearance/ Personality/ Relationship to the Sitter/ Objects Linked to Spirit Loved One/ Scenes Linked to Spirit Loved One/ Words/ Health and Well Being/ Death/ Work/ Special Interests, Talents, Dreams/ History of Spirit Loved One/ Religion or Spiritual Practice

_____
_____
_____
_____
_____

II Guidance: Information from a Spirit Loved One that is Relevant to the Sitter's Life:
Fill in the details given by the medium. _____
_____
_____
_____
_____
_____

III Record 1-2 things that you like about the experience:
_____

Guided Meditation: Your Spirit Family Reunion

In this meditation, I will lead you to your Spirit Family Reunion in the spirit world where you will visit with your spirit loved ones. Your spirit guide will go with you.

Prayer
Let us begin with a prayer.

Infinite Spirit!

Be with us as we journey to reunite with our spirit loved ones on a higher plane of life.

We are grateful for all we have been given by our families – the blessings and the challenges, and we give thanks for this chance to visit them in the spirit realm.

We ask that our spirit guide draws near and help us on our way.

*Open our hearts and minds to your love and light,
now and always.*

Amen

Prepare
As you move into a state of relaxation, make yourself comfortable and free from distractions in your sacred space. Close your eyes and be aware of your breath. Relax. … Breathe in the pure energy of the unseen world around you. Feel its life as you take it into your lungs. Relax. … Breathe out any concerns or tensions . …Let them go. … Relax. Be at peace. …

Now sense this energy as it moves down into your lower body and fills every cell with perfect peace. Relax. … See it flowing like a liquid light as it moves down to your feet and into the earth. Relax. … Notice your breath and let it draw up this energy from the earth into your feet and up your body. Feel the life and light flowing in you back to your chest. … How relaxing!

Let this fluid light move up into your upper body. Relax. See and sense it as it moves into your shoulders, neck, arms and out to your fingertips. Be at peace. … Let this energy flow into your jaw, face and head filling every cell with life and light. Feel it in your mind and let it flow out the top of your head. Feel the lightness of your body and relax. … Now as you breathe, draw the vital energy from the sky into your head and let it flow gently back to your lungs. Feel the peace within. …

My Spirit Self
In this relaxed state, move upward now into your spirit state. Let your self be released from your earthly body. … Reach up … open your soul senses and move up into the etheric dimension. Notice how light and free you are as you float up into this peaceful place! … Keep floating up … and up … and become aware of yourself as your spirit. … Look around. What do you see? … Perhaps a misty space? … Pastel colors? … Light? … You may hear ethereal music as you float up … or a deepening of the silence. … Moving upwards, notice how you are releasing yourself from the earthly energies … and embracing finer and purer vibrations. … How wondrous you feel in your spirit self!

My Spirit Guide
Now as you look ahead and upward … a luminous presence is approaching from a distance … your spirit guide who comes to be at your side. As your guide draws near, what is your first impression? …

What do you see? … Sense? … Hear? … perhaps even smell or taste? … You may notice too how your thoughts and feelings seem more uplifted, your mind clearer, and you have a new sense of joy and love. Perhaps your guide, accustomed to this higher vibration, is able to convey its beneficial essence to you or it may be that you are attuning to the atmosphere of the higher plane in your unfolding sensitivity.

Greet each other and notice how you feel reunited with your guide. … Sitting or moving together, take time to talk. First listen to what your spirit guide has to say. … I leave you to do this. … Now ask your questions of this wise soul … perhaps about your spirit loved ones … about the spirit world. … about your mediumship … about other things … Notice how you commune … thought-to-thought … soul-to-soul … or just plain talk that you hear with your soul ear. …

The Place of My Spirit Family Reunion
Looking ahead, your guide points to what looks like a heavenly place in the distance, but even from here, you can see that it is full of divine light and beauty, and you can sense its love. Drawing closer and closer now, you realize that you're descending into a magnificent scene. … Gradually you feel your feet on the ground and you look around. You are in the middle of a meadow full of flowers, trees and streams, hills and valleys with the sounds of birds and glimpses of animals. It's like earth yet it is a heavenly earth: the colors are translucent, movement is effortless and the air is filled with a loving harmony. You realize you could never feel fear or sorrow here; pain and suffering don't exist. Take in the wonder of this place. …

My Spirit Loved Ones
Now, Spirit takes your arm and shows you your spirit loved ones who have been expecting your arrival. Approach them … and notice how happy and young they are. … Their love is overwhelming. … Who is here? … What do you see? … Greet each other and notice how you feel with your loved ones right here with you in spirit. … Perhaps it's indescribable – your sense of elation, of an ethereal quality to it all, and of connecting like this. … It may seem too good to be true. … Yet you know it's very real … their voices, familiar faces and even pets, what they're wearing. … Yet at the same time, feel the unusual newness of life. There is no sense of deadness or oldness here with your spirit loved ones. You realize that you too are revitalized; you look youthful, more who you really are … You are more fully your soul. …

You have much to say to each other. I leave you now to spend time with your spirit loved ones in the ways that you wish – walking with them or sitting down and getting reacquainted. You have your questions to ask too. Be with your spirit loved ones in this spirit place of loving peace. Enjoy this blessed reunion. …

My Special Messages
Your spirit family has prepared special messages for you to take back with you that help you in your daily life and your learning how to become a medium. A place has been reserved for you to sit with your spirit guide at your side to receive these messages. … Now notice as different spirit loved ones – by themselves or in groups – come forward and

bring you messages of love, insight, comfort, encouragement, direction, information or whatever your soul seeks at this time.

Sit and embrace the the members of your spirit family who bring their special messages. They may communicate directly to you or they may convey their words, thoughts or feelings through imagery and symbols in a space before you. Open your soul senses and let your spirit guide assist you as you receive the wonderful wisdom of your loving family and friends in spirit. …

In a moment, you will leave your spirit family. Is there anything else you want to express or hear before you return? … As you wrap up your visit, know that you can return here again. … Know too that you are never far away from each other in truth: you are always linked in the ever present life of the unseen dimension. This reunion has reconnected you soul-to-soul so you can call on your loved ones more easily in the future – the channel between you is strengthened. It is time to say your goodbyes and give thanks to your spirit family. …

Return

You're ready to leave, and with the help of your spirit guide, who has been with you in the background throughout your visit, you find yourself moving away from your place of your Spirit Family Reunion as your spirit loved ones, too, disperse to their own homes. Now you're floating once more in the ethereal sky feeling uplifted and exuberant from your encounter. … Come back. … And now come down … down ever so gently … slowly … floating down in your spirit self. …

Gradually sense yourself in your earthly body. … Perhaps you feel a little heavier as you move back to your sacred place and your chair. You are in your earthly body yet you retain your uplifted state of life. Revitalized and at peace, you feel centered and whole as never before. … Give thanks to your spirit guide who now leaves, having helped you return to your earthly home.

▸ *My Experience:*

My Spirit Self: _____

_____

_____

_____

My Spirit Guide: _____

_____

_____

_____

The Place of My Spirit Family Reunion: _____

_____

_____

_____

My Spirit Loved Ones: _____

My Special Messages:

Reflections on My Experience:

PART III BE AN INSTRUMENT OF YOUR SPIRIT GUIDES AND TEACHERS

The thing at which we are aiming – access to the great ocean of spiritual influence – must, for lack of a better term, be called spiritual contact and permeation. ... Assume for the moment ... that we are living in, surrounded by, a finer more powerful substance. You can call it what you please – ether, electric field, or spiritual vibrations. When we are accessible, we are permeated by it and obtain from it various elements of expansion and growth.

This contact and permeation can be brought about by ... a genuine energy of desire. We must want to reach out in harmony with spiritual forces. ...

The Invisibles, the Spirit Guides of Betty, *The Betty Book: Excursions into the World of Other-Consciousness*, by Stewart Edward White, 40.

Free Your Soul To Contact Spirit

It is 7:00 o'clock and I have prepared the room for 'class and circle'. I've set up a circle of chairs, lit a candle in the center, and put in a CD of music selected for tonight. I pray, relax and call my spirit guides and teachers to draw near and take me onto higher ground where I can be an instrument of their infinite love and light. I ask that the higher presences come to help the spiritual seekers who will be here shortly. I pray that everyone will feel at-one with themselves, spirit and their fellow students. I continue to reach up and open to God and Spirit.

As I do this, I see the misty vibrations of higher spirit presences that surround the circle and I feel a holiness in this space. I too am changed. My mind is lucid, I feel a new spiritual strength and love. I know that Spirit is uplifting me from deep within and preparing me for the circle. I need only let them work through me. I go the door to greet the students. They have been guided on this path by Spirit just as I have. This gives me comfort for I know the higher powers are working with us.

As the evening progresses, the vibrations in the room become finer and brighter. Each student unfolds in his or her unique way, each a channel for Spirit. I have selected a guided meditation where they will make contact with a spirit guide and be shown the higher planes. I begin, and as they reach up with their hearts and minds, open with their soul senses, then allow the spiritual influences to move them, I sense the power of Spirit lifting the circle upwards. We move towards the heights of the planes beyond this world. I continue and I know they are receiving their own teaching as they communicate with their special spirits. I open my eyes to a circle of shining faces, some with tears and others glowing with the inner light.

When we return, we sit without speaking. Then I ask for feedback. 'I didn't want to come back …', ' It was so beautiful!', 'I felt so good … such love … ' and 'I wanted to stay forever'. Many nods of agreement. They had connected with the higher planes and the spirit presences that inhabit them.

The Law of Attraction

It seems amazing that we can visit magnificent realms beyond the earth plane and contact spirit beings who want to guide and teach us. How is this possible?

In Part I you learned that you could attune to Spirit because you too were of the spirit, and once you realized your soul nature through prayer, relaxation and meditation, you could open to the unseen. With your gifts, you could perceive and gain information from it with the help of your spirit guide. In Part II, you were able to use your gifts to perceive spirit loved ones; in particular, you learned to identify them according to the vibrations they emanated as you communicated through the guidance of your spirit guide.

Here in Part III, you learn how to contact your spirit guide to become a channel or *instrument* of communication between two worlds. This requires a special relationship between you where your vibrational systems work together to ensure that the information comes from the spirit world. This kind of connection and spiritual work is possible through the *law of attraction.*

The law of attraction states that the soul desires, above all, to be close to God and Spirit. Often described as 'like attracts like', it means that as souls we are drawn naturally to higher ground where we experience the fullness of our true nature. When I first introduced this law in class, Nan's hand shot up, 'But don't opposites attract?' she asked. My reply: 'Yes they do in the physical world, but in the unseen dimension, like attracts like.' Let's look at some illustrations. Later, on your own, talk to Spirit. Test it out.

Again, the most fundamental expression of this law is the desire of the soul for God, for oneness, for fulfillment. For example, in the guided meditation in my story above, we were drawn to higher ground to our home, where we experienced our wholeness, our truth. The law applies to our spirit guides and teachers; that is, we seek contact with these higher powers to be close to them, to grow spiritually in the same way a flower seeks the light. While they are more evolved, our soul nature is compatible with theirs. We sense this likeness and are uplifted in our higher selves where we feel close and comfortable deep within. When we connect with their love, wisdom, goodness and beauty that surpasses our normal experience, we don't want to leave their presence. Our soul is fed by these spiritual qualities.

Alternatively, the law works from the perspective of Spirit too. Our spirit guides and teachers are attracted to us through the principle of likeness: the kinds of spirit entities working with us are exactly right for our development as mediums. They are also drawn to vibrations that resonate with the higher planes: For the class and circle, I created an environment that was uplifting and harmonious to draw Spirit. I cleansed and prepared my own inner states to be closer to my spirit teachers, and I helped those who came to the circle to raise their vibrations, awaken their souls and open with their soul senses to attract and move closer to Spirit. You do this in your daily practice and have relied on the law in the exercises you have done. You also rely on this law as mediums when you give messages in a circle. Spirit uses the law of attraction to draw us to the person for whom the message is intended.

In readings too, the law is at work. Sitters are drawn to us through the operation of unseen influences or vibrations. Throughout the session, the spirit loved ones that come through and the messages given, all happen in accordance with the principle of attraction. As you allow the law to work, contact with Spirit and service as an instrument to become a medium will be a natural experience full of wonder and delight. As we proceed, you will see how the law helps you to become a medium in each of these areas of your unfoldment.

Awaken Your Soul's Desire in Your Seven Centers

I will lead you in an exercise that helps your soul to emerge more fully within. Here we look at your soul as expressing its life in seven areas in your consciousness – your *chakras* or *centers*. As you learn to focus on each one, your soul comes to life, and the law of attraction is free to work with more spiritual power. This greater force helps you to create the conditions needed to contact Spirit: You clear away blocks so that you can reach beyond yourself, and your desire for higher ground can find its natural expression. Often referred to as *energy centers,* they are used in many spiritual and religious practices to awaken the life energy (called *kundalini* in the east) and bring about states of enlightenment. (For a fuller understanding of this system, see *Chakras* by C.W. Leadbeader and *Hands of Light: A Guide to Healing through the Human Energy Field* by Barbara Brennan who offer different treatments of the subject.)

Although the chakras aren't physically identifiable, we experience them along our spine and in our head, close to certain organs and glands. Your spirit guide will work closely with you to locate and open each center. At the same time, I will lead you step-by-step, to experience your soul as it expresses in each center. Some of you may have learned to sense them through colors, feelings or sensations (For example, with the first or root center, you may have focused on the color red, the energy of physical vitality and the feeling of warmth.) In this exercise, let the chakra speak for itself. Allow the life within you to express itself in each case as you focus on it with your soul senses. It may well be that your experience fits a classical approach, but the key is to come to it through your direct awareness. In the same way that you opened to a color and another symbol to connect to its meaning and life, here too, we do the same.

The aim here is to experience the divine life that exists within you in each center. In this way, you become aware of your spiritual nature at a deep level of your consciousness. You feel the immense support and power of your spirit that exists right within you and that enables you to contact Spirit and create a close relationship with your spirit guides and teachers. You need only become aware of each center with your soul senses, guided by your spirit guide, for your path to clear and your soul to emerge and open naturally through the law of attraction. As you move from one chakra to the next, notice that the divine energy is different. You may be aware of similarities too.

Let yourself see, sense and hear whatever emerges – colors, sensations, scenes, feelings, thoughts, words, voices, symbols – and trust that Spirit is helping you to discover a deeper layer of your higher self. Feel free to call on your spirit guide to illumine a center at any time. Just ask.

Because this is a long exercise where you need to stay focused, you may want to do it in two stages. For example, end it after the heart center and return when you are refreshed. Begin again to complete the last three chakras. Read the exercise carefully and have your pen ready to record your experience as you go along.

➤ Exercise: Awaken Your Soul Centers

Prepare
In your sacred place, sit comfortably with your spine upright. Close your eyes and pray. Relax and focus within. Become aware of your breath and relax. As you inhale, notice how soothing your breath feels. … As you exhale, release all your concerns. … Relax. Continue to breathe in and out. … Relax. Be at peace. …

As you sit in a relaxed state, look up above your head and see a light that glows with a heavenly love. Open to this light and feel it shining into your head and streaming down into your entire being. Notice now that in its presence, your soul senses have become bright and clear. And as you look at the loving light, you sense the presence of your spirit guide emerging in its aura. … Sit in the uplifting vibration of your guide and notice how you feel. … Now with the loving light of Spirit flowing through you and guiding you, open your soul senses to begin.

Awaken Your Root Center
Focus on the tip of your spine and your root center. Project the loving light of your spirit guide into this center and notice its energy. What is your first impression? … What do you sense as you continue to experience your root center? … What do you see? … Do you hear anything? … Do you have thoughts or sensations? … What word or phrase would you use to describe your experience? … Feel free to talk with your spirit guide as you awaken to your soul in your first chakra.

When you are ready, let the life energy spread out and flow into your surrounding area. … Be aware of it moving up your spine. … What do you sense? … See? … Hear? …Open your eyes and record your experience.

Awaken Your Second Center
Focus just below your navel in the center of your spine to your second center. Project the loving light of your spirit guide into this center and notice its energy. What is your first impression? … What do you sense as you continue to experience your second center? … What do you see? … Do you hear anything? … Do you have thoughts or sensations? … What word or phrase would you use to describe your experience? … Feel free to talk with your spirit guide as you awaken to your soul in your second chakra. When you are ready, let the life energy spread out and flow into your surrounding area. … Be aware of it moving up your spine. … What do you sense? … See? … Hear? …Open your eyes and record your experience.

_____

_____

_____

Awaken Your Third Center
Focus on the upper area of your solar plexus in the center of your spine and your third center. Project the loving light of your spirit guide into this center and notice its energy. What is your first impression? … What do you sense as you continue to experience your third center? … What do you see? … Do you hear anything? … Do you have thoughts or sensations? … What word or phrase would you use to describe your experience? … Feel free to talk with your spirit guide as you awaken to your soul in your third chakra. When you are ready, let the life energy spread out and flow into your surrounding area. … Be aware of it moving up your spine. … What do you sense? … See? … Hear? …Open your eyes and record your experience.

_____

_____

_____

Awaken Your Fourth Center
Focus on your heart near the center of your spine and your fourth center. Project the loving light of your spirit guide into this center and notice its energy. What is your first impression? … What do you sense as you continue to experience your fourth center? … What do you see? … Do you hear anything? … Do you have thoughts or sensations? … What word or phrase would you use to describe your experience? … Feel free to talk with your spirit guide as you awaken to your soul in your fourth chakra. When you are ready, let the life energy spread out and flow into your surrounding area. … Be aware of it moving up your spine. … What do you sense? … See? … Hear? …Open your eyes and record your experience.

_____

_____

_____

Awaken Your Fifth Center
Focus on your throat at the base of your neck and your fifth center. Project the loving light of your spirit guide into this center and notice its energy. What is your first impression? … What do you sense as you continue to experience your fifth center? … What do you see? … Do you hear anything? … Do you have thoughts or sensations? … What word or phrase would you use to describe your experience? … Feel free to talk with your spirit guide as you awaken to your soul in your fifth chakra. When you are ready, let the life energy spread out and flow into your surrounding area. … Be

aware of it moving up your neck. ... What do you sense? ... See? ... Hear? ...Open your eyes and record your experience.

Awaken Your Sixth Center

Focus on your forehead above your brow in the center of your head and your sixth center or third eye. Project the loving light of your spirit guide into this center and notice its energy. What is your first impression? ... What do you sense as you continue to experience your sixth center? ... What do you see? ... Do you hear anything? ... Do you have thoughts or sensations? ... What word or phrase would you use to describe your experience? ... Feel free to talk with your spirit guide as you awaken to your soul in your sixth chakra. When you are ready, let the life energy spread out and flow into your surrounding area. ... Be aware of it moving upwards in your head. ... What do you sense? ... See? ... Hear? ...Open your eyes and record your experience.

Awaken Your Seventh Center

Focus on the area above your forehead in the center of your head and your seventh or crown center. Project the loving light of your spirit guide into this center and notice its energy. What is your first impression? ... What do you sense as you continue to experience your seventh center? ... What do you see? ... Do you hear anything? ... Do you have thoughts or sensations? ... What word or phrase would you use to describe your experience? ... Feel free to talk with your spirit guide as you awaken to your soul in your seventh chakra. When you are ready, let the life energy spread out and flow into your surrounding area. ... Be aware of it moving up and out into the realms above. ... What do you sense? ... See? ... Hear? ...Open your eyes and record your experience.

Now be aware of the loving light of spirit still shining above your head. Open to it with your soul senses and sense it flowing down in and around you. Focus on each divine center as the loving light moves back into your crown, third eye, throat, heart, solar plexus, navel and root chakras. As you wind down, notice what you experience. ... Harmony? ... Power? ... Energy? ... Love? ... Peace? ... Stay a moment in your higher state. When you're ready to return, thank your spirit guide and notice that the light recedes. Open your eyes and become fully aware of sitting in your chair in your sacred place.

> *My Experience:*

_____

_____

_____

Stir the Active and Receptive Modes of Your Soul's Desire

The longing of the soul is both an active and passive principle. Contact with God and Spirit involves these two modes.

- *Active Seeking:* We reach up with our soul's desire beyond the familiar boundaries of the self to be close to a higher power, and

- *Receptive Allowing*: We open our soul to receive the vibrational influence of the spiritual presence in our desire to be at one with God and Spirit.

The Presence of God

The prayer, *Sense the Presence of God,* that you learned in Chapter One, demonstrates these two sides of the law of attraction. Let us pray and experience the beauty of this method in drawing close to God.

Sit in your sacred place, with your eyes closed, and take a few deep breaths as you relax. Open your heart and reach up beyond your self to seek God's presence. Focus your mind on a divine quality such as love or goodness. As you keep your focus, repeat the word; for example, Divine Love … Love … Love. … Then relax your reaching and open to receive. … In this passive state, sense God's love flowing into you. As you allow the divine quality of God to infuse in you, and notice that you feel more of your higher nature, more godlike in your love – more fully your soul. Give thanks and open your eyes.

My Experience of the Presence of God:

_____

_____

_____

The Presence of Spirit

You have used the active and receptive mode of connecting to Spirit in many meditations, but this is an opportunity to experience it with awareness in order to strengthen your ability to make contact with your spirit guides and teachers.

Prepare
In your sacred place, sit comfortably with your spine upright. Close your eyes and pray. Relax and focus within. Become aware of your breath and relax. As you inhale, notice how soothing your breath feels. … As you exhale, release all your concern. … Relax. Continue to breathe in and out. … Relax. Be at peace. …

Active Seeking
As you sit in a relaxed state, look up above your head and notice the light of Spirit in the distant ethereal sky. Be prepared to make an effort with your soul's desire to move beyond your familiar self to be close to the light. Reach up with

your soul heart and mind, and open your soul senses to focus upward on the light. Notice that your focusing requires an active energy to seek higher ground.

Continue to reach. ... Ask to be drawn up. ... Be aware that the energies in your system begin to shift from a sense of yourself as an earth being to a spirit one. How does this feel? ... As you make this shift, you move into an atmosphere of higher vibration. Here your soul senses may work more easily and you feel more natural. Notice how you feel and what you perceive. ... Now, notice that the light has drawn closer. It glows with a heavenly love. ... As you look at the loving light, you sense the presence of your spirit guide emerging from it.

Receptive Allowing

Be aware of the presence that appears before you. ... Let your soul senses take in its pure, fine vibrations ... Allow yourself to be affected by its emanations and notice how you feel. ... At any time, if you are not receiving from Spirit, reach higher in your active mode and then wait. Take your time. ... Now, ask to be shown a special quality that your guide possesses and which your soul needs at this time for your progress as a medium.

Stay in a quiet passive mode and open to the spiritual presence of your guide. ... Let yourself feel the higher nature of your spirit guide – its Love ... Light ... Peace ... Joy ... Understanding ... Strength ... Patience ... Confidence ... Purity ... Clarity ... Tolerance ... Wisdom ... or any other quality your soul desires. ... Let this divine energy flow into you and touch your soul. Continue to receive it and let yourself be enhanced by it. ... Open and receive. ...

Before you end your visit, open to your spirit guide to receive a brief message about what you received. ...

Return
When you're ready to return, thank your spirit guide who also leaves. Gradually come back to your sacred place. Open your eyes and feel yourself revitalized and more fully yourself.

▸ *My Experience:*

My Active Seeking: _____

_____

_____

_____

My Receptive Allowing: _____

_____

_____

_____

My Message: _____

_____

_____

_____

Final Reflections _____

_____

_____

The Difference between God and Our Spirit Guides and Teachers

In both exercises, you invoked the presence of a higher power. Still there is a big difference between our relation to God and to our spirit guides and teachers. We pray to God, but not to the spirits who we invoke and relate to as spirit entities or *discarnates* (beings who are not *incarnated* or who don't live on earth at this time. Our spirit loved ones too are sometimes described as discarnates.)

In your daily practice, ask your spirit guide to explain the difference to you and gain your own intimate understanding of this important distinction. I think of them as *messengers of God* who pray to God as I do, and who are progressing on the higher planes of life through their spiritual service.

My understanding of the difference between God and my spirit guides and teachers:

_____

_____

_____

Our Desire for God

Let us recognize our desire for God (however we understand this Supreme Being,) and how our souls move upwards under its influence. As we seek, we create the conditions that attract the higher powers for they require the soul's vital life energy to work with us as our guides and teachers. The law of attraction shows then, the power of our soul to gain access to the spiritual heights we seek and to become the mediums we envision. In your daily practice, ask your spirit guide to continue to ignite your desire for God and to discuss it with you.

How I continue to ignite my desire for God with Spirit's help and guidance:

_____

_____

_____

10

Get to Know Your Spirit Guides and Teachers

Why Do They Come?

Our spirit guides and teachers come to us as we seek to develop as mediums. It is amazing to fully grasp the startling fact that spirit entities come from the higher spheres of the unseen world to communicate with us in order to guide and teach us. The law of attraction is at work in our relationship with them. They have special talents that are exactly suited to our needs as we unfold our mediumship. Their minds, personalities, view of life, spiritual purpose, and emotional nature are similar to ours and what we aspire to be. Our spirit guides and teachers appeal to us vibrationally, and their influence extends to our personal lives.

Here are some illustrations of this.

Sam is a jolly man who loves music and plays the guitar. His spirit guide is a Norwegian sailor who communicates with him in humorous ways, singing and humming songs. Sam's messages are bright and sunny, and they heal through laughter. His guide's strong presence and optimism helped Sam to overcome a deeply rooted pain that lay behind his joviality most of his life.

In contrast, Leti, a short thin student has a spirit guide who is a serious priest from Medieval France. Like Leti, he exudes a quiet rational mind and high ethical values. He has helped her find security in the ordered goodness of the unseen world. Her messages are clear, thoughtful, and spoken in a level tone without fanfare. Leti's integrity strengthens as her mediumship develops and people trust her words because of it.

Consider James, a strong big boned young man with a loud voice and a very direct way of speaking. His guide is a Native American Indian called Brown Bear. James' messages carry the power of 'bear' energy and the sitter always knows that the truth will be given without any hedging. His spirit guide has helped him to use his assertiveness to uplift and teach others, and in the process, it has reinforced his own self esteem.

Then there is Alice whose spirit guide is Blossom, a young girl with a sweet, innocent slant on life. Many sitters are glad to hear from their spirit loved ones with her messages that are pure and gentle. Blossom's presence has dissolved Alice's timidity and strengthened her soul with a renewed sense of life.

The guides of Anna and Bob come in shimmering robes with translucent colors, and have opened their minds to a new understanding of the progression of spirit loved ones on the higher planes. This teaching has infused their messages with inspiration and motivated them to write and speak as channels of Spirit.

In a message or reading, the kind of evidence and the way it is given, the philosophy, beliefs and higher understanding conveyed, the focus on certain topics more than others, the way in which a sitter is touched, all are reflections of our spirit guides – who they are, where they come from, our relationship with them, and their particular way of expressing their higher nature such as compassion, intelligence, goodness, power, humor and joy. Our part is to make ourselves a channel for these wondrous presences and to create a close and compatible relationship with them as we trust in their guidance and act on it.

A Common Purpose

Ultimately, you and your spirit guides and teachers are drawn together by a common purpose – to bring knowledge of eternal life from the spirit world to the earth plane. You can do this in different ways as a medium. For example, messages and readings are the most familiar forms of mediumship. We have examined the kinds of spirit guides and teachers who come to work with us in that capacity.

There are other less familiar ways in which Spirit brings knowledge of eternal life from the spirit world. Through inspirational writing and speaking certain kinds of spirits, especially suited to this particular work, influence your soul's gifts to bring higher understanding that is different from the knowledge received in messages and readings. Absent healing and prophecy are yet other forms of mental mediumship – each has its unique set of soul gifts that are utilized by spirits with special talents. The kinds and numbers of spirits that work with us vary from medium to medium. Seek as honestly and whole heartedly as you can, and you will attract the spirits you need to fulfill your heart's desire.

Your relationship with your spirit guides and teachers operates on the inner level of consciousness. This allows the gifts of your soul to be awakened beyond your normal capacity. Besides psychic and mediumistic abilities, they include a caring and compassionate attitude, a joyous and happy spirit, an inner peace, higher understanding, insight, and inspiration.

Who They Are

Who are they? Spirit guides and teachers come in many forms – people from past lives whom we may or may not have known, spirit loved ones, pets, non-domestic animals and other creatures, non-human entities such as angels, color rays, forces, spirits of natural things, fairies and nature spirits.

Also, people who lived in enlightened societies of the past help the modern medium to serve. For example, North American Indian, East Indian, Celtic, Asian, Egyptian, Mayan, Greek and Persian souls return as spirit workers to serve. Often they bring their teachings to enlighten us and our world.

Their Roles

The following offers the traditional view of the group of spirit guides and teachers who work with us to give messages and readings. The modern medium may or may not experience their spirit guides and teachers in this way – the focus, numbers and roles may vary. Let's look at this standard description first, then explore it for ourselves later.

A *medium's band or group* consists of many kinds of spirits who fulfill different roles in our readings (and messages). A band is said to be 9 – 12 in number with the following key members.

A *gatekeeper* or *control* is in charge of the process and ensures that the spirit entities enter in a way that is beneficial to the sitter in accordance with the growth of his or her soul.

A *protector* and/or *guardian angel* protects, uplifts and guides the medium with loving care.

A *runner* or *messenger* is a youthful spirit who runs off into the spirit realms to bring spirits to the session or conveys messages from them.

A *chemist* works with the medium's body to create the chemical and energetic conditions suitable for spirit communication.

Teachers provide knowledge, philosophy, practical guidance and understanding on many levels and subjects. One or more spirit teachers, advanced in their spiritual growth, guide the medium's progress from a higher perspective than the other members of the band.

Other Spirits guide the medium including doctors, psychologists, therapists, ministers, priests, priestesses, speakers, inspirational thinkers, business people, historians, mechanics, social workers, scientists, writers, cooks, computer experts, creative artists, contractors and gardeners. Also, all kinds of additional spirit guides can help out, such as, joy spirits, healers and light workers.

Often you will be aware of working with one main spirit guide in giving a message or reading – your gatekeeper or control – with periodic visitations from different spirits who are needed for the task at hand. Usually there is one spokesperson for a band who expresses the mind of the spirit group. (On the higher planes, the thoughts of its members blend harmoniously with one another.)

Where do they come from?

They inhabit the *higher planes*. Many of us first learn about the higher planes through the loss of a loved one. We feel a sense of comfort and happiness knowing they are in a better place. As we develop as mediums and we are initially drawn to the unseen by God and Spirit, we begin to experience the same world of immense beauty, goodness, love and wisdom. Our souls are moved. We want to explore this spiritual universe that feels so true and right.

Ancient teachings describe the unseen as made up of higher planes, or dimensions, where a different vibrational influence determines the kind of life that exists there. As we learn about these planes of existence, and attune to their vibrations, we can more fully grasp the kind of spirit beings who communicate with us. They are able to help us because they have evolved to higher states of consciousness traversing these planes in the unseen world. So too, our own soul's journey involves our progression beyond the earth plane to life in the higher planes.

Descriptions differ according to philosophies and belief systems. Usually the unseen is divided into seven planes of existence characterized by a physical, emotional, mental, celestial dimension, and three realms of nirvana. (For descriptions of these planes, see *Man Visible and Invisible,* by C.W. Leadbeader who offers the view of Theosophy, plate II following p 22; and *Arthur Conan Doyle's Book of the Beyond* who offers his Spiritualist version with eleven planes, p 42. Typical of their day, both authors describe the earth plane in a negative light that most of us would not agree with today.

The Seven Higher Planes

Let's take a brief look at each of these planes.

- The spiritual dimension of the physical or earth plane is the *etheric*. This is the dimension of the unseen in which we live as earthly beings. When you relax by noticing your breath, you are revitalized in every part of your body because you breathe in its life giving vibrations. We all have an *etheric double:* It is our spirit that can be seen clairvoyantly as a translucent bluish white energy that is a replica of our physical body yet in its more youthful and pain free state. This is the 'body' in which we make the transition from this plane to the next. You can perceive a thin band of it around your hands. Hold up your hand against a dark background with your fingers spread out. Take a moment to relax, and focus on the half inch space around your fingers. Relax your gaze, and as you persist, you will see the clear etheric energy.

- The next plane is the emotional or *astral*. It means 'starry' and refers to its luminous appearance which results from its rapid rate of vibration. This is where most of us go when we pass from the earth plane at the end of this life and where our spirit loved ones can progress spiritually. Activities here include healing, counseling, teaching and loving service directed to people on the earth and the astral planes. As mediums, we can learn about life on the astral plane from those who communicate in messages and readings. *Summer-Land* was coined by Andrew Jackson Davis to capture a heavenly place in the upper astral plane and the happy condition of life there, free from pain and strife. (See his account of his explorations – in lucid states of higher consciousness – of the unseen dimensions in his book *Death and The After-Life*.) It stands in stark contrast to the *Winter-Land* that is his depiction of earthly life.

- The *mental plane* has two kinds of activity – practical thinking and abstract thought. We hear fragments of information about this dimension, such as the 'halls of learning' or 'temples of wisdom' (from Arthur Ford in Ruth Montgomery's *A World Beyond*) and 'places of higher contemplation' (from Silver Birch in *The Teachings of Silver Birch)*. Here enlightened spirit teachers inspire and illumine the soul with their gentle compassion and understanding. We're told that the earth's inventions and cultural achievements are first created here. Spirit intelligences from this plane point out the faults of earth – our cruel treatment of criminals, the futility of war, and our religious intolerance that separate us as a humanity.

- The next plane, the *celestial* or *Buddhic,* is where we learn to be of greatest service to others and gain states of true bliss. The self, as we know it, experiences an increasing awareness of selflessness.

- The next, *nirvanic* plane, is the highest conceivable spiritual attainment. Here one is no longer a human form. Peace, harmony and bliss are experienced beyond our conception.

- Two even higher planes exist about which little is known.

Spirit Guidance and Teachings Come from Higher Planes

Our spirit guides and teachers live on these higher planes of life. We can learn a great deal about them by attuning to their vibrations. As they ascend, the planes are more luminous and uplifting, and the vibrations are finer. The colors that spirits express when they come to us often reflect the plane on which they exist or the kind of expertise they bring. But the planes are complex – each is said to have seven levels within it – and the nature of existence is hard for us to conceive. The information, then, may not be specific or quite what we expect; but if you keep an open mind to new understanding, your spirit guides and teachers will teach you what you seek.

There are other ways that Spirit helps us to gain information from the spirit realms. While we can't live on these planes until we have progressed to them, we can visit them in dreams. Higher understanding comes to us through the influence of our spirit teachers who take us to places of learning in this dimension. You may not be aware of your experience, but you may gain the insight you wanted or a piece of information seems to magically fall into place upon waking. You also visit these spheres in guided meditations.

As we open to the higher vibrations through contact with our spirit guides and teachers, we can transcend our limitations and the challenges of earthly life. Our increased awareness of the higher planes deepens our relationship with Spirit and our mediumship as an instrument of service.

Communicate With a Member of Your Spirit Band

To determine what spirits are with you, it's important to find out yourself. This search will bring you wonderful discoveries, and help to refine your gifts as you reach into the higher realms and await the compassionate intelligences who come to guide and teach you. We begin our search by communicating with a member of your band to discover who they are, where they come from and their purpose with you.

In the following exercise you will contact a specific member of your band – your protector or guardian angel. I have selected this particular guide because we tend to invoke this spirit's help in the course of our lives whether we are mediums or not. For example, you may have a sense of its protective influence during difficult driving conditions or other dangerous situations, and you give thanks to it though you may not have known who or what it is. In less critical conditions, we find comfort by calling on this presence who seems to strengthen and support us in the face of challenges, or keeps us safely cocooned in its fine vibrations of loving light and goodness when we feel vulnerable, even though we may not perceive this spirit directly.

As a medium, your needs for protection are linked to your ability to work as a channel for spirit. You want to be able to raise your vibrations and communicate in your soul's higher state of consciousness in a safe environment; that is, where no intruding influences distract your focus. Your protector helps you to do this. You will find out more now from your guide.

→ Exercise: Contact Your Protector or Guardian Angel

In this meditation, notice how you are guided to use the active mode of your soul to reach up to Spirit, and your receptive mode to become aware of the higher vibrations that your spirit guide expresses. (It will be familiar to you from the meditation *The Presence of Spirit* in Chapter Nine.) Your spirit guide, who protects you, may be a guardian angel, a human being or even an animal or bird, but whatever it is, I will use the word 'protector' to refer to your guide. And while your specific protector may be a he, she or it, I will use 'it' or the singular 'they' to refer to this divine presence. I will continue to refer to any spirit guide or teacher this way throughout the book.

Have a pen ready so you can record your experience during your meditation, or at the end when you're still in a partially elevated state of consciousness. For some of you, writing during the exercise may help you to focus; for others it may interrupt your connection to Spirit.

Prepare
In your sacred place, sit comfortably with your spine upright. Close your eyes and pray. Relax and focus within. Become aware of your breath and relax. … As you inhale, notice how soothing your breath feels. … As you exhale, release all your concerns. Relax. Continue to breathe in and out. … Relax. Be at peace. …

Reach up to Spirit
Reach up with your soul heart and mind into the higher realms of the unseen. Look up from within and call on your spirit protector to draw near. Open your soul senses, and as you focus upward become aware of the shimmering light of a spirit presence far off in the etheric sky. Feel your soul's desire to be closer to the light. …

Be Your Spirit Self
Let yourself float up and up. … Let go. … Feel yourself releasing your earthly body. … Notice a sense of your spirit self. … Let go. … Become lighter as your spirit moves up into the etheric sky. Your soul senses are clear and bright. Notice how you feel … and what you perceive. …

Your Protector

Now, the light draws closer. … It glows with a heavenly love. As you look at the loving light, see your spirit guide emerging in its aura. … Be aware of the divine presence that appears before you. … With your soul senses, take in the uplifting vibrations emanating from your protector. … Open to its fine spiritual influences and notice how you feel. …

What is your first impression of your spirit protector? _____

_____

_____

What do you see? _____

_____

_____

What do you sense? _____

_____

_____

What do you hear? _____

_____

Do you smell or taste anything? _____

_____

_____

How else would you describe your spirit protector? _____

_____

_____

Your Common Purpose

As you greet each other, notice how you feel with your spirit protector. … Open your soul senses, and in particular your soul ear, and listen to your protector as your conversation unfolds. You may grasp the words as sounds or as mental hearing, or you may communicate thought-to-thought or by an intuitive knowing. Sometimes you may receive information through messages from your guide that you can pick up with your sight or sense. Enjoy your connection. …

Spirit begins with opening words: _____

_____

_____

Next, your protector answers your questions:

Who are you? _____
_____
_____

Why have you come to me? _____
_____
_____

Where do you come from? _____
_____
_____

How You Are Protected

As you talk, you are surrounded by a magnificent vibration that has been created by the presence of your protector. You find yourself sitting in its divine influence. … Your spirit guide demonstrates its protective power. Know that it can be used any time of the day, during daily practice, and to prepare for service as a medium:

Protection within

Open to the fine vibration of your guide's protective influence. Its spiritual energy pours down into your entire body and fills you with divine light, love and life. … Feel the power of these spiritual vibrations flowing in you and extending from within into the space around you to create a strong sense of your own being. Feel it. Know the power within that is you. …

Protection around you

Looking up above your head, see and sense its divine vibration in a translucent color that cascades down around you and surrounds you as a protective energy of light and love. …

Protection for a specific a situation

Now, Spirit shows you the situation unfolding before you. Step into that scene feeling spirit's protection in and around you. Be your new self of power and spiritual strength. Notice how the situation changes and unfolds in a positive way. … Notice how strong you are in your higher self. …

Protection in times of stress

Your protector now bathes you in divine light, love and life of protection and you feel completely released from anxiety.

How to Identify Your Protector

How will I know you're with me in the future? _____
_____
_____

What is your name or what can I call you? _____

_____

_____

Know that you can call on your spirit protector at any time. You can also return to this meditation when you choose.

Return
It's time to leave. Thank your guide for coming and helping you. When you're ready, you both depart. You find yourself floating gently down and becoming heavier and more aware of the vibrations of earth. ... Yet you retain the same sense of your bright uplifted soul; your consciousness is still bathed in the light of the higher realms and this stays with you. Now, slowly come back to your awareness of your comfortable chair. Take a few deep breaths to center and ground yourself. ... Open your eyes feeling renewed and comforted in your knowledge that a higher presence is with you helping to protect and uplift you on your earthly path and in your spiritual work.

You can use this exercise to get to know other spirit guides and teachers in your band. Feel free to adapt it to your use. Embrace the new learning each one brings to enhance your spiritual unfoldment. For another account of your spirit guides and teachers and how to communicate with them, see *So You Want to Be a Medium?* by Rose Vanden Eyden.

Be an Instrument of Your Spirit Control

Three Ways to Be with Spirit

The Presence of Spirit

From the very beginning (Chapter Two), you began to be aware of the presence of Spirit. Some of you felt an uplifting vibration around you, others felt peace, still others sensed clarity of mind or saw an ethereal light. As you unfolded your gifts, you may have noticed that your awareness of the presence of Spirit has become enhanced – Spirit seems to draw near with less effort and this experience feels more and more natural. Most importantly, as you become more aware of the presence of Spirit, you will be able to use your gifts more easily: Your soul sight becomes clearer, your inner ear picks up sounds more readily and your inner sense is more acute. Your evidence becomes more accurate and precise, your guidance more relevant.

For some mediums, awareness of the higher vibrations of Spirit's presence is all they need to do good work whether they are giving a message, a reading, writing or speaking inspirationally, or healing. Whether your experience of the presence of Spirit is subtle and hardly noticeable, or dramatic and vivid, continue to call on Spirit to draw near as a presence. Ask for whatever you need – a clear mind, a loving heart, a renewed spirit. Reach up, open to the higher powers and wait for what you seek.

Information about Spirit

Most of us also want to know who our spirit guides and teachers are: We want to spend time with them and benefit from their knowledge. We want to see them and talk with them face-to-face. You have done this in the guided meditations, *Meet Your Spirit Guide in Your Sanctuary* (Chapter Four), and *Communicate with a Member of Your Spirit Band* (Chapter Ten). You have learned to pray, relax and meditate in order to raise your consciousness and draw close to your spirit guides and teachers as they lower their vibrational rate to meet with you.

Next, you have used your soul senses to contact and perceive them – you can see what they look like, sense who they are, hear what they say. You will find too, as you continue to seek guidance and higher understanding from them, that you are communicating soul-to-soul, mind-to-mind and heart-to-heart. You are close to them, uplifted and at-one with them. You can find out their names, their history and all you want to know for your soul's growth and mediumship.

You will have many opportunities to be with Spirit in this way and to find what you seek. Your ability to perceive them and develop a close relationship with them will evolve in time. Continue to attune to them, keeping in mind that they come to teach you how to unfold your true self and become a medium. As you learn from them and trust them, they guide you to higher ground where you can envision this world and the next from their perspective. To receive the precious gifts of the spirit, make a practice of communing with them during your daily practice in the restful quiet of your sacred place.

An Instrument of Spirit

When we give a reading, a message, a talk or we write inspirationally, heal at a distance, or attempt to prophesy we always work as *an instrument* of a spirit guide or teacher. Our aim is to communicate with the spirit world to bring knowledge of eternal life, and as you know, we do it through our spirit guides and teachers. And as we discussed in Chapter Ten, one guide or teacher in particular works with us as our *spirit control* (or *gatekeeper*) to direct the proceedings while members of the group support the process from afar. Through the spiritual law of the unseen dimension, we attract a spirit control who is best suited to work with us given our abilities, interests, and life purpose.

As an instrument of our spirit control, we combine both ways of being with our spirit guides and teachers described above. We use our soul senses to become aware of the presence of our spirit control. We may see an ethereal light, a symbol, a color, or glimpse spirit's face or appearance. We may sense an immense peace or love, hear sweet music, a gentle voice, or a name. We may feel transported to a quiet place. Some of us may sense heat or cold or notice our hands are very big; we may be very tall when we stand up and sense spirit's vibrations in and around us. We may feel unusually light-weight, happy or free from any concerns.

Any one of these signs of spirit's presence acts as a *trigger* that moves us deep within. It is a powerful way to open our soul to higher presences who teach us how to work with them. We feel an immediate connection with Spirit and are drawn up to an elevated state of consciousness where we are attuned to the spirit world. The infusion of Spirit's fine, uplifting vibrations flows into us and we experience the fullness of our true selves and a blending of our spiritual energies with our spirit control. In this state, we feel the power to serve as an instrument of Spirit.

The trigger by which we recognize the presence of our spirit guide or control and are drawn up to the higher planes, differs from one medium to the next. Whatever the indicators by which Spirit helps you to work as an instrument, trust that they are exactly what moves you beyond your normal reach. We may not receive a distinct trigger – Spirit may work with us in a fluid way where we have a feeling of everything falling into place, or a sense of a veil lifted or a deep state of peace. Sometimes we may just jump in and realize that we were ready all along! Finally, a medium can work very well as an instrument and not distinguish her vibrations from those of her spirit control except to be aware that she is elevated beyond her normal capacity.

Be an Instrument of Your Spirit Control

As an instrument of Spirit, you participate in a higher order that unfolds wondrously around and within you. You and your spirit control have your parts to play.

You prepare through prayer, relaxation and meditation. Clear and cleanse your system of any concerns. Raise your vibrations, awaken your soul and open your soul senses for your guide's higher influence. Open your heart with compassion and a desire to serve. (You will be given more guidance about this in Part IV.) Spirit can work better when you are uplifted in your soul. You want to create an atmosphere where the vibrations are spiritually uplifting so that your messages and readings will come from a pure source of love and truth.

Your spirit control and your spirit group prepare the etheric space for the events of the reading. They open the way for a sitter's spirit loved ones to come and communicate. Through the vibrational influence of your spirit control and the visiting spirits, evidence and guidance are given to benefit the soul of the receiver. All this is carried out in tandem with the spiritual forces operating in the unseen dimension.

⤺ Exercise: Become an Instrument of Spirit

Here you will learn how to identify your spirit control and experience its presence in order to work as an instrument. Now that you know how to prepare and move up in your soul to meet a spirit guide in the spirit world, I guide you here with simple directions to be with your spirit control as an instrument.

Prepare:
- Sit quietly in your sacred place. Pray, relax, meditate and raise your vibrations. …

- Call on your spirit guides and teachers, and ask them to help you move into your soul's higher states. …

- Wait and notice how you begin to feel released from the concerns of this world and from the sense of your physical body. Let yourself be drawn up into the higher realms and be free of your ego. …

- Open your soul senses, reach up and focus into the unseen with them. Ask that you may be of service as a medium. Continue to sit in harmony. …

Become an Instrument of Spirit:
- Now, ask for your spirit control to draw near and teach you how to be an instrument. Allow the law of attraction to work and begin to notice a difference in the atmosphere around you and in your inner state.

- Stay open with your inner senses and gradually become aware of your control. The finer and more elevated vibrations of this guide are beginning to influence you within and without.

- How are you aware of the presence of your spirit control near you? Is the light in the room brighter with the spirit's influence? Do you sense your spirit's presence? In what ways? Perhaps you hear your control? Or do you see something that is an indication of your guide's presence? Does your spirit control show you a symbol, or color or a scene that moves you? You may feel hot or cold, or a wind; your hands may be large or energized; you may be unusually tall when you stand up or your breath feels revitalized. By what trigger are you aware of your control and drawn up to a higher state where you feel connected soul-to-soul with your guide?

- If you haven't received an indication of your spirit control's higher vibrational presence with you, ask for one. Wait for a sign and be receptive to the guidance you receive. …

Experience Your Elevated State
- Welcome your spirit control. Become aware now of an elevated state that is being created by a sense of your control's divine vibrations infusing in you. Experience a new power in you where you feel confident that you can give a message.

- You're connected as an instrument of Spirit, and in particular, of your control. With this, you may experience a greater clarity of mind and perception as if you are an enhanced version of your normal self. You feel good!

- You may also feel an enriched sense of compassion, tolerance, empathy, understanding and vitality. How do you feel as an instrument of your spirit control?

> *My Experience:*

My Preparation: _____

_____

_____

_____

My Experience as an Instrument: _____

_____

_____

_____

My Elevated State: _____

_____

_____

_____

Give a Medium's Message as an Instrument of Spirit (Partners)

Follow the same procedure for giving and receiving a medium's message with feedback, as you did in Chapter Eight. This time, you will work as an instrument of your spirit control. Notice the difference and record it below on your worksheet *Give a Medium's Message- Feedback by Medium*. Compare your feedback with your previous experience. Also, aim to improve your message in whatever way you are guided by Spirit. Perhaps you want to receive more precise evidence, hear from several spirit loved ones, or offer more detailed guidance that is relevant to your sitter's life. Recognize that this is a learning situation where you give loving support to yourself and each other. No judgment enters here – only acceptance and desire for your own and your partner's success. Review your feedback sheets *Give a Medium's Message – Feedback by Sitter* is familiar. *Give a Medium's Message – Feedback by Medium* is new: It empowers you to appreciate and pursue your progress as a medium.

Medium:

1. Prepare to give a medium's message. Pray. Take your time to call on your spirit control to draw near. Open your soul senses and let this divine presence infuse you and draw you up to your elevated states where you connect soul-to-soul. Determine how you want to improve your message and receive a sense of the spirit's power to help you do this. When you are ready, invite your partner to sit in the chair in front of you as your sitter.

2. As you begin your message, stay strongly connected to your control's presence as an instrument.

3. Throughout the process, maintain your link to your spirit control. Notice how your spirit's presence brings more life to your soul senses, more clarity and more accuracy to your message. Ask for this.

4. Don't hesitate to close your eyes to reinforce your contact with your control and receive information. Trust in the higher forces. Trust in yourself and the power bestowed upon you.

5. Relax in this learning environment and feel the loving support from your partner and the spirits from the planes beyond. Rejoice in this opportunity to work closely with your spirit control!

Sitter:

1. Prepare with prayer, relaxation and meditation. Call on your spirit guides and teachers to be with you. Then, open to your spirit loved ones and ask for them to draw near. The more aware you are of them and the spirit world, the easier it is for your partner to communicate and give an uplifting and accurate message.

2. As a sitter, be relaxed yet alert. The medium is helped by your elevated soul states and your higher vibrations.

3. Be ready to accept what is given and record what you receive in a positive and kindly way. Ask your spirit guides to help you with the feedback for your partner on *Give a Medium's Message – Feedback by Sitter*.

4. When the message is finished, take a few minutes to fill in Section III as the medium records her own feedback.

5. Offer your feedback. Exchange roles and repeat the process.

Give a Medium's Message – Feedback by Sitter

I Evidence: Information That Identifies My Spirit Loved Ones
Circle the kinds of evidence the medium gives, and fill in the details below.

Physical Appearance/Personality/Relationship to the Sitter/ Objects Linked to Spirit Loved One/ Scenes Linked to Spirit Loved One/Words/Health and Well Being/Death/Work/Special Interests, Talents, Dreams/History of Spirit Loved One/ Religion or Spiritual Practice

_____
_____
_____
_____
_____
_____

II Guidance: Information from the Spirit World That is Relevant to My Life
Fill in the details given by the medium.

_____
_____
_____
_____
_____

III Record 1-2 Things I Liked About My Message.
_____
_____
_____
_____
_____

Give a Medium's Message – Feedback by Medium

I **My Experience:** *Immediately following your message, record your feedback.*

What I liked about my mediumship: _____
_____
_____

What I would like to improve: _____
_____
_____

How my work as an instrument of my spirit control improved or affected my mediumship: _____
_____
_____

II **Feedback from My Spirit Control:** *Later, in your sacred place, ask your spirit control for insight into your mediumship and give thanks.*

Please give me feedback about my message. _____
_____
_____
_____

Help me to understand these things about the message. (Specify what puzzles or confuses you, if anything). _____
_____
_____
_____

How will you continue to help me unfold my mediumship?

Help Others Know Their Spirit Guides and Teachers

Just as you help others develop a closer connection to their spirit loved ones when you communicate with them, you can help others get to know their spirit guides and teachers by communicating with them. In both cases, you open your soul senses to the spirit world, and with the guidance of your spirit guide, bring through information that helps your sitter know who has come and why.

When you perceive your partner's spirit guide or teacher, you will want to find out what they look like and how you feel with them, who they are, why they come and where they come from. You will also want to hear from them with messages that help your sitter in some way. (You are familiar with this from your meditation with your spirit protector.)

Above all, in both kinds of spirit communication, you will want to help your partner awaken to a vibrational connection with the presence of a spirit, and to experience its spiritually uplifting and transforming quality. (This is also what you seek to do for your sitter when you give a message.) In the following exercise, you will have the opportunity to explore a new way to communicate with another's spirit guide or teacher. Instead of sharing what you perceive with your partner through words, you will do it through *art*.

Draw the Spirit Guide or Teacher of Another

Spirit art or *spirit drawing* is a form of mediumship where spirit influences the medium to produce a visual portrait of a spirit loved one that accurately portrays how he or she looked on earth. (For illustrations and a description of spirit drawing as a form of mediumship, see *The Complete Idiot's Guide to Communicating with Spirit, 119*.) This is a wonderful way to receive an evidential message that confirms the continuing existence of a loved one on the other side of life.

Spirit art is also loosely used to describe other kinds of visual information from the spirit world that are not forms of mediumship (strictly speaking), because the art doesn't provide evidence. Still, these artistic ways of receiving information from the spirit realms through art are invaluable ways to learn and grow as mediums.

One of these ways is to draw a spirit guide or teacher as one perceives him or her with the soul senses guided by Spirit. Sometimes in my daily practice, I will be impressed to draw a spirit presence (as I write with my pen), and I'm surprised at how its life comes through on the page. It's a wonderful validation of my inner perception.

➔ Exercise: Draw Your Partner's Spirit Guide or Teacher

As always, read over the exercise before you begin. Don't be intimidated by the idea of *drawing* Spirit. I have done this with hundreds of students and everyone has provided a rendition of a spirit that delighted and inspired their partner. Do it in your way and be proud of your creation. This is an opportunity to free up your inner censor and let Spirit influence you with form and color. Some of you may draw a swirl of colors or a symbol instead of an image of a spirit. Follow your creative instincts and let yourself be guided. Enjoy!

The aim of this exercise:

- to help your partner confirm and expand her knowledge of her spirit band, and
- to provide insight into her spiritual progress, and
- to experience one form of spirit art.

I will guide you step-by-step through the exercise including the process of drawing what you perceive. Here music is used to help you meditate and easily connect to Spirit with your soul senses to perceive your partner's spirit guide or teacher. This is a very uplifting experience because you are influenced by the vibrations of the spirit as it comes to life on the page. And since you and your partner are connecting to a higher presence at the same time, your heightened state is intensified.

Have ready: Sheets of white paper, pastel crayons, felt nib pens or whatever materials you wish. Also, have a pen ready to record Spirit's messages. You and your partner will do this exercise at the same time, and then take turns to share your drawings and messages.

Prepare:
Sit facing each other. Close your eyes, call on your spirit band and ask any member to draw near for your partner to clearly perceive. (Don't stipulate who.) Ask a question about your spiritual progress that you would like answered. Record it, but don't tell your partner what it is.

My question: _____

_____

Music Meditation
Play quiet music that you both find inspiring. Silently pray and relax each in your own way. Continue to relax and allow the music to lift you upwards into your purer self where you feel free from your earthly body and busy mind. Let yourself drift up as the music helps you to float upwards into the higher reaches of the ethereal sky. … Feel the peace, sense the quiet. … Let yourself be free. Open to the love and harmony that surrounds you. Be at peace. …

Your Spirit Guide
As you look around, notice that you are in a clearing and your own spirit guide is approaching. You greet each other and sense the uplifting vibrations of this spirit entity from a higher plane of life. … How do you feel with your spirit guide? … What do you see? … Notice who has come … someone new or perhaps familiar. … Listen to a message from your spirit guide … and embrace the teachings. …

Now you are directed to a seat, your guide sits beside you and you see an empty space in front of you where your partner's spirit guide or teacher will appear before you. You feel confident and excited about what's to come.

Draw a Member of Your Partner's Band:
Open your soul senses now to perceive a presence that is emerging before you on the stage. How magnificent it is! You could never have anticipated the feeling you have as you attune to this higher being who expresses such divine qualities. This is your partner's spirit guide or teacher.

Draw Spirit
Notice what this guide looks like and observe the colors that emanate from its presence. ... Focus on the details of the spirit before you. ... When you feel ready, ask your spirit guide for help to draw its form and colors. To do this, stay in your elevated state attuned to your partner's spirit, and open your eyes to pick the colors to capture what you perceive on the paper before you.

Relax and enjoy the freedom to express your soul by drawing your partner's spirit guide. ... Let your arm and hand be moved by Spirit and continue to sketch the spirit you perceive within. ... Close your eyes when you need to reconnect with your partner's spirit. ... Feel your close contact with your own spirit guide as you work together and play with your work of art. ... I will leave you now to do this. ...

Messages from Your Partner's Guide or Teacher
As you attune to this divine presence, reach up with your soul and ask the following questions. Let the answers come through your soul senses in symbols, conversation, thought or just a knowing.

Who are you? _____

_____

_____

Why have you come? _____

_____

_____

Where do you come from? _____

_____

_____

What is your answer to my partner's question about her spiritual progress? ... Write the answer in a corner or on the back of your drawing. _____

_____

_____

What word or phrase describes my partner's essence? ... Write this at the top or bottom of your drawing. _____

_____

_____

What attracts you and my partner? (By the law of attraction.) ... In a word or phrase, write your answer in another corner of your drawing. _____

Return
Feel the power of your partner's spirit begin to fade. Give thanks to this presence who now retreats. Linger a moment with your own guide for a final message. … Ask your spirit guide to stay with you as you give and receive feedback with your partner. Gently return to the room. Retain your elevated state to the best of your ability. Silently say a prayer of thanks.

Share:
Take turns to share your drawings and messages. Try to sustain your higher consciousness and link to the presence of your spirit guides as you do this in the same way that you do in a development circle. Exchange your drawings and thank your partner. Silently express your gratitude to your spirit guide for coming as you take your leave.

▸ *My Experience:*

My Spirit Guide _____

_____

_____

My Opening Message _____

_____

_____

My Closing Message _____

_____

_____

Additional Thoughts, Insights, Feelings _____

_____

_____

Perceive Another's Spirit Guide or Teacher

(To do in a separate sitting from the exercise above). Proceed the same way as you would if you were drawing your partner's spirit guide or teacher only instead of drawing, record your perceptions and the answers to your questions. You may receive the information in symbols, abstract visual images or colors, or merely with words and sounds rather than a literal perception. Trust that Spirit is communicating in whatever way is right for you and your partner to receive at this time.

→ Exercise: Perceive Your Partner's Spirit Guide or Teacher and Record What You Receive

As always, read over the exercise before you begin. Like spirit art, don't be intimidated by the idea of perceiving another's spirit guide or teacher. This is an opportunity to free up your inner censor and let Spirit help you to perceive the magnificence of a higher being who comes to help you and your partner. Enjoy the freedom to explore the unseen in your own way.

The aim of this exercise:

- to help your partner get to know another member of his band,
- to give him insight into his spiritual progress, and
- to contact and communicate with another's spirit guide or teacher.

I will guide you step-by-step through the exercise. Again, music is used to help you meditate and easily connect to Spirit with your soul senses to perceive your partner's spirit guide or teacher. This is a very uplifting experience since you and your partner are connecting to Spirit at the same time, like in the previous exercise.

Have paper and a pen ready. You and your partner will do this exercise at the same time, and then take turns to share what you received.

Prepare
Sit facing each other. Close your eyes, call on your spirit band and ask any member to draw near for your partner to clearly perceive. (Don't stipulate who.) Ask a question about your spiritual progress that you would like answered. Record it, but don't tell your partner what it is.

My question: _____

Music Meditation
Play quiet music that you both find inspiring. Silently pray and relax each in your own way. … Continue to relax and allow the music to lift you upwards into your purer self where you feel free from your earthly body and busy mind. Let yourself drift up as the music helps you to float upwards into the higher reaches of the ethereal sky. … Feel the peace, sense the quiet. … Let yourself be free. Open to the love and harmony that surrounds you. Be at peace. …

Your Spirit Guide
As you look around, notice that you are in a clearing and your own spirit guide is approaching. You greet each other and sense the uplifting vibrations of a spirit entity from a higher plane of life. … How do you feel with your spirit guide? … What do you see? … Notice who has come … someone new or perhaps familiar . … Listen to a message from your spirit guide … and embrace the teachings. …

Now you are directed to a seat, your guide sits beside you and you see an empty space in front of you where your partner's spirit guide or teacher will appear before you. You feel confident and excited about what's to come.

Perceive a Member of Your Partner's Band
Open your soul senses now to perceive a presence that is emerging before you on the stage. How magnificent it is! You could never have anticipated the feeling you have as you attune to this higher being who expresses such divine qualities. … This is your partner's spirit guide or teacher.

Describe Spirit

Notice what this spirit looks like and sense the vibrations that emanate from its presence. ... Open your soul senses now and with the help of your spirit guide beside you, record below what you perceive. Close your eyes when you need to reconnect with your partner's spirit guide or teacher. ... Feel a close contact with your spirit guide as you work together. ...

My Partner's Spirit Guide or Teacher

My First Impression _____

_____

_____

What I See _____

_____

_____

What I Sense _____

_____

_____

What I Hear _____

_____

_____

What I Smell or Taste (if anything) _____

_____

_____

Special Features _____

_____

_____

Messages from Your Partner's Guide or Teacher

As you attune to this divine presence, reach up with your heart and soul, and ask the following questions. With your guide's influence and support let the answers come through your soul senses in symbols, conversation, thought or just knowing.

Who are you? _____

_____

_____

Why have you come? _____

Where do you come from? _____

What is your answer to my partner's question about her spiritual progress? _____

What word or phrase describes my partner's soul or essence? _____

What attracts you and my partner? (By the law of attraction)? _____

Do you have any other message for my partner? _____

Return
Feel the power of your partner's spirit guide begin to fade. Give thanks to this presence who now leaves. Linger a moment with your own guide for a final message. … Ask your own spirit guide to stay with you as you give and receive feedback with your partner. Gently return to the room. Retain your elevated state to the best of your ability. Silently say a prayer of thanks.

Share
Take turns to share what you received. Try to sustain your higher consciousness and link to the presence of your spirit guide as you do this, in the same way that you aim to do in a development circle. Thank your partner. Silently express your gratitude to your spirit guide for coming as you take your leave.

› *My Experience:*

My Spirit Guide _____

My Opening Message _____

My Closing Message _____

Additional Thoughts, Insights, Feelings _____

Feedback
Fill in your partner's feedback as she shares it with you so you will have a record of it.

My Spirit Guide or Teacher: (Perceived by My Partner)

My Partner's First Impression _____

My Partner Sees _____

My Partner Senses _____

My Partner Hears _____

My Partner Smells or Tastes (if anything) _____

Other Features _____

Messages from My Guide or Teacher (Perceived by My Partner)

Who are you? _____
_____
_____

Why have you come? _____
_____
_____

Where do you come from? _____
_____
_____

What is your answer to my question about my spiritual progress? _____
_____
_____

What word or phrase expresses my soul or essence? _____
_____
_____

What attracts us? (By the law of attraction.) _____
_____
_____

Do you have any other message for me? _____
_____
_____

Thank you.

Perceive and Draw a Member of Your Own Spirit Group: (Optional)
Proceed the same way as you would with a partner. Call on a guide that will help you during this exercise, listen to a message and sit together to perceive a member of your own spirit group. Draw this presence and ask the same questions. Give thanks for the opportunity to get to know another member of your spirit band.

Guided Meditation: Teachers on the Higher Planes

In this meditation, I will guide you to meet an animal spirit guide who brings you unusual insight, and then to a higher plane where a spirit teacher enlightens you about your spiritual journey as a medium. This is a long meditation, so some of you may want to do it in two parts where you communicate with your animal spirit teacher in one and go directly to your spirit teacher for the second.

Have your pen ready to record what you receive from Spirit. Some of you may want to open your eyes to write during the meditation in the space provided, or you may want to wait until the end of the meditation to do so.

Prayer
Let us begin with a prayer.

Divine Spirit!

We give thanks for the opportunity to learn from our spirit teachers from the unseen world.

Shine your light upon us as we seek higher understanding.

We ask that what we learn helps others as well as ourselves.

Amen.

Prepare
Sit in your sacred place. Close your eyes. Focus on your breath and relax. … Imagine yourself surrounded by an infinite loving life. As you breathe in, let this life energy flow into your lungs and relax. … Be at peace. As you breathe out, let go of any tension within. Relax. … Continue to breathe in and out, and let the loving breath of life flow into every part of your body. … Relax. Breathe it into every cell and fill every part of your being with its soothing light. … Relax.

The Etheric Plane
Gently open your soul senses and see your sacred place opening to a natural scene. You step into it and realize that this place is like the earth, yet it seems brighter, more alive. Everything glows with a translucent life. … This is the etheric plane of existence where you are attuned to the spirit of the earth.

Looking around you, what do you see? … How do the colors look? … What do you hear in this earthly paradise? … Are the sounds different than usual? … What do you sense here? … Do you sense more vividly here? … Do you smell? … Taste? … Do you feel warm or is it a crisp day? … Be aware of how sensitive you are to the influences around you … perhaps the life of trees, the vibration of water, or the energy of the sun. … Enjoy this world as you continue to explore its wonders. …

My Animal Spirit Guide
Now, begin to notice wildlife here – animals, birds and even insects – yet you are not afraid. … In your spirit self, you are at-one with all life around you. No harm can come to you. And every living thing is a spirit here and is in harmony with one another. Sense the wonder of being at peace with all creatures and to move among them freely with love. …

Become aware of an animal, bird or other natural creature coming toward you looking like it does on earth, but alive with its spirit. What creature do you attract to teach you today? … What is it doing? … Notice its appearance and behavior. ... What do you sense with its presence? ... What is it teaching you just by showing you its magnificent ways? ... Your animal spirit guide prepares to communicate with you. ... Listen with your inner ear and use your soul senses to pick up its teachings. ... Perhaps you connect with your thoughts telepathically or with your heart. ... You may hear words or sense the meaning of the message. Relax with this beautiful creature and learn from it. Open to receive new insight that surprises you. I leave you to do this. ... Your animal spirit guide is here to teach you whenever you are in need. Just ask. Thank your teacher and prepare to move on as it too returns to its own life.

A Higher Plane

You move on and feel a new freedom from the pull of earthly forces. As you focus into the expanse of the infinite, you're drawn upward . Let yourself go and reach up with your desire to be on higher ground. Your heart quickens as you see a silvery halo of light ahead. Moving towards it, you float effortlessly into a fine, pure vibration where you feel a sublime elevation. ... Coming closer to this shimmering aura, you feel immense calm mixed with a brightness of mind, and your heart feels like a newly opened flower. You know that you are close to the presence of spirit beings of higher intelligence and compassion. You have arrived on a higher plane. ...

A Loving Welcome

Looking up, a kindly presence greets you and takes your hand. This is your spirit teacher. What an amazing presence! Notice how you feel as your teacher welcomes you. ... Open your soul senses and be aware of your spirit teacher's finer vibrations. ... What qualities do you sense in your teacher? ... What do you see?... Open your ear and listen to your teacher's words. ... How do you feel with them? ... Are they soothing ... uplifting? ... What else do you experience in spirit's presence? ... Perhaps you feel love or a gentle strength and wisdom you've not known before. ... How enlightening your contact with your teacher is! ...

My Spirit Band

Next you move with your teacher into an assembly where your spirit band has gathered. A bright yet soothing light emanates from the group and lifts you into your higher consciousness where your soul senses are completely clear and lucid. ... Realize now that your spirit guides and teachers are drawing near; they smile with love and exude a happiness that draws you up into a state completely free of many of the thoughts that occupy you on earth. Your mind is open and clear.

Here with your spirit band, you are not concerned about your mediumship in any way: You feel close to them, a sense of being naturally drawn to them and them to you, and this gives you a new buoyancy, a sense of things being taken care of from their side. You're not alone as a medium, and you need have no doubts about your gifts and how to work with your spirit band to unfold them.

My Spirit Teacher

You walk among these uplifting souls with your teacher who gently ushers you to a secluded place of sacred teaching. Spirit begins with a brief opening message as you settle in and listen. ... Your teacher may connect with words, thoughts, symbols, images or even demonstrations to help you learn; you may link soul-to-soul, mind-to-mind or heart-to-heart. Open with your soul senses and trust in how the teachings are given.

Opening Message

You want to know more about your teacher who now sees your thoughts and answers your questions.

Who are you? _____

_____

_____

Why have you come to help me? _____
_____
_____

How is the law of attraction at work here? _____
_____
_____

What is this higher plane? _____
_____
_____

How will I know you are with me when you visit? _____
_____
_____

Teachings

Your teacher has much to say about your spiritual journey to become a medium. Listen to the wise and compassionate teachings that are offered to you. Spirit first addresses your strengths and challenges as a medium.

Your strengths as a medium _____
_____
_____

How to develop your strengths _____
_____
_____

Your challenges as a medium _____
_____
_____

How to overcome your challenges _____
_____
_____

Your spirit teacher now brings higher understanding that is relevant to you at this time. Notice how easy it is to hear spirit's communication in this realm! Embrace the teachings that enlighten you. …

Higher Understanding: _____

Return

You sense the session drawing to a close. How amazing to receive knowledge from a spirit intelligence who inhabits a realm beyond your present conception! Thank your spirit teacher for all you have received and prepare to return. Know that you can come here when you seek higher understanding from your spirit teacher. Know too that you will now be more familiar with your spirit teacher's presence when you are called here for higher learning. As you open to Spirit on the higher planes, you are helped to be a stronger channel, your soul senses become more purified and your higher mind more illumined.

You move gently down, down towards your earthly home. Feel its pull as you slowly return to your sacred place. With gratitude, notice how alive and bright you feel in your soul, and confident in your spiritual journey as a medium.

▸ *My Experience:*

The Etheric Plane _____

My Animal Spirit Teacher _____

A Higher Plane _____

A Loving Welcome _____

My Spirit Band _____

_____
_____
_____

My Spirit Teacher _____

_____
_____
_____

Reflections On My Experiences _____

_____
_____
_____
_____
_____
_____
_____

PART IV GIVE A READING AND A PUBLIC MESSAGE

For nearly fifty years he put his mediumship at the disposal of humanity without asking for reward or praise. Many have obtained an enlarged outlook, and received renewed hope and comfort, because he lived. In all humbleness and modesty he gave freely and expected nothing.

On the Edge of the Etheric or Survival after Death Scientifically Explained, by Arthur Findlay, in memory of John Campbell Sloan, the medium whose service as an instrument of Spirit was the foundation of Arthur Findlay's research.

13

Be Of Service

A couple has arrived half an hour early for a reading and sit in the shade under an old maple tree in front of my house. In the summer, mediums in Lily Dale create their waiting rooms outside. These are sacred spaces in natural surroundings with flowers and artifacts where sitters feel the quiet serenity of this spiritual community.

I am in my reading room about to prepare to give readings. I relax and as I play soft music, I become engrossed in my own happiness. The day is sunny and still, and I realize that I really don't want to disturb this sense of being, content just where I am. I hear the people outside and go to the front door to let them know I'll be ready at the appointed time. As I open it, I'm startled to see a deep despair and hopelessness on their faces. They make no attempt to hide their grief – it hangs everywhere around them – and I know they have lost a child.

I return to my reading room, light a candle, smell the fresh flowers, and as I begin to relax, I realize that I can help this couple as an instrument of Spirit, only if I reach beyond my present sense of myself and use my inner happiness and love of God and Spirit to become a vehicle of service. Even with a deep compassion for their suffering, I know that I cannot help them without my spirit guides and teachers. Not the way a medium can.

I pray urgently. I reach up with a new desire to be close to Spirit. I pray to be able to be an instrument. I pray for help for this couple. I invoke Spirit to draw me up and to draw near. Please be with me … Please take me up …

Then I see the blessed light of my spirit group illuminating my reading room in a soft spirit glow. I feel those elated states I've become familiar with as I experience Spirit's infused presence. My inner gifts are heightened and as I look out at the world, I sense with their vision, the way they perceive it – illumined, brighter, alive.

I wonder how I could not have wanted to break out of my old self! How could I have not wanted to seek, to reach into the higher planes! Here all is well. Even in the face of misery and suffering, still one knows that all is well. We are of the spirit – eternal. And those who have passed on can link with us closely, intimately soul-to-soul. I sit and give thanks.

I know that in this state, working as an instrument – at one with my spirit guides and teachers – I can help the grieving couple find relief from their terrible suffering. Spirit can reach into their hearts and convey what is needed.

I open the door to greet them, ready at last to serve. As I invite them into my reading room, I pray that their souls will be touched and their awareness of their child's living spirit will lift them up and light their way.

The Law of Loving Service:

Let us remind ourselves that the laws we're talking about aren't imposed upon us. We may resist them as I did, but it's because we forget to listen to our soul's yearnings. They are forces intrinsic to the soul. They're spiritual – natural to the soul – and function on the unseen levels of consciousness.

The law of loving service is such an inner force of our soul. It's our soul nature to love others; that is, given a healthy environment where our soul is free to express its real nature, we care deeply for the well-being of others. Within us lies an infinite capacity for compassion for our fellow humans and for all living things. Especially if another is suffering are we drawn to reach out with love. Even when a stranger is in need, we are moved to ease their pain.

As mediums, we help others in the capacity of instruments of our spirit guide and teachers. This is how mediums *serve*: we communicate with higher spirit beings who bring information from the spirit world that proves the eternal nature of the soul and an understanding of what this means for the sitter in this life and the next. In my story above, I realized how powerless I was to truly help a grieving couple because I hadn't taken on the mantle of *service*. As my soul was touched by the despair of my sitters, the law of loving service moved me to connect with my spirit control and function as a channel from my soul self that is capable of true compassion and selflessness.

Strength in the Law

The law helps us to draw on our soul's natural love for others and to reach out to help. In this way our soul is strengthened so that we can overcome any obstacles that interfere with our mediumship. A classic example is in *The Wizard of Oz*: the cowardly lion overcomes his fear when his love of Dorothy and his desire to save her from the wicked witch moves him to risk his own life for her.

While this may seem an extreme illustration – we're not risking our lives to give a reading or a message—it may seem so as we prepare for a sitter or a crowd of seekers, all who have high expectations of our ability to communicate with Spirit and in particular with their spirit loved ones. The whole thing may seem daunting if we let fear take hold. Even in a circle, the situation can be intimidating: our message may seem so meager, so silly, 'How can I possibly give it out and survive?'

But we do survive. And as we allow our love to express to those who seek guidance from us, we realize that with loving service, all is well. For we serve Spirit, and as we learn to trust in the higher powers, we are aware that we are supported by magnificent beings whose compassion for us and for all humanity is boundless.

→ Exercise: Use the Law to Overcome Fear

It seems strange that we don't embrace higher states of our soul's fulfillment, as in my story, even when we know in some part of ourselves, that we can. One way to grasp this is to realize that we're human as well as spirit beings; that to become a medium we need to learn from our human foibles and with the help of Spirit, become stronger, more tolerant and compassionate. For example, the fearful lion in *The Wizard of Oz* learns how to be courageous and become more fully his true self. Think of a situation where you felt fear or some other state that interfered with your ability to work effectively as a medium, such as before giving a reading, a message in a circle, or a public demonstration (for those of you who are more experienced). Describe it.

My Situation: _____

_____

_____

Prepare
Sit quietly in your sacred place and with your eyes closed, pray, relax and meditate. ... As you continue to sit, open to the higher planes and call on Spirit, in particular, your spirit control to draw near. ... Feel your earthly concerns dissolve as you move up higher and higher into the etheric atmosphere. ... Be at peace and relax. ...

A Message from My Spirit Guide
Your spirit control comes close and you open your soul senses to this etheric presence. Talk with your spirit guide about your fear in the situation you've identified. Ask Spirit to help you understand how the law of loving service can help you to overcome this challenge. Listen to the insight and guidance you receive.

Understand the Power of Love to Overcome Fear
Imagine yourself in that situation feeling that fear. Let yourself be aware of this feeling and your sense of being immersed in it. You may feel you can't change it.

Then, picture the person(s) in that situation who seeks help from you as a medium and feeling the love of your guide in and around you, open to this person with your loving soul. Pour out your love to those who seek – let it pour out from your heart and sense your soul-to-soul connection. Let Spirit help you to understand the power of love to overcome fear. You can tap into your soul's reservoir of love anytime you feel fear.

New Strength as an Instrument of Service
Now ask your spirit control to come near to strengthen you as an instrument of service as you continue to focus on the situation. Be aware of the presence your guide. Sense a fine spiritual vibration infusing you and carrying you upwards. You feel more your soul self. Your inner senses are open and sensitive to the spirit world as you realize a new connection to Spirit and a power, that comes with a close link with your spirit control. You are in an elevated state of readiness to work as a medium. You are ready to serve.

Now you look out at your sitter(s) and know that in your higher state of oneness with your spirit control, you feel compassion beyond your normal capacity and as spirit's messages flow through you as a channel, you want only to serve. You have experienced the law of loving service expressing through your soul. Talk to your spirit control as you reflect on the power of this law to transform your fear into new strength.

Return
Prepare to return to your normal consciousness. Give thanks to your spirit control and come back gently to your sacred place.

▸ *My Experience:*

My Message: _____

_____

_____

The Power of Love to Overcome Fear: _____

_____

_____

New Strength as an Instrument of Spirit: _____

You may prefer to do the exercise where you have more distance from your fear. Instead of experiencing the situation, perceive yourself in front of you in a clearing or on a stage, and with spirit guidance, see yourself learning how to use the law to overcome your challenge.

You can do this exercise using any attitude or concern that interferes with your effectiveness as a medium. Here are some examples from my own and my students' experience: self-doubt and lack of confidence, over confidence and inflated self-esteem, intolerance and a critical mind, and self-righteousness and a know-it-all attitude.

Use the Law to Uplift Another with Prayer

Throughout this course, you have been guided to begin any spiritual activity with a prayer. It draws God's pure and loving vibrations into your awareness, clears away the debris of interfering influences and creates a spiritual space for your soul's growth. Also you have been asked to thank the higher powers at the end of the activity. This brings closure that prepares you to return to the normal events of the day. The same principle applies to mediumship. When you give a reading, you begin and end with a prayer. But now your prayers are *spoken aloud*. Here, as an instrument of loving service, you pray for your sitter. Your words create an awareness of the sense of the presence of God and Spirit that uplifts you and your sitter in a cocoon of spiritual well being. There's nothing so moving as listening to someone pray for you with a loving heart and a genuine desire for your happiness.

A Medium's Prayer

With the help of God and Spirit, create your *medium's prayer* that feels right for you to open your readings. This is the prayer that came to me (over time) as I asked for inspiration to help those who heard it – including myself!

Divine Spirit! Infinite Intelligence!

We give thanks for all our blessings.
Please draw near to help us on our journey.

We ask that spirit loved ones, guides, teachers and angelic messengers be with us at this time
and bring whatever is needed – comfort, guidance, inspiration and information.

Open our hearts and minds to your love and light,
now and always

Amen.

➔ Exercise: Receive Your Medium's Prayer

Before you begin, review the discussion of God in Chapter One, and renew your connection with God in a leisurely way. Revisit the section on prayer and enjoy your communication with God through different kinds of prayer. Know that inspiration often needs time to gel. Enjoy the process. Have your pen ready.

Prepare
Sit in your sacred place and close your eyes. Relax using an exercise of your choice. ... Be at peace. ...

Commune with God and Spirit
Sit and silently call on God and Spirit to draw near and bring inspiration in the form of a prayer. ... Reach up with your soul senses and your mind, and continue to ask for their help. ... Feel yourself become lighter, leaving your sense of yourself as a physical body, and more your spirit self. Enjoy your freedom to float up and up without effort and relax. ....

Now open to the presence of God and Spirit. Allow their uplifting vibrations to infuse your soul and bring you to a higher state of peace and oneness. Notice how bright your mind is, how loving your heart, how clear your eye and ear and sense!

Receive Your Inspiration
You are ready to receive your inspiration for your prayer. Feel yourself as a channel for God and Spirit. Perhaps you want to imagine yourself with a sitter before a reading. Ask to be given what you need. Let it come in its own time and write down what you receive. Perhaps thoughts come that move you, or you hear words, or you just write what you sense and need. Trust and record what moves you, know that whatever touches you will also reach into the heart of another and bring them to an awareness of their own divinity. You may change what you receive or fix it as you go along. Some of you may talk with God and Spirit as you go along. Do whatever suits you. Stay connected to the best of your ability.

My Medium's Prayer: _____

_____

_____

_____

_____

_____

_____

_____

_____

_____

Your prayer may be a draft that you revise over several sittings. Or you may feel pleased with it as it has come to you today. You will find that as you use your medium's prayer, it will immediately trigger a higher state of spiritual awareness in you: It becomes a beacon for God and Spirit to draw near.

Return
When you are ready, give thanks to God and Spirit. Return slowly to your sacred place and gently open your eyes.

▸ *My Experience:*

_____

Receive Your Closing Prayer

Your *closing prayer* is a brief thanks and request for blessings as your sitter goes on her way. You don't want to distract your sitter from her elevated experience, but you want to bring a quick and reassuring closure, so she can make a transition to her day.

Here is an example.

Infinite Spirit!

We give thanks for what we have received.

*Be with us, keep us in your love and light,
now and forever,*

Amen.

In order to receive your closing prayer, you may want to repeat the exercise above. Or, you can simply sit in prayer with your pen and ask for your inspiration.

My Closing Prayer: _____

➤ *My Experience:*

These prayers can also be used in other spiritual activities. For example, in an unfoldment circle, all members can create their prayers and take turns to open and close it. Also, these prayers are powerful tools for leading spiritual services and ceremonies.

Give and Receive a Mini-Reading

To prepare to give a mini-reading, let's look at some definitions.

A *reading* is a 30 minute session where a medium gives a collection of messages to a sitter, in private, and usually includes a brief question and answer period. Generally, the information received by the medium is more detailed and personal than messages given in a circle or in a public demonstration.

A *mini-reading* is a 10 -15 minute session where the medium gives several messages to the sitter and answers one question. You may have noticed that when you do this service, you expend a kind of energy that you haven't used before. Mini-readings help you to build your stamina and focus before you move to longer and more complex ones. Mediums often begin their public work with mini-readings as a service to organizations or churches for fund raising events.

You have learned to give messages where you received evidential information from the spirit world that describes another's spirit loved one and that also brings guidance that is relevant information about the sitter's life. I have encouraged you to be open to receive whatever Spirit brings and to share it without censoring or restricting the flow of the communication. It's important to continue to do this even now as you hone your medium' skills.

Evidence: Review and Enhance Your Skills

When we serve Spirit as an instrument, we allow the law of loving service to operate through us so that our soul senses can perceive the precise nature of the evidence presented to us. When the evidence clearly identifies a spirit loved one, the sitter reconnects with his or her familiar loved one, and also becomes aware that their loved one is a spirit living in another dimension of reality. The sitter is opened to the unseen, and with it, to a sense of his or her own soul and of being a part of something quite out of the ordinary, something holy, sacred.

It can all seem so easy and magical – to the medium and sitter alike – especially as one becomes practiced in giving readings. But, as a rule, to serve Spirit with consistently accurate and uplifting readings requires discipline and practice.

Here are some ways to refine your gifts on your own, before you give a reading, to help you get off to a good start on your journey of loving service.

→ Exercise: How Are You Perceiving Spirit Loved Ones?

Have a pen ready and be prepared to open and close your eyes to do the exercise. As always, read it before you begin. Retrieve the exercise from Part II Chapter Seven *Evidence to Identify a Spirit Loved One* to refresh your mind about the many ways that you can identify a spirit loved one.

Prepare: Sit in your sacred place. Pray, relax and meditate in ways that you wish. ... Call on Spirit as you open with your soul senses. ... Relax. Let yourself move up into a higher state of consciousness and feel your soul self. Let go and be free in your higher self. ... Enjoy!

Be with Spirit: Call on your spirit control or other guide or teacher. Reach up with your soul's desire to be close to Spirit. ... Open your soul senses and move upwards. Feel at peace and complete in yourself. ... Now see a spirit presence approaching. Greet each other and sense the fine vibrations of this divine being. ... Is this a new guide or someone you're familiar with? Listen to Spirit's words. ...

Kinds of Evidence Perceived: With Spirit as your guide and teacher, reread the *Evidence to Identify a Spirit Loved One* and notice the kinds of evidence you have received in your messages. For example, you may have perceived the *Physical Appearances* of spirit loved ones and their *Health and Well Being*. Or you've sensed their *Personalities, Interests* and *History*. Close your eyes and discuss the kinds of evidence that you have perceived so far. When you're ready list them below.

Soul Senses Used: Read your list of evidence and reflect on the soul senses you used to perceive each kind. For example, you may have perceived the *Physical Appearance* of a spirit loved one and used sight entirely to pick up every detail. Or perhaps you also sensed some aspects of the spirit. Or you may have heard a description of the loved one. Talk with your spirit guide or teacher about this and when you're ready, list them below.

Kinds of Evidence I've Perceived	Soul Senses Used
1.	
2.	
3.	
4.	

Value Your Messages: Reflect on the chart above and notice what you like about your gifts and the evidence you've perceived with them. ... Close your eyes, and open to a white screen before you. Your spirit guide shows you your gifts and the evidence you perceive in shining light, love and life. Look at yourself as a medium now. What do you see? ... Sense? ... Hear? ... Listen to the teachings of your spirit guide. ...

Return: Give thanks to your spirit guide. Return slowly and gently to your sacred place and open your eyes, refreshed and pleased with your progress.

▸ *My Experience:*

My Perception of Myself as a Medium _____

_____

_____

Teachings from Spirit _____

_____

_____

_____

➤ Exercise: What New Kinds Of Evidence Do I Want To Perceive?

Review the fact sheet *Kinds of Evidence* once again, and become aware of the areas that you would like to perceive that you're not familiar with. Spirit can help you refine your soul senses to pick up a new kind of evidence on your own before giving a reading. You increase your familiarity with spirit loved ones in the spirit world and you can then access information more readily during a reading.

Let's look at one example – *Relation of the Spirit Loved One to the Sitter*. Knowledge of the relation of a spirit loved one to your sitter often opens the way to a flood of information to further identify the communicating spirit. But developing mediums often find it difficult to do. This is one way to help yourself.

Here you learn to familiarize yourself with the different possible kinds of relations by focusing on each, and with the influence of your spirit control or other guide, identify it with your soul senses. For example, focus on *mother* – Do you pick up a motherly vibration with your soul sense? Or you may see a color that shows you a mother presence ... or hear the word. ... Perhaps you just know. ... Let Spirit show you how to pick up the distinct vibration of each relation.

Have your pen ready to record your experience as you go along. Go with your first impression and move from one relation to the next quickly without second guessing what you receive. Prepare as you did in the exercise above. Wait until you feel uplifted in the presence of your spirit control or guide. Then go down the list and with your soul senses open, ask to be shown how to pick up the vibration of each relation. When you are ready, begin.

Relation of the Spirit Loved One to the Sitter	See, Sense, or Hear the Vibration
Mother	
Father	

Grandmother- Mother's Side	
Grandmother- Father's Side	
Grandfather- Mother's Side	
Grandfather- Father's Side	
Brother	
Sister	
In-Law	
Aunt- Mother's Side	
Aunt- Father's Side	
Uncle- Mother's Side	
Uncle- Father's Side	
Friend	
Cousin	
Child	
Pet	
Teacher and Mentor	
Religious and Spiritual Influence	
Neighbor	

Work Associate	
Acquaintance	
Step-Family Member	
Other Relations	

Ask for Further Help

Your spirit control creates an order to your readings by bringing through communicating spirits in ways that will get the most beneficial results. Ask for further insight regarding the relation of the spirit loved ones to the sitter listed above. When students have asked for further insight, they were often guided to see these relations in a pattern around the sitter. For example, imagine yourself facing your sitter and see a map of all the relations positioned around him or her. On the right, visualize mother's side of the family: mother is roughly in the middle, grandparents above, aunts and uncle parallel to mother but further to the right, cousins lower down and so on. See the same map unfold for father's side on the left. Brothers, sisters and spouses can be viewed closer to the sitter in various ways. Also, in-laws and step-families can be worked into the scenario. Children are lowest in the picture, close to the sitter's legs.

This doesn't suit everyone. For some, their own spirit loved ones come through to clarify the relationship of the spirit to the sitter. For others, the spirit loved one simply identifies their relationship to the sitter themselves. Still others don't work very often with this kind of evidence. What system is best for you? Open to your spirit guide with your soul senses for guidance.

Guidance Received

When you are ready, thank Spirit for all that you have received and return as you did in the above exercise.

_____

_____

_____

Reuse this Exercise

Consider another kind of evidence that you would like to develop from the fact sheet. For example, *Death* and list six to eight ways in which people pass or are ill. As you go down the list, open to Spirit's influence as you pick up the vibration of each illness with your soul sense and notice how amazing it is to distinguish each one in the light of the unseen world. You may want to make a random list of male and female names and notice how Spirit works with you. In this way, you can get over the intimidation so many feel with names. You can extend this to places spirit loved ones were born, the names of streets they lived on, countries that are significant to them. And then there are occupations, interests, houses and history.

Know that you can use this exercise whenever you wish to sharpen your evidential messages. Each time it will be easier and full of delightful surprises, and you'll be pleased at how you progress when guided and taught by your wise and supportive spirit guides and trachers from the higher planes.

Guidance: Review and Enhance Your Skills

As you know, in a message, once you have brought through evidence for a sitter to prove that their spirit loved one is still alive on the next plane of life, you will receive information relevant to the sitter's life that benefits them in some way. Let's review the kinds of conditions and guidance you have received from Spirit so far in your messages. Since you're familiar with this exercise from *Evidence: Review and Enhance your Skills*, above, sit in your sacred place and prepare on your own. Open to your spirit guide as you fill in the chart below as best you can. You may want to review your feedback sheets of the messages you gave a partner.

Kinds of Conditions and Guidance for My Sitter	Soul Senses Used
1.	
2.	
3.	
4.	

Talk to Spirit about your results, and listen to the uplifting guidance that you receive about your progress.

Guidance from My Spirit Guide: _____

_____

_____

Give thanks and ask Spirit to stay with you and help you with the next exercise.

→ Exercise: Sharpen Your Ability to Bring Information Relevant to Your Sitter's Life

On the left is a list of the most common conditions relevant to your sitter's life. Read over the list and become familiar with the many kinds of situations that can come up in a reading that concerns the sitter in his or her daily life. Think back to the conditions for which you received guidance in Part I Chapter Four. While some of your issues may not be included here, such as *Self Concept,* or *Emotional or Mental Health*, many subjects are the same. You may wish to add these and other conditions to the list beside *Other*.

Now that you have a general grasp of the range of issues that can concern a sitter, you want to be able to distinguish the condition that Spirit's message is directed to. One way to do this is to ask your spirit guide or control to give you a symbol or a piece of information by which you can quickly know the condition that is the subject of their message. It may be in the form of a soul sense, sight, sound, smell or taste from the unseen. For example, Spirit shows you a conflict. You may sense, see or hear it, but you don't know whether it has to do with the sitter's marriage, workplace, or family. If you know that the symbol for a marriage is an image of a heart, and Spirit shows you this, then you know that there is conflict in your sitter's marriage. You can then hone in on the sitter's marriage and open to guidance from Spirit to help your sitter.

A list can't capture the richness of your experience of a condition as it's brought to you from the spirit world to guide the sitter in his daily life. But it can be used to fine tune your messages. This is one way to sharpen your ability to *distinguish* the conditions to which Spirit is referring in order to bring through the guidance that is relevant to it. Since this is also similar to the exercise you did with evidence, prepare on your own in your sacred place and call on Spirit to bring the insight you seek. Open to receive whatever you are given from your spirit guide or control and keep moving without double guessing your results. The ability to tune into a condition of the sitter (to which a piece of information applies) will help you with your readings.

On the right side of the list is a space to write in the symbol or sign by which Spirit will distinguish each condition. To receive this guidance, sit quietly in your sacred place and prepare yourself to communicate with your spirit control. When you sense your spirit control with you, ask for a symbol or indicator for each condition as you go down the list. Open your eyes to record what you receive beside its condition.

Stay elevated in your higher state of consciousness and close your eyes to receive the next sign or message. Continue down the list. If you're stuck, move on and return another time when you are fresh and can receive Spirit's help. Don't force it. Enjoy the messages you receive.

Conditions Relevant to the Sitter's Life	Soul Senses Used to Identify a Condition
Dreams and Goals	
Family and Friends	
Finances	
General State of a Person's Life	
Geographic Connections	
Health	

Hobbies and Interests	
House and Home	
Love Relationship and Marriage	
Personality	
Spiritual and Personal Growth	
Spiritual Path	
Stages in Life	
Study and Education	
Talents and Opportunities	
Travel	
Work and Career	
Other:	

(*An important note about 'Health': A medium isn't licensed to prescribe, diagnose or overrule medical or therapeutic advice. See a fuller discussion of this subject in the next chapter.*)

Ask your spirit control for any further help you need.

Guidance Received: _____

_____

_____

_____

A Mini Reading

You are now ready to give a mini-reading. In fact, when you gave a message as an instrument of your spirit control in Chapter Eleven, you were pretty close to doing just that. To review, when you give a mini-reading you want to communicate with your spirit control or guide to receive

- evidence that identifies 1 – 2 spirit loved ones for the sitter,
- guidance that is relevant to the sitter's life, and
- the answer to a question from the sitter.

Remember that when you open to the law of loving service as an instrument of your spirit control or guide, you experience the support of your spirit band and the power of love to overcome any fears or blocks that concern you. Release them to the higher powers and enjoy your soul's natural desire to uplift another.

➔ Exercise: Give and Receive a Mini-Reading

Decide who will be the *medium* and *sitter*. Go over the material together and be clear about your roles. Change places at the end of the reading.

Medium

Read *Give a Mini-Reading*.

Prepare An introduction for your sitter. Create a *brief talk* that will orient your sitter to what a medium does and what to expect from you. Think of what mediums have said to you before their reading. Call on Spirit to inspire you. Here is a sample:

As a medium, I communicate with the spirit world to bring evidence that our spirit loved ones are still alive and well – on a higher plane. In a minute, I'll say a prayer and then bring pieces of evidence to show you who is here from the other side. Guidance, too, will be given to help you with a situation in your life. Please don't give me any information, but I may ask for a 'yes' or 'no' to make sure you're with me. I'll take a question at the end. Are you good with this?

My Talk: _____

_____

_____

_____

_____

_____

- Have your medium's opening and closing prayers ready. Since this is a learning situation, feel free to read them and see if they express God's presence the way you want. Relax and feel the loving support of God, your spirit control, and your partner as you seek to do your best to serve. Embrace your new stage of giving a reading.

Sitter

Read *Feedback for Mini-Reading*.

Here are some guidelines for you, the sitter.

- Like your partner, prepare for the reading before it begins. Following your prayer and relaxation, call on your spirit control or guide to be with you to help you as a sitter. Ask your spirit loved ones to draw near to help your partner bring evidence that identifies them. Also, ask for guidance that is relevant to you. The more you are aware of your spirit loved ones and the spirit world, the easier it is for your partner to communicate and give an accurate and uplifting mini-reading.

- As a sitter, be relaxed yet alert. The medium is helped by your elevated soul states and your higher vibrations.

- Your attitude is important: Be open to receive. Be encouraging by accepting what is given whether you can identify it at the moment or not. When you say *I'll take it*, you indicate that you can't clearly identify the presence, but acknowledge that you may later when you think about it or check with a family member. Alternatively, if you say *No*, the beginning medium can be jarred by it and find it difficult to retain his or her openness.

- Whether it's information about a spirit loved one or your life, be kind and sensitive to your partner. A simple smile, a *Thank you* for something that's helpful, or a *Yes* if something is particularly relevant can lend support to your partner's need to trust what he or she is receiving.

- Prepare a question that you want answered by Spirit. Don't let your partner see it ahead of time.

My Question:_____

_____

_____

Record what you receive in a positive way. When the mini-reading is finished, take a few minute to fill in Section IV as the medium records his or her own feedback. When you are both ready, offer your feedback

Medium and Sitter

Follow the worksheets *Give a Mini-Reading* and *Feedback for a Mini-Reading*, and when you are ready, give and receive a mini-reading. Take your time to record feedback. Then share it. When you are finished exchange roles.

Give a Mini-Reading

Procedure for the Medium:

Prepare for the reading with ½ to 1 hour of prayer, relaxation, meditation and communication with your spirit control before you come to give your mini-reading. Take 5-10 minutes just before you begin to prepare: Pray, relax and call on your spirit control to draw near. Reach up and continue to ask until you sense spirit's presence and you are elevated in your spirit with your soul senses open and clear. Stay connected as you greet your sitter.

Greet your sitter and be sure that he or she is comfortable. Sit facing each other in a space that is quiet and free from any distractions.

Explain briefly what he or she can expect from you as a medium using the notes you have prepared.

Pray aloud to begin your reading using your medium's prayer.

Identify 1 – 2 spirit loved ones for your sitter, with evidence, as you work closely with your spirit control or guides. Begin by closing your eyes, taking a few deep breaths to relax. Reconnect with the spirit world and call on your spirit control to be with you. Sense the presence of your spirit control as you are drawn up to a higher state. … Open your soul senses and ask to be shown a spirit loved one for your sitter. … Notice what you see … sense … hear … smell … and taste … and give out what you receive. … Open your eyes when you choose. Retain your inner connection to your spirit control and your elevated state.

Ask for help when you need it. Don't hesitate to close your eyes and reach up to your spirit control to focus within to receive more information. Take your time. Then when you're ready, open them to give out what you have received.

Confirm your evidence with the sitter if you are guided by Spirit. Do it sparingly – perhaps once or twice during the reading. You may ask, 'Do you understand?' If the answer is No, stop and ask Spirit for more details to the best of your ability. Do what feels comfortable: You may not want confirmation until the end, or you may want it early on.

Offer guidance for 1 – 2 conditions in the sitter's life as you stay open to your spirit control with your soul senses. Stay elevated and linked to Spirit during this part of your reading and watch that you don't slip into your own opinion. Also keep in mind how your evidence and guidance can merge where you can receive beautiful insight into a condition through the symbolic interpretation of the evidence.

Open to a question from the sitter and let Spirit bring you the answer. It may be given in symbols, or refer to a physical event. It may be a yes/no response; you may hear words spoken or sense an answer. Remember to trust what you receive. It's easy to be thrown if your sitter is confused or uncertain with your answer. If this is the case, check back with your spirit control for more details and confirmation.

Maintain a professional yet warm attitude throughout. Avoid getting chatty with your sitter: Keep your consciousness elevated and your soul senses clear. Don't allow interruptions to the flow of your reading and your connection to your spirit guides and teachers. In this way you best serve God, Spirit and your sitter.

Pray aloud to end the session with your closing prayer. Give thanks silently to God and your spirit guides and teachers for the opportunity to serve.

What I Liked _____

_____

_____

What I'd Like to Improve. _____

_____

_____

I encourage you to give mini-readings whenever you have the opportunity. This is the way to become a medium at this stage. The most important thing you need now is experience, and this is one way to get it. Also, a mini-reading helps to build your energetic system that you need in order to sustain the longer and more complex full reading described in the next chapter.

Feedback for a Mini-Reading

To Be Filled in by the Sitter:

I Evidence That Identifies My Spirit Loved One(s) _____
_____
_____
_____
_____
_____

II Guidance That is Relevant to My Life _____
_____
_____
_____
_____
_____

III Answer to My Question _____
_____
_____
_____
_____
_____

IV What I Liked about My Mini-Reading _____
_____
_____
_____
_____

Mini-Reading Given By _____*(Name of Medium)*
Feedback Given By _____*(Name of Sitter)*

Give and Receive a Full Reading

What Makes You a Good Medium?

Definition of Mediumship Revisited: A medium communicates with the spirit world in order to prove that life is eternal. In an elevated state of consciousness, she receives information from her spirit guides and teachers that is not available to her physical senses. In messages, a medium demonstrates the continuity of life with evidence that identifies a spirit loved one to the sitter. In readings, she gives proof of life after death in a more detailed and personal way than in messages. In both kinds of mediumship, Spirit also offers guidance to benefit the sitter in her daily life.

A Good Medium

When you have a strong desire to become a *good medium*, you may be inclined to impose standards— what you ought and ought not to do – upon yourself. But if your internal censor is too strong, or if it goes against your soul's natural inclinations, you may lose touch with your own spark of life with which Spirit is able to work. Your messages become mechanical; you are using your limited mind rather than your soul mind that is a channel to the higher powers. It's easy to be influenced by other's opinions, and an unexpected rejection can throw even an experienced medium into self-doubt.

How can you make your way and become the medium you want to be? Work with Spirit. Ask for help. Be receptive to God and Spirit first, and in that higher awareness, learn how to find what you seek. Spirit doesn't judge or reject, but offers guidance that nurtures your soul. Trust in how Spirit is guiding you on your path to accomplish in your unique way. Then, your mediumship will meet the highest standards, for you will be intimately at one with Spirit and the beyond.

So, within the basic framework of mediumship, a good medium is true to her soul, herself. Your own talents, interests, history, personality, beliefs, preferences, attitudes, values and dreams are the content of your soul. Seek an enlightened view of these things in your daily practice, and Spirit will integrate them into your mediumship. Touching deep within, Spirit awakens the soul and helps the medium, on a personal and professional level, to become fully oneself.

Finally, rely on the law of loving service. When you embrace it and let your spirit guides and teachers work through you, you express your mediumship in your individual way. This is an ongoing process where your soul emerges as you reach out with love to uplift others as you too have been helped. Yet we each have our own ways of being good; for example, some of us are more honest, others more thoughtful, some have big hearts, others inner strength. Your ideal medium has a virtue that appeals especially to you because you too have it within you. As you work closely with Spirit, you become more virtuous than you might have believed possible.

→ Exercise: I Am a Good Medium

Prepare
Sit in your sacred place. Close your eyes and pray. ... Relax and meditate. Call on your spirit control or guide. Let yourself be drawn up into the etheric sky. Feel yourself moving away from the pull of the earth and into a finer vibration. Sense the lightness of your soul and be free. ... Float up and relax. ...

Meet Spirit
Look ahead and see your spirit guide or teacher approach. Who has come to teach you? Your control, another guide or a teacher? Perhaps a spirit loved one? Greet each other now and sit down together. ... Listen as this spirit presence talks to you about being a good medium. Open to these words of insight.

Spirit Insight: _____

_____

_____

Your Ideal Medium
Next, with the help of your spirit guide or teacher, see a screen or a space in front of you and picture your ideal medium: Let Spirit help you to envision your perfect medium. Notice what you really like about this presence. ... What are his or her unique qualities? ...

Qualities I Really Like about My Ideal Medium: _____

_____

_____

Become Your Vision
See yourself moving into center stage on the screen or space, and step into your vision of your ideal medium. As you do, your soul begins to shine more and more brightly within, and you sense your soul awakening to new life. Stay with this good feeling and notice how open your heart center is as it flows with love; how clear your soul senses are as your third eye center opens to the spirit world. Ask Spirit to open you even more to the higher realms and infuse their fine uplifting vibration into you from the crown of your head. Embrace your ideal medium in you.

▸ *My Experience:*

_____

_____

_____

Be a Good Medium
One by one, open to experience each of the qualities of your perfect medium listed above. Claim it with an affirmation – *I am*_____(Say the quality such as *confident* or *accurate* or *spiritual*.) Feel each quality seep into your being as you own it.

When you have finished, affirm *I am a good medium,* and stay in your power as long as you can. Keep this sense of your soul self as a good medium close to your heart. Remember that this is who you truly are and nothing can ever diminish it. Remember that when you trust your own way and seek as you are guided by higher intelligences of compassion and goodness, you fulfill your soul's vision.

▸ *My Experience:*

_____

_____

_____

Qualities of Other Good Mediums

As you gain more experience through your readings, you will become your ideal medium more fully. You may also add more traits to your repertoire. These are some qualities that developing mediums have included in their list that you may want to consider.

Spiritual

- Loving, serves God and Spirit, inspirational

When your sitter senses your genuine love and the presence of spiritual forces, they are uplifted with an awareness of the sacred nature of your reading. Everything is enhanced by these purer vibrations.

Skilled

- Accurate, relevant and wise

When your evidence is strong, the guidance is relevant, and you present things with a knowing or wisdom, your sitter feels confident and the reading flows with a mutual trust and respect.

Aware

- Tolerant, empathic, non-judgmental

When you accept your sitter as they are and your critical judgment falls away, they experience a healing in the same way that you do in the presence of Spirit. They feel confirmed as a person – a soul – and you are attuned to their needs.

Ethical

- Honest, pure intentions, responsible

A sitter may feel vulnerable sitting for a reading and relies on your honesty and responsibility in all you do and say as a medium. With pure intentions, you are less likely to succumb to flattery and other ego issues. (A discussion of accountability is given below.)

Refine Your Readings

Sensitive Issues and How to Handle Them

In all you do, you want to help your sitter realize that life is eternal: this truth is evident through communication with their loved ones and in their daily lives as it buoys them up and moves them ahead on their earthly journey. They learn this through your spirit guidance that confirms this truth again and again – they are spirit beings, we are all spirit beings. Through this knowledge we find our way to the fulfillment of our life's divine purpose.

As you work as an instrument of your spirit control with compassion for the one who seeks your help, know and trust that the guidance from Spirit is the way to truly help another. Spirit's teaching is beyond our ordinary understanding. We are drawn into an awareness of Spirit's way and our sitter often glimpses a supernal order of life beyond his former conception. Not all guidance is so lofty, but when you rely on Spirit in accordance with the law of loving service, you will handle any issue effectively. Still, there are some subjects that may arise in a reading where the medium needs to tread with care. These are *sensitive issues* for the sitter and, as a rule, need to be handled delicately.

Death

Predicting the death of the sitter or someone known to the sitter is a subject a medium is usually advised to exclude from discussion. Most often, it arises when a sitter wants to know when someone else will die, such as 'My mother is very ill. Do you see her passing soon?' or 'When will my grandfather die?'. The questions are well meaning and a date would help the family to know when they should gather to say their goodbyes. But death is a very intimate thing. Often when a dying person or a spirit wants others to know, they send a message in a dream or an intuitive thought.

Sometimes a situation arises that is perplexing. For example, in one of my early readings, a woman walked into my reading room who exuded a gray color and I knew instantly she was about to die. I had never seen this before nor have I since. I was startled. She was well groomed, bright and confident. She seemed oblivious to her condition as she sat down. What was I to do? As I began to ask Spirit, she said 'I'm about to die. I'm not here for myself. I know that I will pass on soon to the next world. I'm here to get advice to help my children face my death.' I still feel admiration for this courageous woman who embraced her own death and spent her last days teaching her children to do the same. Spirit may advise you to make exceptions to the exclusion rule. For example, in the case above, Spirit wanted me to see her condition and to help her to prepare her children. Some beautiful spirit loved ones came through to teach her exactly what she needed.

Suppose you're shown an accident that could mean death for your sitter. Why has Spirit shown you this situation? Who is it coming from? What are you being asked to do with it? No matter the situation that arises, be assured that your spirit control is close by to advise you in the best way possible, and usually in ways far beyond your present understanding. You will discover this yourself.

Health

The health of your sitter or someone known to him or her is another sensitive subject. In many areas, the law prohibits non-health care professionals from diagnosing or prescribing medical or therapeutic advice. Suppose Spirit shows you a flashing red light over the heart of your sitter as you are communicating with his father who passed with a heart attack. You know as you verify this with your spirit control that your sitter has a heart problem.

Some mediums exclude the subject of health, like death, from the reading entirely. Others preempt their remarks with a disclaimer such as 'I do not diagnose or prescribe …. ….'. Then, if guided to do so by Spirit, and in this case also father in the spirit world, the medium says something like 'If I were you, I would have my heart checked out by a specialist especially since father always encouraged you to look after your heart.' Or you may be quite direct. Following the disclaimer, you share what you see with your sitter and your interpretation, and recommend a check-up. Perhaps you go into detail as you see and sense the heart's condition.

In the past, mediums were often sought out for their medical advice by sitters and doctors alike. Then and now, a medium's spirit band often includes a medical doctor and psychologist. Know that here, too, you will receive the advice that helps you to handle this sensitive issue in just the right way when you discuss it with your spirit guides and teachers.

Socially Sensitive Issues

Some issues have a stigma attached to them by society, and you may or may not want to address them. They range from alcoholism, abuse and mental illness, to suicide and abortion. The issues can be about the sitter, someone close to the sitter or a spirit loved one. Your sitter may be uncomfortable with them, or on the other hand, may want to use the reading as an opportunity to get something off their chest. For example, how does your sitter feel about her brother committing suicide? Perhaps no one is talking about it. Yet Spirit's acceptance and enlightened understanding that her brother has been welcomed into the light of the beyond may bring the comfort her soul has been seeking.

As a rule, Spirit is able to bring healing, comfort and relief to the sitter who has carried a concern like a heavy weight throughout his or her life. As a medium, you are not a therapist, but you are ministering to the suffering of the ones who seek your help as a voice of Spirit. Trust what you're given and take time on your own to find answers to the questions that puzzle you, and resolutions to the concerns that perhaps still weigh upon your heart. Every problem can be brought into the light and love of your ministering spirit guides and teachers. And here, with your soul open to these compassionate intelligences, you will find your healing.

↠ Exercise: Receive Guidance about Some Sensitive Issues

In your sacred place, prepare on your own to receive guidance from you spirit control, guide or teacher. Notice who comes to you to help you with these issues. When you are ready open to receive answers to the following questions.

- How should I handle the sensitive issue of death?

Advice: _____

_____

_____

- How should I handle the sensitive issue of health?

Advice: _____

_____

_____

Think of an issue in your own life that has troubled you and which you haven't yet resolved. It may be about yourself, someone close to you here or in spirit. It may be from the past or present. Would you feel comfortable talking about it in a reading? Ask Spirit how to find relief.

- Please help me with my own sensitive issue.

Advice: _____

_____

_____

And a final question:

- How should I handle socially sensitive issues?

Advice: _____

_____

_____

Reflections on the guidance I received _____

_____

_____

Your Sitter's Soul Needs

We don't know the sitter's specific soul needs but Spirit does. That is the beauty of giving readings – they unfold in wondrous ways that we could never orchestrate on our own.

Still, you have been addressing three kinds of information in a reading that already speak to the soul of your sitter. Let's look at them in order to understand how they can meet your sitter's needs.

- Evidence: Your sitter needs to be certain that their spirit loved one(s) is (are) present and to feel a connection to them.

- Guidance: There's also some reason they need to know this at this time and it is often linked to a condition in their life and the need for guidance with it.

- A Sense of the Presence of Spirit: Finally, your sitter's soul seeks a sense of the presence of Spirit, or an awareness of spiritual forces at work during the reading.

Ways in which the soul is touched varies from sitter to sitter and depends on their individual needs at the time received from the spirit world with different kinds and amounts of *evidence, guidance and Spirit influence.*

Illustrations of the Variety of the Needs of the Soul Addressed in a Reading

A sitter who is familiar with a spirit loved one may require only a few pieces of evidence to be certain of the presence of their spirit loved one, as in these examples, but they seek a close connection with their spirit loved one(s), for their own reasons, at this particular time.

- Medium: I see a man standing behind a microphone speaking to a large audience …

- Sitter: That's my father. He always comes that way.

Or

- Medium: Pansies are all around you and a basket of them is handed you. …

- Sitter: It's my sister who had pansies everywhere …

Once you've begun to identify a spirit loved one, then continue to bring through what is needed to fulfill your sitter's needs at the time. In the first example, the sitter wants to connect with father because she's worried about her younger sister who father doted on. She fears for her sister and feels alone in her sense of responsibility. She needs to be certain of father's spirit presence and she needs his loving support.

In the higher wisdom of the spirit world, father takes her back to both fond memories and a difficult move from their family home when her mother became ill and hospitalized. Evidence and guidance come through in a natural flow of conversation. The sitter gradually gains perspective on her sister's situation and also receives healing of old anxiety about her need to be the strong and capable one in the absence of her mother. She came with a desire for some advice from her father and went away with a renewed sense of her higher self and a fresh outlook on life.

In the second case, the sitter came to commune with many members of her family, especially her sister and her mother. She knows her sister is present, but wants to hear more from her. This is the sitter's yearly visit – her special time to renew her connection to her spirit loved ones especially since she is the last one left. So she needs to hear about her sister's favorite activities, her home and how she loved bright colors everywhere. She also needs her sister to know that her (the sister's) cat is doing well and is delighted to hear that her sister knows all the cat's recent ups and downs. And then she wants to link closely with her mother around different issues. Again, evidence and guidance mingle together in the natural course of the reading as information is brought through from the spirit world.

A sitter who is unfamiliar with readings and communication with their spirit loved ones often needs a lot of evidence to be absolutely sure they are in contact with their spirit loved one. They need a strong connection which they haven't known before. They may need to linger with their spirit loved ones to feel assuaged in their souls.

For example, Betty had lost her husband six months ago and thought that by now she would feel comforted with her religious understanding that all was well with him. But she was restless and didn't feel assured. She landed on my doorstep after I had read for the day and I was about to say 'No' when my spirit control said 'Welcome her in for a reading'. Her husband came through playing music in a country band, laughing and looking exactly as she knew him. With this her heart began to lighten up.

Information about how he died and the family arrangements were given and all of it continued to comfort her. The reading was lively and her husband came through easily bringing up all the things they loved to do together, what they said and what they found funny. They were a happy, loving couple and despite her loss, Betty was enjoying herself and him. And so was I. We continued past the half hour and by that time he felt very much like a live presence in the room.

Yet others – some new to a reading – may make contact with very little evidence and don't want to linger. Sometimes it's because the evidence is very specific and that's all they needed. For example, a young man came looking disheveled and distraught with alcohol on his breath. Before I could say anything, he said 'I need to hear from my fiancé who just passed in a car accident.' I was impressed by Spirit to proceed despite the alcohol. As I began, I asked Spirit to help me and I saw a perfect buttercup – a sweet delicate thing in soft yellow sunlight – and said 'I see a *buttercup*' and … He leaped up with a smile on his face 'That's what I came for! '*Buttercup*' was my pet name for her and no one else knew.' And he was out the door.

While this is extreme, let's look at other examples of very specific evidence that speaks to a strongly felt need.

- Medium: A large dog, looks like a light brown color, is very happy to see you.

Or

- Medium: A dog, a retriever, bounds in to greet you, wagging her tail and jumping up on you to lick your face. She has shinny long hair that is a chestnut color and a pink collar.

A sitter has come to find out that his dog is happy on the other side of life. Both the above descriptions are true, but the second one, with its specific details, will better meet his soul needs for reassurance that his devoted pet is alive and well. And it better prepares the way for his soul's healing since the details establish a close tie with the spirit of his loved one.

Events or behavior that are specific and familiar help the sitter to identify a spirit loved one through an emotional connection that touches the soul deeply and brings beautiful healing. For example,

- Medium: I hear the song 'O Danny Boy. ….' for a mother who lost her son, Danny, in the war and this was the song played at his Irish wake.

Some kinds of specific evidence may seem sufficient – they *seem* to identify a particular person—but more information is needed for a sitter to know with certainty. For example,

- Medium: I have your *mother* here.

Or

- Medium: A man by the name of *Bob* comes in.

These are both good starts. But more is needed for the sitter to know that it's *her* mother, or the person *he or she* knows as Bob.

With some sitters, a lot of spirits come through and with others, one or two spirits present themselves. Trust Spirit who knows what is needed.

Learn to sense when your sitter has not yet been touched in the way that Spirit aims to do. They don't yet seem to be satisfied even though you've brought many spirits through and much guidance has been given. Relax and go deeper or higher. Be still, go within and ask Spirit. If you still have a sense of your sitter's deepest need not being touched, you may ask directly what it is that they still seek.

Know that some people are easier to read than others. On the odd occasion, you will not have a rapport with your sitter – everything you bring is rejected. If it continues, kindly indicate that it's not working between you, and end the reading after 10 minutes.

Yet most of us discover through readings, the beauty in every soul and learn from our sitters how to be better people ourselves. We learn from their courage, humility, their struggles and their overcoming, their laughter and tears. We learn from their trust in us and in the spirit world. And there is nothing more thrilling than to see your sitters bathed more and more in the light and glow of their soul that Spirit has ignited in the course of communication over the years. They develop new strength, inner peace and optimism from the knowledge awakened in them of eternal life.

You will find too that as you grow and deal with your own issues, your sitters will be going through similar things; what you learn from Spirit and how you grow spiritually will benefit them. As you progress, Spirit uses you to be a channel for their higher teachings.

A Regular Reading

When you read over the procedure for giving a reading, it may seem too rigid. My aim has been to make clear what is expected in a reading. However, it doesn't capture the flow and wondrous nature of spirit communication, the ways our spirit guides and teachers uplift and inspire as they teach the truth about eternal life. It doesn't reflect how the souls of your sitters are touched by the presences of spirit loved ones who come through in an infinite number of ways that move them and remind them of their essence.

Up until now, I have encouraged you to be spontaneous and let whatever information you receive to be given out freely. The aim was to release the tendency to restrict or censor your communication with Spirit and to reinforce the free flow of information. Continue to let yourself be open to perceive the spirit loved ones that your spirit control brings, and to trust in who comes, when and how, in keeping with the workings of your spirit band.

However, you may find that your spirit control begins to bring through information in a regular order each time you give a message or a reading. For example, you may find you want the evidence to come in a certain order where you identify the spirit loved one as a male or female, their relation to your sitter and then their appearance. Or you may sense how they passed and their health and well-being during their life. Or it may be that your sitter's most pressing need will be addressed by the spirit loved one who comes first.

On the other hand you may find that the information comes through spontaneously in no particular order and that works well for you. Let Spirit help you to develop a way that suits you.

As you do this, you will find that there is a beautiful mingling of evidence and guidance. Let the conversation move along naturally and one will flow into the other. For example, grandfather whose grandson is named after him identifies himself and talks about how he 'watches over' the young boy and lets his son, the sitter, know how much he knows about the boy's schooling and little league activities. Or mother offers insight for her daughter, the sitter, about her upcoming promotion and the conversation includes memories and details that reinforce their loving connection.

Accountability

Some developing mediums are worried that they might give out advice from the spirit world that misleads the sitter because it isn't accurate enough. As an instrument of Spirit you need to trust the information that comes through and as you let the law of loving service express through you, you won't have any reason to doubt the truth of what you say.

But further, the reading is not a passive interaction; the sitter too is elevated in her own higher self. As a rule, Spirit helps your sitter to see, know or feel something from a higher state of understanding so they can make more enlightened decisions.

Still there are times when you want to remind the sitter that you are fallible, especially where a big decision is at stake such as the sale of a home, a marriage or change of job. State with clarity what Spirit is giving you. Then suggest that your sitter prays and opens to the spirit realm to be confident with his or her decision.

➔ Exercise: Give a Reading and Receive Feedback (Partners)

A reading is an expanded version of a mini reading. You are familiar with the procedure. Only now, you will provide a longer, more detailed reading. You're well prepared to do it. You just need to practice and gain the experience needed to become an accomplished medium. Spirit knows your every need and desire. Rely on these intelligences from the higher planes to support and guide you throughout the reading, and enjoy the opportunity to serve with love.

With your partner, decide who is the *medium* and *sitter*. Continue the same way you did in giving and receiving a mini-reading and exchange places at the end. Together read over the exercise and the worksheets *Give a Regular Reading* and *Feedback for a Regular Reading to* be clear about your roles.

Medium

The procedure for *Give a Regular Reading* is basically the same as a mini-reading. The difference is that here you will bring through more detailed and complex information from the spirit world. Aim to identify more spirit loved ones and offer more guidance that is relevant for your partner. You will be guided by your spirit control.

Also, your partner will offer you feedback on several new issues that were discussed at the beginning of the chapter. Know that as you allow the law of loving service to express through you as an instrument of your spirit control, you will find your natural way of giving a reading. In your elevated state of contact with the spirit world, you will shine and experience the joy of selfless service. Trust that you are being guided in all you do.

Following your reading, reflect on your experience as a reader, and record what you liked and what you want to improve. Then you can compare your insights with your sitter's evaluation.

Sitter

Notice the difference in the feedback worksheet, *Feedback for a Regular Reading*. There are additional questions to answer that help your partner with the material covered in this chapter, including

- how the medium dealt with *sensitive issues* (if there were any), and
- whether the reading was *spiritually uplifting*.

Like all feedback, this is intended to be helpful and to enlighten the medium. Listen to Spirit when you record your evaluation. Focus on the positive and stay open to Spirit as you share your experience in an uplifting and supportive way.

Medium and Sitter

When you are both ready, follow the worksheets to give and receive a reading. Enjoy this opportunity to express your higher level of skill as you work closely with your spirit control and feel the joy of loving service. Also, embrace this time to pray for your partner,.

Remember it is important for both of you to prepare for the reading. If you need reminders, reread the guidelines given for giving and receiving a mini-reading in Chapter Fourteen. End the reading after 30 minutes.

Give a Regular Reading

Procedure

For the Medium: Prepare for the reading with ½ to 1 hour of prayer, relaxation, meditation and communication with your spirit control before you come to give your reading. Take 5-10 minutes just before you begin to prepare: Pray, relax and call on your spirit control to draw near. Reach up and continue to ask until you sense your spirit's presence and you are elevated in your soul with your soul senses open and clear. Stay connected as you greet your sitter.

Greet your sitter and be sure that he or she is comfortable. Sit facing each other in a space that is quiet and free from any distractions.

Explain briefly what he or she can expect from you as a medium.

Pray aloud to begin your reading using your medium's prayer.

Identify 1 – 3 spirit loved ones for your sitter, with evidence, as you work closely with your spirit control or guides. Begin by closing your eyes, taking a few deep breaths to relax. … Reconnect with the spirit world and call on your spirit control to be with you. Sense the presence of your spirit control as you are drawn up to a higher state. Open your soul senses and ask to be shown a spirit loved one for your sitter. Notice what you see … sense … hear … smell … and taste … and give out what you receive. Open your eyes when you choose. Retain your inner connection to your spirit control and your elevated state.

Ask for help when you need it, and don't hesitate to close your eyes, reach up to your spirit control to focus within to receive more information, and when you're ready, open them to give out what you have received.

Trust Spirit to guide you in the order in which spirit loved ones come through and the information that you receive. Let the reading unfold spontaneously.

Confirm your evidence with the sitter if and when you are guided by Spirit. You may ask *Do you understand?* If the answer is *No*, stop and ask your spirit control for more details to the best of your ability. Do what feels comfortable: You may not want confirmation until the end, or you may want it as you go along.

Offer guidance for 1 – 3 conditions in the sitter's life as you stay open to Spirit with your soul senses. Stay elevated and linked to your spirit control during this part of your reading, and watch that you don't slip into your own opinion. Keep in mind too, how your evidence and guidance can merge so you can receive beautiful insight into a condition through the symbolic interpretation of the evidence.

Open to questions from the sitter near the end of the reading, and let your control bring you the answers. They may be given in symbols, or refer to a physical event. They may be *yes/no* responses; you may hear words spoken or sense an answer. Remember to trust what you receive. It's easy to be thrown if your sitter is confused or uncertain. Check back with your spirit control for more details and confirmation.

Maintain a professional yet warm attitude throughout. Avoid getting chatty with your sitter: Keep your consciousness elevated and your soul senses clear. Don't allow interruptions to the flow of your reading and your connection to your spirit guides and teachers. In this way you best serve God, Spirit and your sitter.

Pray aloud to end the session with your closing prayer. Give thanks silently to God and your spirit guides and teachers for the opportunity to serve.

▸ *My Experience:*

What I Liked _____

_____

_____

What I'd Like to Improve. _____

_____

_____

Now that you have given a regular reading, continue to seek out opportunities to develop your mediumship this way. Use each experience to learn how to be a loving and clear instrument for your spirit control and other guides and teachers. (For a sample reading and an account of evidential mediumship see *Where Two Worlds Meet* by Janet Nohavec with Suzanne Giesemann.

Feedback for A Regular Reading

To Be Filled in by the Sitter:

I Evidence That Identifies My Spirit Loved One(s)

_____
_____
_____
_____
_____
_____
_____
_____

II Guidance That is Relevant to My Life

_____
_____
_____
_____
_____
_____
_____
_____

III Answers to My Questions

_____
_____
_____
_____
_____
_____
_____
_____

IV Likable Qualities of the Medium That I Value

_____
_____
_____
_____

V How Sensitive Issues Were Handled

_____
_____
_____
_____

VI What Was Spiritually Uplifting about the Reading?

_____
_____
_____
_____

VII What Other Things I Liked about My Reading

_____
_____
_____
_____

Reading Given By_____(Name of Medium)

Feedback Given By_____(Name of Sitter)

Thank You for the Opportunity to Serve Spirit

I was walking to an outdoor service where I would give my very first public message to demonstrate the continuity of life to an audience I hadn't seen before. There would be about a hundred people there. I was a student and I would be called up by the chairperson to give three messages after the experienced mediums who were 'registered' had given theirs. This was free to the public and mediums came voluntarily to serve Spirit.

In the past, I enjoyed coming to these services as a sitter. As I had taken my seat facing the front, I had looked up at tall old growth elms, rich and green, and beyond to the sky. The sun streamed down here and there on shining faces, pure and expectant. Voices were hushed and like others around me it seemed, I was aware of the holiness of this place.

The event began with a prayer by the chairperson. Then the mediums one-by-one gave their messages. I was refreshed to be in a group of people who all seemed to be spiritual seekers of some kind. The messages were meaningful; they were about things that mattered. Whether they were directed to me or not, they touched my soul's longing for a connection to the Infinite, to life. And this seemed to be true for all of us – whatever the particular needs of a sitter, Spirit reached in to offer it, whether from the evidence of a spirit loved one's continuing existence, or guidance about a person's everyday concerns. We felt the presence of a higher power; we sensed the wisdom and love of something greater than ourselves as each medium gave out the messages of her communicating spirits.

When each medium ended, he or she said to the chair and the audience, 'Thank you for the opportunity to serve Spirit.' The gratitude expressed moved us all. It seemed that Spirit too was pleased by this opportunity for they appeared to sprinkle a fine vibration over us all as the medium came back down the aisle. The last time I sat in the audience, I had been puzzling over where to go next in my life. A medium had come to me and honed right in on my quest – Before long, you will be up here giving messages just as I am, she said. Although I had known this, I needed to hear it stated in a matter of fact way to take action.

So here I was, about to do just that. Earlier in the day I had prepared for this service and I felt my spirit guides and teachers close; their light shone within my mind and my inner senses were acute and ready. Or so I thought.

As I walked along, suddenly I was aware of a spirit beside me – he was unusually short and appeared quite earthy, in dark brown colors, unlike my spirits in white robes and shining light. I told him to please leave. I want-

ed to retain my inner focus with my own spirit control. But he didn't go. He ran along beside me trying to keep up with my fast pace. I was upset that my inner calm was disturbed. As I tried to ignore him, he said 'Go to the man in the red sweater'. I paid no attention and he repeated it again and added. 'He'll be standing to your right.' I thought 'Right, only one red sweater in the audience'. As if he read my mind, he said ' He'll be the only one in a red sweater.' Now I wasn't sure what to think or do. I thought 'I'll keep this in the back of my mind just in case.' Finally, he said 'His father just passed and he wants to let his son know that he's happy and well on the other side of life.' By this time, I was alert.

When I was called up to give my messages, I felt overwhelmed by so many people who all seemed to want a message. I was relieved to see a young man standing on my right with a bright red sweater—the only one in the group – and latching on to the little man's words, I attuned to the man in the red sweater and asked 'May I come to you?' He nodded and I saw his father standing beside him beaming with happiness. The message flowed easily and I was grateful to my mysterious guide. With this connection to the spirit world, I was able to bring messages to others as I was guided by my own spirit control.

Following the service, the young man thanked me – He had been worried about his father's wellbeing just as the small man had told me, and had driven several hours to come to the service for that reason.

I looked for my walking companion, but he wasn't around. Later my spirit guides told me he was a well-respected guide of a medium who had since passed. He gained wisdom when he lived on the earth plane because of the intolerance he faced for his small size and the challenges he faced in an adult world. He wanted to assist me in my initiation into public work, and to help the young man and his father.

As I reflected on my experience, I became acutely aware of my earlier attitude – my ego – in the face of such a wise and compassionate soul. As I asked forgiveness from the little man in Spirit, I felt humble. I prayed that I may grow through this learning and become a better person and medium.

(My story describes an outdoor service in Lily Dale where mediums publicly demonstrate the continuity of life.)

Commitment to Serve Spirit

('Spirit' refers to both 'God and Spirit' in this context, where the presence of God is implied.)

A *commitment to serve Spirit* strengthens our resolve and buoys us up when we face challenges along our way as mediums. It's a decision that comes from within; it also involves action. It means giving messages in circle. It means giving readings. And it means giving messages that demonstrate the continuity of life in a public or group setting. Each step seems difficult, like a giant leap, an impossible feat.

But think back to when you gave your first message in a circle or with a friend. Many of us held back, hesitant in the face of ridicule or rejection. What if it sounds silly? What if everyone laughs? What if it's rejected?

Yet despite your anxiety, you made an internal decision – a commitment to serve. You called for the help of your spirit guides and teachers, trusted in the message you received, and you did it! And you probably felt elated. Also, most of you were strengthened by your resolve to work with Spirit even in the face of failure.

When you make a commitment to serve Spirit, you are supported through your ups and downs as mediums. And probably someone will think that what you say is silly, another may laugh at you, and without doubt, you will face rejection on occasion. But when you work as one with your spirit control, you are aligned with your truth and grounded in your soul, and your concerns about the judgments of others no longer have power to stop you.

→ Exercise: Examine Your Commitment to Serve Spirit

As you continue to serve as a medium, it's important to examine your ongoing commitment to serve Spirit. Why? Because it is an indication of your soul's investment in your mediumship. You can't force yourself to want to serve. Rather, it comes as you desire it with your soul heart and mind.

In order to embrace mediumship fully and to develop a strong commitment, let's go back to Chapter One where you recorded your long term reason for taking this course. Your answer identifies your soul's higher purpose (or an aspect of it) for becoming a medium. (Perhaps your short term goal does too.)

How you give messages and readings reflects your purpose. For example, some of you may find that you approach your readings with a desire that your sitter is healed. Your sitter is touched by who and how a spirit comes through in a way that heals. Or perhaps your focus is on your sitter's life path. Ultimately the information is to help your sitter progress this way. For others the purpose in connecting to family is for the sitter to have a secure happy life. For some of you, to express compassion so your sitter feels the love of spirit is key, and for others, bringing comfort in the face of grief is your focus. Whatever moves you deep within to be a medium is the spark that fuels your desire to serve Spirit.

Prepare
Sit in your sacred place. Pray, relax, meditate and call on your spirit control, or another guide or perhaps a teacher, to help you. … Talk to your spirit guide about your commitment.

Connect with Spirit
I will leave you to connect with Spirit on your own and receive answers to the following questions.

What moves me deep within to be a medium? How does this motivate me to serve Spirit? _____

_____

_____

How committed am I? _____

_____

_____

How can I become more committed? _____

_____

_____

Know that as you grow, your commitment will deepen in beautiful and unexpected ways.

Teachings Along the Way
As you stay firm in your commitment, Spirit will teach you in unexpected ways and the universe will show you your way. It may not always be easy, but it's always growth and it's always good—like my humbling experience.

Rejection

One of my students, Beth, had given some beautiful public demonstrations of the continuity of life at the outdoor services. She asked for my feedback. Sitting at the service, I observed her go to large man in the audience with an evidential message about his brother in Spirit. I could see it was accurate, but as she spoke in a quiet small voice, he crossed his arms, sat back and gruffly refused to accept it. She was thrown by his rejection; it was so clear to her.

Later, as we walked in the serenity of the woods, we discussed some of the ways to treat *rejection*. If it happens, stop, close your eyes and ask Spirit for help. Then respond to the receiver accordingly. For example, it may be that the sitter needs more information. So give out more details and see if he or she can identify their loved one. If not, bring through another spirit or end the contact. Or, for example, the person may not know the spirit you bring through. This may be Spirit's way to get a message to a family member. So you suggest that the sitter ask his relatives about it.

Many of us have had the experience of going blank when we receive a message. We disconnect with it and we feel embarrassed because we can't remember anything. As the medium, give out what you receive and suggest that your sitter think about it later. Sometimes we can't do anything about rejection and it's best to not dally. I observed a seasoned medium describe a little white spirit dog that ran down the aisle and jumped into a woman's lap. The woman didn't want a message from her dog – she wanted to hear from someone else. She rejected the message whereupon the medium moved on with a 'Thank you'.

One thing we should always do – stand strong in what we've been given and do our best to inform the sitter. Then, as long as you are confident in the truth of a message, don't take it back because your sitter refuses it. You can say 'I feel solid with the truth of this message. Spirit shows it to me very clearly. I leave it with you.'

At the same time, when messages are not as clear as you would like, be honest and do the best you can. People usually will relax with your open acceptance of your limitations.

Beth and I agreed that she could learn from her experience – to reexamine and affirm her commitment to serve Spirit. Then, she discovered that when she delivered her messages in front of a group, she could project her voice, stand firm in her truth and she was less likely to face rejection. But even if she did, with her new inner strength, she could handle it with ease.

Fishing

If a medium asks the sitter for information instead of getting it from the spirit world, she is *fishing*. Have you heard someone say, 'Do you have a mother in spirit?' The reply was 'Yes!' The medium says, 'Because I have a woman here in spirit who says she is your mother'. It sounds like the message is evidential, but she fished for the answer before she actually gave it out. Another example: The medium says 'There is a Jim standing beside you.' So far so good. But then 'Who is this to you, please?' The reply 'My father!'. This may seem like wonderful evidence – Jim is his father! But the evidence that the spirit is a father was got by fishing.

Fishing is different from confirming. Consider 'I have a grandfather here on father's side of the family. I sense he suffered from emphysema and. … Can you take this?' Here the medium gives out the evidence she receives, and then asks if the receiver can recognize the spirit. I believe a medium fishes when she wants to protect herself from the possibility that she is wrong. It seems to occur under stress such as intimidation by a large crowd or a skeptical sitter. It can also be a habit that one is unaware of.

'Negative' Information

We all want to hear that our lives are unfolding beautifully and that our dreams are coming true – happiness, success, fulfillment are ours. From Spirit's perspective, this is true. There is no such thing as *negative information*. The world is of the spirit and so are we. The sole message from the spirit world teaches us this. It underlies all spirit communication as they help us to discover this through our unique path.

If we see something 'negative' – a house doesn't sell, a child has an accident – ask Spirit to frame the message from their perspective. When you give out such a message, you are not covering up reality; you aren't watering down the truth; you are providing a glimpse into another reality—the unseen world, the way of the soul.

For example, a sitter asks 'Will my daughter be happy?' and pictures a rosy life of ease. Spirit wants to help the parent to understand the child's life on different terms, such as the happiness of learning her life's lessons, working hard, using her talent – even doing without. This may seem 'negative' but it's not. We worry about things that spirit sloughs off as unimportant. We see troubles and they teach us how to embrace challenges with optimism. We forget that we are eternal souls and they remind us that everything we ever truly wanted is ours.

Public Demonstration of the Continuity of Life

You already know how to give a medium's message that demonstrates the continuity of life. You learned this in Part II and have been practicing ever since. To give a public demonstration, you need only learn how to give your messages standing before a group. In readings and public messages alike, the expression of the law of loving service makes a big difference to the positive results you seek: When you open to your sitter with a warm heart and truly care for his or her well-being, you establish an intimate and trusting rapport. In a public setting when you have a limited time to give a message, this is especially valuable. Also, since this is a public forum, you need to be especially sensitive to the privacy of the individual. If you have something that can't be said without embarrassing your sitter, suggest that you meet following the demonstration and offer it then.

As you begin this kind of service, recognize that no matter how well you do, some interactions will flow more easily than others. Know that as long as you do your best as an instrument of your spirit group, you are doing a service that uplifts the world in some way. Often we don't understand the workings of the higher orders of life, but as we seek, they are revealed to us when we are ready to grasp them.

Getting Started
Read over the exercise *Demonstrate the Continuity of Life* to become familiar with the standard procedure.

Your Development Circle: You can ease your way into public demonstration of the continuity of life by starting in your development circle. Begin by standing up to give regular messages to members of the circle. Stand in front of your chair only when you are ready to give a message.

When you are comfortable with this step, open a small space at the 'front' of the circle. When you are ready, go to the front and give your message. As you continue to do this, be aware of how you are standing and projecting your voice. Imagine that you are in an unfamiliar larger group, and give your messages with your public persona. Finally, stand at the front of the circle and ask Spirit to show you who to go to, ask for the message and give it out.

Create a Theater Style Setting: Next, with your familiar group, set up the chairs in a theater style with several rows facing the front. Come up to the front and look at the group. Notice how you feel. You may want to talk about it. The next time you get up, ask Spirit to show you who to go to, ask for a message and give it out. It doesn't matter how small or seemingly trivial. Do it just as you did when you began giving messages. Be pleased that you gave your first message in this setting. Continue in this format.

Follow the Guidance: Select a chairperson to run the session with your same group. Now proceed according to the guidance given in the exercise, but give only one message. When you can, give two, then three messages. Continue giving messages until you feel comfortable and ready to give a public demonstration of the continuity of life to a group where you don't know the audience. Ask for Spirit's advice in your daily practice to determine how you're doing and when to take each step. Also, ask the sitters for a brief confirmation of your messages following each step, since it's too interruptive during your demonstration.

Training Wheels: At any time during these steps, you may want to use *training wheels* or *aids* from your spirit control to get you started. For example, you may ask Spirit to show you a color around a person that helps you to pick up something about them – information about their personality or a condition in their life. Or you may ask for a symbol that reveals something about the person, their interests or their life. Or you may hold an item belonging to a member of the group to gain information. Usually these aids are psychic ways to get started with evidential messages.

Training wheels can also be used as aids to perceive spirit loved ones. If you're having trouble getting started with spirit communication, ask spirit for a color, symbol, sound or sense for a spirit to come in on. For example, you may ask for a particular place a spirit liked, or the color of a spirit's favorite dress.

Once you feel comfortable with these aids, ask for your spirit control to help you to identify spirit loved ones without them.

→ Exercise: Demonstrate the Continuity of Life

Often in spiritual centers or churches, students are invited to get up before its members to give public messages. Wait until you have some experience before you get up in front of a group outside your own center or group. Don't do public work for large groups until you are guided by your spirit control. When you are invited to demonstrate the continuity of life, find out what your responsibilities are and the protocol you're expected to follow such as dress code, number of messages to give, the group's expectations, if any (for example, that everyone gets a message) and how you will be introduced.

Give a Public Message

Procedure
Medium: Prepare to serve. Pray, relax and meditate. Call on Spirit and open your soul senses. Contact, identify and sense the presence of your spirit control in and around you, as you already have done.

As you walk up to the front of the group, thank the chairperson. You are now in charge of the audience. Greet them. Close your eyes, open to your spirit control with your soul senses and sense the power in you. Experience your elevated state and the infusion of Spirit's presence in you.

There are two standard ways to give an evidential message for someone in the group. The first is common practice in the west though we are gradually adopting both approaches. The second method is used by mediums in the British Isles.

First Method
As you stand before the audience, you 'go to' a particular person and ask 'May I come to you?' just like you have done in circle. How do you know who to 'go to'? Follow the same inner guidance; for example, ask and Spirit shows you a light, a feeling of attraction, or some other method. As you're drawn to the individual or even before, perceive a spirit loved one with your soul senses. When the sitter replies 'Yes', give out the evidence that identifies the spirit as your spirit control continues to impress your inner senses with information.

Second Method

Your spirit control may bring you a spirit loved one before you come to the front of the room or clearing, or even before you arrive at the service. You may be given the information earlier in the day, in meditation, as you prepare for the service in your sacred place or as you stand before the group. Call on your spirit control, open to perceive a spirit loved one, and ask for several pieces of evidence. Also ask to be shown a general area where the message belongs. Then as you stand before the audience, give out the message that partially or fully identifies a spirit loved one and ask 'Who can take this?' If several people can 'take it' ask your spirit control for more information until you can narrow it down to one person. Spirit may show you the person it's intended for. When someone responds, you say "May I come to you?" or something similar, and continue the message.

This is not fishing since you are not asking for information from the sitter, but merely trying to link up the spirit loved one with its owner. Don't ask a person's name or touch someone in the group for this is a 'kind of' fishing since you are using the sitter to help make your connection. (However, these are common practices in many places and don't seem to detract from the excellent messages and readings that the mediums give.)

For Both Methods

As you make contact with a member of the group, stay in tune with your spirit control as an instrument and feel a spiritual connection to this person. In an elevated atmosphere, you see, hear, sense, smell, and taste with clarity and love for both the spirit loved one and the sitter.

Next, ask for guidance from the spirit world that is relevant to the sitter's life and give it out. As you work with Spirit, allow your message to flow spontaneously and you will give exactly what is needed.

Close your connection to your sitter with 'I'll leave that with you with God's blessing' or something similar. As a rule, you're expected to give more than one message. Move on, then, to your next person.

When you've finished, address both the chairperson and your audience with something like 'Thank you for the opportunity to serve Spirit'. You have now given back control of the group to the chair. Give thanks to God and Spirit silently as you leave the front or the podium.

Feedback for a Public Message

For the Sitter: (To be given to the medium following a public message given in a development circle or learning group)

I Evidence That Identifies My Spirit Loved One(s) _____
_____
_____
_____
_____

II Guidance That is Relevant to My Life _____
_____
_____
_____
_____

III What I Liked about My Message _____
_____
_____
_____
_____

IV What I Liked about the Way the Medium Served _____
_____
_____
_____
_____

Message Given By_____(Name of Medium)

Feedback Given By_____(Name of Sitter)

Guided Meditation: Your Garden of Love

I will guide you to your Garden of Love where you communicate with its loving creatures and meet a wise and compassionate spirit guide who answers your questions on mediumship and offers you teachings on love and service.

Prayer
We begin with a prayer.

Infinite Loving God

How grateful we are to be with you in your loving presence, to feel you in our hearts!

Open us to the outpouring of your gentle Spirit as it flows in and around us. Help us to hold fast to your love in all we do. Keep us supported always in your love.

We come to you today to learn to be of loving service as mediums, so that we may uplift others. Teach us to touch their souls with your loving spirit, so they may know the truth of eternal life and its joyous message.

Please send your messengers of compassion – our spirit guides and teachers – to deepen our desire to care for the happiness of others. Show us the way of loving service.

Thank you for all our blessings.

Amen

Prepare
Sit quietly, close your eyes and relax. Take a few deep breaths and feel your entire body winding down. Relax. … Focus with your soul senses on your feet and become aware of how sensitive the soles of your feet are. Feel the energy here. Now open to the spirit of the earth and let its vibrations touch the bottom of your feet. What do you sense? … What do you see? … Do you hear anything from the spirit of the earth? …

Let this spiritual energy move into your feet; feel it streaming up your legs and relax. Sense its life flowing upwards into your pelvic area. Relax. … Notice the life at the tip of your spine awaken now and join this life energy as it flows up your spine. It spreads out to all the organs of your body. … Relax. Be at peace. … Feel it as it moves into your heart area. Relax in its loving support. …

Now focus with your soul senses on your head and become aware of how sensitive the top of your head is. Relax. …Feel the energy here. Open to the spirit of the sky and as you do, imagine stretching your arms up into its vast heights.… Notice how your hands – your palms and the tips of your fingers – are especially sensitive to the influences around them. Let the spiritual vibration of the sky touch into your crown and hands. What do you sense? … What do you see? … Do you hear any thing? …

Feel the revitalizing power of this fine influence from above as it pours down into your head and hands. Relax. … Be at peace. Feel this life energy move into your third eye, arms and neck, … and as it does, feel its relaxing vibration spreading into all your organs and cells. Relax. ... Down it flows into your spinal column, chest and heart. Now let your heart be full of loving life. ... Feel the love in every part of your being. Be at peace in your wholeness. ...

My Path
In this loving state, feel your self being lifted upward along a path. Notice as you move along it, what you sense. ... How does it feel on your feet? ... Overhead the sun shines, though it is not the sun of the earthly world. Feel its spiritual warmth, its manna. ... The path too is different – more ethereal. How healing it is on this path. Notice your surroundings as you move up ... and up on your path. ... How free and happy you feel! ...

My Butterfly
As you continue, a butterfly flies towards you. Notice how you feel in its presence. ... What does it look like? What do you sense with it? ... Listen to its sound. ... Open and communicate with this divine being of the unseen world. ... What is it doing here? ... Let your soul open to its presence; let it bring you its teachings. ...

My Garden Gate
You realize that you have been led by the butterfly to your garden. See its shimmering light ahead and sense of love. Moving towards it, you see the gate of your garden of love. Stand before it and notice it in every detail. ... How do you feel with it?...

My Garden of Love
Open your gate now and step into your divine garden. Look around your garden of love. ... What is your first impression? ... How do you feel here? ... Your garden may be full of flowers with trees and shrubs, it may be a desert or a mystical place. It may be a place you've never seen before, or the unseen dimension of a familiar back yard or quiet space. Embrace the beauty and love in your garden. ... What do you see? ... Sense? ... Hear? ... Smell? ... Taste? ...

Messages from the Creatures in My Garden
Your butterfly may guide you around your garden now or it may leave you at the gate. Begin to walk about and notice what attracts you. What is it—a flower, a bird, a nature spirit—that draws you to it? ... Open all your soul senses to it. Attune to its love. ... Commune with it. ... How does this wonderous creature express love? ... And how does it serve? ... Listen and open to the teachings you are being given. ...

When you are ready, move on to another living thing that attracts you. It may be a tree, a stone or jewel, an animal, or insect. Even the sky, sun, water, and fairies too, are living expressions of God's love. Communicate with them as you stroll through your garden. Notice the love you feel in their presence and how each expresses it in its own way. ... Seek insight about the law of loving service: discover the unique way each creature serves in your own garden of love. ... I leave you now to explore your garden of love. ...

My Spirit Guide
Now as you look ahead, you see a bench and nearing it, you read your name on it. You sit and enjoy your garden. Such harmony, such love surrounds you in this magnificent place! You feel completely relaxed as if you could stay here forever. ... Sitting in this relaxed state, you have a sense of a spirit presence who you don't yet perceive, but looking up, you notice a light in the distance moving towards you and even at this distance, you feel immense love exuding from it. ... It comes near you and gradually the figure of a spirit guide or teacher emerges – a magnificent spirit – shining and supernal in its other worldly vibrations. You feel in awe as this spirit intelligence stands before you and greets you. ... What does this spirit look like? ...

Be aware of all the features of this spirit entity and how you feel in its presence. ... As you greet your spirit guide, notice how you feel as you communicate. Do you hear the spoken words or are you connecting thought-to-thought? ... Soul-to-soul? ... Or do you just speak without words? Notice how easy it is to feel at-one with this spirit who has come to guide and teach you. ... What is your spirit guide's opening message? ...

Conversation with Spirit

You ask Spirit questions and receive answers. Who are you? ...   Why have you come to me? ...   What should I call you? ...   Where have you come from? ... You stroll together in your garden and your spirit guide talks to you about many things that you have had on your mind and in some cases didn't even realize. Without you having to inquire, your guide helps you to understand your mediumship and how it is a part of your divine purpose. ... Take time now to ask any other questions of your spirit guide. ...

Teachings from Spirit

Back at the bench, you sit down together to discuss the nature of loving services. 'How can I have more compassion for those who seek help from me as a medium?' you want to know. And 'How can I deepen my commitment to serve God and Spirit?' Finally – In what areas of my life do I need to practice loving kindness and caring for the happiness of others?' You settle in to listen as Spirit inspires and enlightens you with compassion. ... How wonderful to be given these higher teachings from such a wise and loving being! You feel blessed as you now discuss the loving ways of the soul. ... As the conversation continues, you are shown your soul's great capacity for love and its deep longing for service. You discover how the law of loving service truly does lie right within you. Let other teachings come as you commune with your spirit guide. ...

The time has come to prepare to leave this divine presence and your garden. You give thanks for what you have received, say your goodbyes and your spirit guide reminds you that your spirit group is never far away, but is always present when you are in need. With this comfort, you watch as your spirit guide moves away and becomes a shining light that exudes a loving harmony that you sense will always be with you.

Return

You walk back now through your garden of love noting all the creatures who have helped you on this journey, You come to the gate, open it and taking one last glance of your garden to keep close to your heart you leave closing the gate behind you. Your butterfly greets you and shows you the way back along the path You come back...and back... as it stops and flies away with a loving wave and you realize you've arrived back in your sacred place. ...Gently sense yourself in your chair and when you're ready, open your eyes. Look around you and note the vivid nature of the things around you. You feel refreshed and renewed.

▸ *My Experience:*

My Path: _____

_____

_____

My Butterfly: _____

_____

_____

My Gate: _____

_____

My Garden of Love: _____
_____
_____

Messages from the Creatures in My Garden: _____
_____
_____

My Spirit Guide: _____
_____
_____

My Conversation with Spirit: _____
_____
_____

Teachings from Spirit: _____
_____
_____

Further Reflections on my Experience: _____
_____
_____
_____

PART V RESCUE A LOST SOUL

*No Spirit or Angel is too exalted or holy to reach and assist those
who are beneath and none too low to be aided by those above.*

The Guides of Cora Richmond, *Presentation of Spiritualism,* Cora Richmond, Part II.

I Once Was Lost, but Now Am Found

Before falling asleep, I ask Spirit for deeper insight into the rescue of lost souls. The next morning, at four o'clock, I am half awake and without conscious thought or effort, I drift into an experience of a past life in Egypt.

I am hovering around my co-workers who are carving out pieces of sandstone from a wall in a pit in the desert. The world appears to me as it always was – I perceive my friends as I always have. We have been together as artisans for many years; we have a close bond and are proud of our profession. I hear them laughing together and the sounds of their tools scraping and clinking. The sun is bright, the sky blue and the air is clear.

But I'm troubled. No one seems to see me or hear my words. No one seems to know I'm here. I'm confused … What is going on? I continue to try to make contact with my friends for what seems to be a long time.

Finally, I have a sudden insight. I'll go to the court where my old priest and mentor, Elba, lives. I seem to know instinctively that of anyone, he can help me. As I see him in my mind's eye, I realize how different he is from most people – there's a brightness around him that my friends don't share – and I'm drawn to it. In a flash, I'm there in the presence of my beloved teacher. He sees me! What a wonderful feeling! It is as if my existence, my very being had been in question. Now I'm real.

He speaks to me kindly and directly. At first he asks what I can remember about my recent past before this new strange experience. I feel calm and secure with him as he helps me recall an accident where I suddenly blanked out, and I know now … I died! I am no longer living on earth. I'm not who I was – I am my spirit self.

At first I don't want to leave my friends and my familiar world. He talks gently to me about my life and my spiritual journey. He describes the beauty and magnificence of the afterlife. And he tells me about my brother who is waiting for me to join him there.

Then the priest, Elba, shows me a brilliant light above … loving … beckoning with its divine purity … its serenity … its love. I'm irresistibly drawn to it. Something inside me yearns to be close … I want to go there … to be in that place beyond.

I feel myself lifting up, feeling free of the earth's forces. Now I see my brother and others behind who have 'died' … how could this be? … They're shining and happy. … Arms extended, they come to guide me home … I feel the light in me ... such a feeling of pure joy ... of complete being ... Can this be true? ... I take the hand of my brother and, glancing back, I thank dear Elba. In an instant, I'm in my new world.

My story illustrates how I was a *lost soul* in a past life and how a priest, who could perceive the unseen, *rescued* me. When he became aware of my presence, he knew that I was lost; that is, that I was unaware that I had died, that I believed I was still in my earthly body and that I didn't know my way *home*. Elba acknowledged my presence and helped me to realize the truth – that I was a soul and that my path was towards the light of the astral plane. To rescue a lost soul means *to awaken the so called dead to his or her true nature or soul*.

To rescue me, the priest didn't have to do anything except help me to change my false belief that I was a material being. When he helped me to understand that I was a living spirit, I was released from my earth bound state and aware of the light and the spirit presences who greeted me from the next plane of life which was my new home. How is it possible that simply by knowing the truth about myself – that I was a soul – I found my way? It can be explained by the law of creative responsibility.

Law of Creative Responsibility

As souls, we have the power to fulfill our divine purpose, to find the path that will bring us happiness, to accomplish our hearts' desires. Built into the very nature of the soul, this law shows us how we can do this: we create our life's conditions with our beliefs, thoughts, feelings and attitudes.

For example, when you learned to attune to Spirit for daily guidance (Part I), you received messages from higher intelligences that awakened your soul and changed your old ways of thinking and believing. From a false sense of lack to a belief in plenty; from a conviction of one's helplessness to a feeling of strength; from a perception of darkness to a vision of light – in a thousand ways you were helped to find your path by embracing your soul and the spirit in all things.

Just as our soul's natural path is towards our fulfillment, so our ongoing journey at 'death' takes us naturally to the next plane of life. But just as we can get waylaid on our earthly path – through illness, disappointments, struggles, conflicts at work and disagreements in relationships – and we lose sight of our inner light and our way, so too the soul journeying to the next world can become side tracked from its intended path and lose its way.

Such a soul is not evil, but lost. It need not be feared, but assisted. It is important as mediums to recognize how we too can lose sight of our own way, lose touch with our soul and feel lost and confused. But when we lose our way, we are supported by our spirit guides and teachers who understand our plight because they have known the same struggles and have overcome them. Further, through their own lessons of spiritual growth, they have compassion for us when we are lost in the darkness, tolerance as they pick us up in our stumbling and wisdom to guide us on our way.

Let us learn from these kind intelligences from a higher order of life, and help another soul in need with the same compassion, tolerance and wisdom. We begin by learning to help *ourselves* when we are lost.

➣ Exercise: Let the Law Help You Find Your Spiritual Path

Let us focus on our spiritual growth as mediums. Students often take classes because they want to know how to find their path. Others need to reconnect with Spirit; some seek to reignite the inner spark of life that seems to have become dim in the course of a busy life. In these kinds of states, we are unable to make contact with our God, Spirit or our soul – we have lost our way and may even doubt our worthiness or ability to be seeking a spiritual path.

In truth, these states of separation from our spiritual sources are part of the very nature of spiritual growth. Through them, we learn how to develop inner strength to overcome the challenges facing a spiritual seeker. And we are then better equipped to comfort and guide others in their darker times where they are lost to themselves, their God and their spirit loved ones, guides and teachers.

Underlying the workings of Spirit and our striving are the spiritual laws. Let's look at the law of creative responsibility and how it helps us to overcome states of separation where we are lost on our spiritual path. Read over the following exercise before you begin and have a pen ready.

Prepare: Sit quietly in your sacred place. Pray and relax using exercises of your own choice. … Reach up and call on your spirit guide or teacher to draw near and be with you during this exercise. … Let yourself move up in your soul and be free from your earthly world. …

Be Aware of a State of Separation: Reflect on your spiritual path as a medium, and be aware of an inner state or condition where you are disconnected to your soul, to God or your spirit guides and teachers. For example, you may want to reach higher, but you can't get there. You're stuck in a lower place. Or you may want to see, hear or sense more clearly with your soul senses but you feel discouraged and restless. Or you feel heavy and resistant to your daily practice. You can't get motivated or focused. In each of these cases, you want to experience your inner life, your soul. You want to be close to your spirit guides and teachers. You don't want to feel cut off from God. These are mild states of feeling lost.

Simply notice the inner state you have identified and sit quietly with it. Don't fight against it or judge yourself; rather accept where you are completely. Just be with yourself in this condition. Breathe and relax. … Accept this state. … This is part of your spiritual growth as a medium. …

How do you feel when you accept this condition? _____

_____

_____

Own Your Soul: As you do this now, realize that the *you* who is aware, the *you* who accepts without judgment, the *you* that sits quietly with yourself, is your soul. Within your lost state, you are still a soul. Nothing can ever change that or take it away. You are eternal – your inner light doesn't die. Take responsibility for this truth – own your soul. Reflect on this now and gain strength from it. Take a few breaths again and relax. …

How do you feel when you own your soul self? _____

_____

_____

Understand Your Inner State: Go back to your inner state and see it from your soul's point of view – see that while your soul is your stable self, this condition is *changeable*. You have believed, for some reason, that it was a fixed part of you. Now take a few moments to explore your thoughts, beliefs and feelings that have created this condition. Deep down, what do you believe about yourself, and your relation to God and Spirit? Discuss them with your spirit guide or teacher.

Write them out, flesh out every detail and follow up any associations that may come to mind from earlier years, such as a childhood understanding of God, a feeling of inadequacy within, a belief that to seek a spiritual path is arrogant, selfish or foolish.

How do you think, feel or believe when you are in this inner state? _____

_____

Let God and Spirit Uplift and Guide You

When you begin to feel familiar with this condition and you're able to identify a thought, belief, or feeling that's contributed to this state, call on your spirit guide or teacher and the presence of God – perhaps an angel or other higher power comes to your rescue – and let their spiritual love, light, wisdom and goodness pour into you in this state of being lost. …

Allow the spiritual forces of the unseen replace your old condition with a newly awakened state of your soul. Let yourself be drawn into the light, up onto higher ground and open your soul senses to your new state. Open your mind to fresh insight, to the guidance of your spirit guide. Open your soul self and let it emerge renewed and transformed. Take responsibility and claim the joyous truth about yourself!

You may experience this change as an 'Aha!' Experience – you see the light with a flash of insight or you wake up to the realization that you are of the light, of the spirit. Sometimes, you may need to ask God in prayer at night and wait until the next day when you will receive an intuitive awareness of the truth that you are a soul and you are always connected to God and Spirit.

What higher power helped me to change my consciousness? What was my experience? _____

_____

_____

An Ongoing Learning: Keep asking and be receptive to change. Trust in the law – it operates deep within. A pitfall for many of us doing spiritual work is that we may be afraid to see our frailties because we think we have to be perfect. People look up to us for answers and guidance. But true mastery of our lives comes from the blending of our human with our spirit selves. And the law shows us the way.

Souls in Transition

The Natural Transition from This World to the Next

Perhaps a medium has said to you, when you have just lost a loved one, 'I will send healing and prayers to their soul *in transition* '. She is referring to a transitional phase between this world and the next where a soul traverses after the change called 'death'. In most religions, the soul is believed to pass through an intermediary stage as it progresses to the beyond; rites are carried out and prayers are offered to help the spirit of the deceased on its journey.

The Spirit Leaves the Body

One of the most well-known accounts of the change called 'death' is provided by Andrew Jackson-Davis in *Death and the After-Life: Eight Evening Lectures on the Summer-Land.* He calls the heavenly sphere where spirit loved ones gather the 'Summer-Land'. Though his language is not modern, he depicts, in specific detail, the way in which the spirit leaves the body and moves upward by the soul's natural pull towards the light of the higher realms. As a medium, he observes how the 'Life Principle' or soul gradually separates from the body and the brain.

The golden emanation which extends up midway to the ceiling, is connected with the brain by a very fine life-thread (silver cord*). Now, the body of the emanation ascends. Then there appears something white and shining like a human head; next, in a few moments, a faint outline of the face divine; then the fair neck and beautiful shoulders; then in rapid succession, come all parts of the new body down to the feet – a bright shining image, a little smaller than this physical body, but a perfect reproduction, without disfigurements (etheric body*). The fine life-thread continues attached to the old brain. The next thing is the withdrawal of the electric principle. When this thread snaps, the spiritual body is free! (p 16) (*My words are added here to explain the death scene.)

A spirit loved one progresses to the beyond in the etheric body.

From Earth to Astral

In the transition from the earth to the next plane of existence, the soul is assisted and guided upward by spiritual forces of the universe, spirit loved ones, spirit guides and teachers, angels and spirit workers. As Davis writes:

There is a golden shaft of celestial light touching this spiritual body near its head. That delicate chain of love-light is sent from above as a guiding power. The spiritual being is asleep – like a just-born, happy babe; the eyes are closed and there seems to be no consciousness of existence. It is an unconscious slumber. In many cases this sleep is long; in others not at all. ... It is surrounded by a beautiful assemblage of guardian friends. They throw their loving arms about the sleeping one, and on they speed to the world of Light! (p 16, 17)

A World of Light
For many souls, their first experience since 'passing' is a 'world of Light' which is the astral plane. Here spirits find themselves in circumstances exactly right for their learning and fulfillment, just as on earth. However, the celestial world is infinitely more beautiful and harmonious, the vibrations are more loving and sweet, and the guidance surrounding the soul on all sides, ultimately wiser and more tolerant.

Experiences Differ
Some souls are completely awake and aware during their passage to the Summer-Land. Accounts of the near death experience (NDE) describe a tunnel through which the soul travels before it sees a divine light, or contacts a presence or senses a heavenly realm. Other souls spend time in a semi dark transitional 'place' before they move towards the light. Still others hover around the earth for a short period of adjustment to their new etheric state prior to taking up residence in their astral home.

Who Needs to Be Rescued?
In Arthur Conan Doyle's *Book of the Beyond*, the spirit guide White Eagle says:

When a soul leaves the physical body, it is in reality passing inward to an inner state of being. Think of the physical life as an outward life, in which you are immersed in matter of a coarse condition. Away from your body your world will be of a finer and more malleable matter, matter more easily responsive to thought and emotion. (p 244)

A Lost Soul is Unaware They Are Dead
Given this new state of consciousness, it is understandable how souls become lost. If a person is unaware of their inner being in life, if they identify themselves with their external self, then they will be confused because their etheric body feels and looks like their earthly one. They don't *feel* dead. Just as I did, they will try to contact their friends and remain in the environment of the earth believing that this is where they still live. When no one responds to them and things aren't the same, they become disoriented and don't know where to go or what to do. They wander about lost until they discover their way to the light.

A Lost Soul is Not Evil
My past life in Egypt was enlightening because I realized from my experience how normal one feels in that state of transition. I wasn't *evil*, I was just lacking in knowledge. I didn't know who I was or what had happened. I was merely puzzled and confused; I just needed insight and guidance.

A Lost Soul Feels a Strong Pull to Earth
Now that they have left their material body, and their inner nature is who they are, their beliefs, thoughts, feelings and attitudes all exert a strong force. They can no longer hide them and manifest themselves immediately. For example, in my case, as soon as I thought of the priest Elba and felt a desire to consult him, I was in his presence. The instant my soul awakened to the light, I was there.

The difficulty for one who is unaware that they are a soul, is that they think they are functioning like their familiar earthly body, but in truth they are hypersensitive to the vibrations of their inner states that now identify them and can affect their conditions in their life.

Emotional and Mental States

- √ A spirit can be drawn to the earth because he or she wants to help those left behind, such as a spouse who is not used to coping on their own, or children who are now trying to manage without their parent.

- √ Sometimes a family member holds a spirit loved one to the pull of the earth because they want them to remain close. They have difficulty letting go and the spirit feels it and wants to assuage their grief.

- √ Concern about things left undone; for example, one's financial affairs or will, can keep a spirit bound for a time to earth.

- √ Also, a spirit may have close attachments to places that hold either fond or troubling memories and not want to move on.

- √ Strong feelings of anger about events before or during their death can cause a soul to remain in transition as well.

Addictions

- √ Obsessive cravings for alcohol, drugs, smoking, food, sex or any such earthly desire can exert a powerful hold on an entity as they progress to the beyond.

The Shock of Sudden Death

- √ The shock of a violent or sudden death from an accident or suicide accounts for the bewilderment of some souls in the lower realms. Soldiers may continue to experience anger or fear of battle for some time before they realize that they no longer need to fight.

False Beliefs

Another category of lost souls is the person whose belief system on earth hasn't prepared them for a natural transition.

- √ Some may shy away from the light because they fear God's judgment.

- √ Others, burdened with guilt and remorse, believe they aren't good enough for higher ground.

- √ Still others may not at first perceive their loved ones or the light because they don't believe in the afterlife.

- √ And some with a fixed idea of how their savior or God will appear, may not realize their direct spiritual link to the light.

Empathy Needed

When we reflect on the times that we have been lost on our own earth journey, we can empathize with the plight of these spirit sojourners who are lost in transition. Let us remind ourselves that just as the struggles we have faced are part of our soul's learning that we have taken on to progress on our path, so too, these souls have taken on this learning for their soul's higher purpose.

Nor can we ever judge from our present circumstances or those around us, just why we may spend time in the lower regions as we transcend our earthly existence. Many help each other, and many spirit workers devote their lives to healing here.

No Need for Fear

Of this we can be sure – *there is nothing to fear either for ourselves or our loved ones.* For our souls are of the light, a light that sustains and supports us, a light that guides us always towards higher ground. And while we may turn away from this light, and in some circumstances, forget it; still we'll discover who we are in our own way. We can't help it. For it is the life – the stuff – of which we're made.

Absent Healing

To rescue a lost soul, we use our natural gift of *absent healing*. In my past life experience, when I was in conversation with Elba, I felt a loving energy coming from him. I knew that he cared for my welfare and was sending me healing during our encounter. My soul was touched and nurtured by it. When I first learned how to do absent healing, I felt a great comfort in knowing that I could do something for someone at a distance who was suffering. I had experienced someone sending me healing in this way and I felt its wondrous power. So I trusted in this method to do the same for others.

A Phase of Mental Mediumship

Absent healing is a phase of mental mediumship. Here the medium is a channel for the healing vibrations of his or her spirit healer. Though it can be used in the presence of someone as well as at a distance, it is distinguished from hands-on healing because there is no touching involved. The healing power of Spirit infuses the medium who allows it to go to the receiver. The medium lets the energy flow through him or her and outwardly through the hands, heart and/or mind. Revisit the absent healing exercise in Chapter One where you used the light of spirit to infuse you as an instrument of its healing power. You may want to do it again in view of its importance in rescue work.

▸ *My Experience*

_____

_____

_____

A Way to Serve

Absent healing is a wonderful way to serve as a medium. I was shown this in my early days of doing it. Sitting in a large audience as the speaker was preparing us for an exercise, I noticed the man in front of me straining his neck from side to side as if to alleviate tension. As I sat, I called on my spirit healer and holding out my hands without drawing attention, I asked Spirit to flow through me and help this man in his neck and shoulders. I felt the beautiful energy move through me to him. He suddenly stopped straining and I could sense him happily relaxing in his chair. At the same time, I realized that my own neck was relaxing. I had forgotten that I too had a stiff neck that had been bothering me. And as I helped him, my own stiffness completely released and I too was healed!

This was an amazing discovery that demonstrated the nature of service – that as we reach out to others we too are helped. In rescue work, and mediumship in general, we attract people with similar issues, and in sharing our loving vibration and care for them, the universe opens a channel to restore our own wholeness as well.

A Medium's Healing Book

You can serve Spirit as a healer by creating a special book where you write in the names of those in need of healing. I write a special prayer in the front of the book and keep it in my sacred place. Sometimes you may want to send healing to specific people in it; at other times, you can simply ask God and Spirit to send their divine love and light.

Some people believe it can be intrusive to send healing without a person's permission. While it is good to ask those you can, I believe that as long as you are working as an instrument of Spirit where your loving energy is sent without self-interest, it is beneficial and good. Ask your spirit healing guides and teachers for their answer that feels right for you.

My Answer: _____
_____
_____

Who You Can Help as an Absent Healer

As an instrument of your spirit healers, you can send healing to your family and friends, and to those who seek guidance from you. You can help persons in another country when you hear of war, famine or a natural disaster. You can help the earth and the living creatures on it. And you can send healing to spirits in transition and on the higher planes. They can all be entered in your healing book and even this act of caring can make a difference. The uplifting vibration in your sacred place and your spiritual practice also helps them.

Who else do you want to include in your healing book? _____
_____
_____

➸ Exercise: Be an Instrument of Your Spirit Healer and Send Healing to Another at a Distance

Prepare
Sit quietly in your sacred place. Pray, relax and meditate using exercises of your own choice. … Think of someone at a distance (or a group) you would like to send healing to. If no one comes to mind, let your spirit healer bring someone to you when you begin the healing. Relax. … Be at peace. …

Call on Your Spirit Healer
Ask your healer to draw near. … Open with your inner senses and reach up with your heart and mind. … Let your soul move up into the higher spheres. Let go. … Let go. … Wait and allow Spirit to come to you. … Looking ahead, a spirit appears (or perhaps several appear) and comes towards you. … What is your first impression? … Open to the magnificent and shining world around you and notice what you see. … What do you sense? … What do you hear? …

Receive a Greeting Message
As you greet, listen to your spirit healer's opening message for you. …

My Opening Message: _____
_____
_____
_____
_____

Be an Instrument
Be aware of a higher vibration above and around you as you sense your spirit healer. Sit together in this energy and enjoy the loving presence of this higher power who has come to teach you to help others through absent healing. …

Notice that you feel the fine uplifting vibrations of your spirit healer infusing in you. Allow the pure healing energy to flow down into your crown and stream into all your centers. … Let it fill your entire system. Now you are transported to a higher state of consciousness. Here you feel completely free … whole … at-one. …

Send Healing Energy to Another at a Distance
In the presence of your spirit healer, picture or sense the person you would like to help. You may perceive them on a screen or in a space in front and above you. Or you may imagine them at a distance. Open your heart and mind, and let your spirit's healing energy move through you to them. Allow it to flow naturally from your heart. …

Hold up your hands, if you're comfortable doing it, and let it also flow from them. … You may want to let uplifting words of healing flow silently from your mouth. Or you may want to be still in the silence. … If you are inclined, use your soul senses to see or sense your receiver in the healing energy of Spirit and give thanks that you can be an instrument for healing. …

Let Spirit Guide You
As you feel the loving, spiritual energy moving through you as a channel, listen to your healing guide for any direction or insight that may be given. … And ask for anything you need. … You may be guided to direct the energy to a particular part of the person, or be encouraged to relax or to trust that the healing has helped.

Bring Your Healing to a Close
With the guidance of your spirit healer, you become aware that the power to send absent healing is leaving you. Give thanks for the opportunity to serve Spirit as an absent healer and send blessings to your receiver.

Your connection to your spirit healer is still strong and you now receive answers to these questions.

By what trigger will I recognize you when we meet again? _____
_____
_____

Who are you and why have you come to help me? _____
_____
_____

Please tell me how to use my gift of absent healing in the future. _____
_____
_____

May I have a final message before you leave? _____
_____
_____

Return

Give thanks to your spirit healer and say your goodbyes. Gradually you find yourself coming back to your earthly state. … Gently you return to your chair in your sacred place and open your eyes. … Notice how invigorated and refreshed you are.

▸ *My Experience*

How did I feel with my spirit healer? _____

_____

_____

How did I feel as an instrument of my spirit healer?:

_____

_____

Who came for healing and how did they change? _____

_____

_____

How did I feel giving absent healing? _____

_____

_____

What new insights did I receive? _____

_____

_____

What did I especially like about my experience? _____

_____

_____

➔ Exercise: To Give Your Partner Absent Healing

Go through the same process of absent healing as above with a partner. Agree to a time that one of you will send absent healing to the other at a distance. Although you may only send the healing for 5 – 10 minutes, sit for half an hour to gain its full impact. You need time to prepare, make contact with your spirit healer, and adjust to the higher vibration as an instrument for healing. Your partner, who is receiving the healing, should sit for half an hour in their sacred place and open to the healing influence.

Then change roles and the partner who was the healer now becomes the receiver. The key here is to have your timing synchronized so that each of you can gain the full benefit of the healing when your partner is sending it. Again, sit for half an hour.

Call each other and give feedback to your partner, who sent you healing at a distance as an instrument of Spirit. You may also want to talk with your spirit healer about your healing and to make a note of your experience serving as a healer.

Feedback for my partner: _____

_____

_____

_____

Feedback from my partner: _____

_____

_____

_____

Rescue a Lost Soul

In What Sense Do We Rescue?

I scheduled an evening class for the rescue of a lost soul. Everyone was excited as I prepared them for it. Then Hallie, a regular member of the group, raised her hand. An outspoken critic of the things we do, she had often stimulated a discussion that helped us all to clarify our thoughts and own our beliefs. Sometimes her remarks were outlandish and the class treated them with light hearted humor. She seemed to entice the class with tongue in cheek and we all enjoyed ourselves. Given our topic that night, I wondered what was to come. Already the class was poised smiling.

'Nobody needs to be rescued!' she asserted. 'What do we think we're doing, rescuing a lost soul?' We heard her out – there was always a good rapport amongst us all – and discussed her point. Eventually, I asked if she was still interested in doing it and seeing for herself. She thought that was a good idea and the class proceeded. Later, as I reflected on her remarks, I realized an important truth in what Hallie had said – there is a sense in which no one can be rescued and the law teaches us this.

Recall from Chapter One, our discussion of the soul or spirit within us – like the seed of a flower, it grows of its own accord, given the nutrients and surroundings that it needs to flourish. A gardener doesn't make the flower grow; he provides the food by which the seed blossoms from within. The law of creative responsibility states this same principle; we create our lives, we fulfill our purpose in accordance with our own consciousness.

Let's apply this principle to rescue work. As a lost soul, I was helped by Elba to awaken to myself as a soul or spirit, but I sought out the light. I wanted to find my way; I allowed his healing, his words, and the light of the beyond to touch me. I could have turned away. We have free choice – we choose our way.

In rescue work – as in other forms of mediumship – we give out what we can as channels of Spirit. But it's up to the sitter, seeker or lost soul to receive it, to take it in. And that person can't just pretend to accept it – when the soul opens to higher knowledge of its eternal nature, a person's life changes. In rescue work, the results are dramatic – as a rescuer, one sees the soul go to the light in a flash, and embrace their loved ones and a new sphere of life. This is the power of the soul that lies within. This is the power we have to make our way to higher ground.

Let's remember then, that while our spirit guides and teachers take our hand to guide us on our way, still, we open to that divine influence by our own will to help us on our path that we have chosen. Similarly, while we reach out, as channels of Spirit, to guide a lost soul on their way, they open to the influence of Spirit expressing through us of their own accord, for help to find the way that they have chosen. As mediums, we help others to help themselves awaken to their souls as they journey on earth and in transition to their lives beyond.

Psychic Self Defense

This same principle applies to the idea that we need to defend ourselves from what is called *psychic attack* or lower vibrations that can influence us in a harmful way. This concern arises when we consider communication with lost souls or earthbound spirits.

The Law of Creative Responsibility is Our Best Defense

Let's apply the law of creative responsibility to this view. As a soul, we are indestructible. Nothing can harm us. As we learn to nurture our souls through daily guidance and our mediumship, and as we practice the law of loving service, we exert an uplifting influence on those around us. With loving thoughts and spiritually enlightened attitudes, we can dispel and transform any harmful forces we may encounter. As we build our inner strength and goodness through service, we can manifest the law in all areas of our lives.

When We are Vulnerable

However, there are times when we are vulnerable and don't have the power to express our positive, loving spirit. In these periods, you want to protect yourself by revitalizing your inner life. Nurture your soul. Take time out to heal. Find out what lies at the root of your condition. Read inspiring books, take long walks, rest and regenerate your spirit. Above all, be kind to yourself.

When Our Energies are Low

When your energies are low, do not do mediumship. Recall that when you gave your first mini-reading, you were advised to not overtax yourself, but to build up your stamina gradually, and as you strengthened your psychic senses and inner power, you could eventually do more and give full readings with ease.

When We are a Developing Medium

Also, as a developing medium, your system is becoming more and more sensitive to the higher vibrations of Spirit that are fine and pure. It's important to keep your environment as peaceful and spiritually uplifting as you can to sustain this beautiful growth within. You are like a delicate flower that needs tender care. Because of this condition you want to protect yourself from stressful and aggressive surroundings. They aren't harmful or bad in themselves, but like a telephone ring in the middle of a reading when you are in a light trance, they can jar your vibrational stability. And if persistent, they can undermine your system.

When We are Doing Rescue Work

As a medium doing rescue work, and as an instrument of your spirit guides and healers, you will be bathed in their uplifting vibrations of loving light. You will find that many other spirit workers will come to help because lost souls are drawn to the light.

At the same time, rescue work is like care giving to someone who is physically weak, emotionally needy or mentally distraught or depressed on this plane: It requires inner strength and a solid sense of your own soul because you are attuning to those who are in great need of your vital energy to support and uplift them. To develop your ability to rescue a lost soul, begin slowly and do it with a group in a rescue circle for support. Prepare well and work closely with your spirit guides and teachers. Ask them for advice regarding this kind of service as a medium.

Realize that as you become a seasoned medium, you will deal with many people with a wide variety of emotional concerns and psychic energies in the course of giving messages and readings. You will learn to discern similar issues with lost souls, and guided by your spirit guides and teachers, you will be able to handle them with ease.

A Rescue Circle

The purpose of a rescue circle is to awaken a lost spirit to his or her true nature that frees them from their earthbound state to progress to their higher existence. When its members have a strong desire to serve in this way, powerful intelligences of immense compassion come near and enhance the gifts of healing and mediumship that extend beyond the capabilities of any individual effort.

Physical Mediumship

One of the best and earliest rescue circles in America was given in Buffalo between 1875 and 1900. It was led by Dr. Carl and Anna Wickland where Anna operated as a physical medium. In such a séance where physical mediumship was practiced, the spirits to be rescued, who were still unaware of their true condition and the possibilities of progression to the spirit world, would enter the aura of the medium through the guidance of her spirit control.

Members of the circle asked the lost souls questions to learn more about their predicament; in turn, the spirits to be rescued were able to converse with them much like a channeled spirit. The lost souls would receive advice, and as the light of the beyond came into focus, they were drawn upwards by their spirit loved ones. And guided by higher intelligences, they went to the astral sphere of life.

As the rescued spirit released their felt need to be earthbound, Anna had to rely on the power of her spirit control to move the entity out of her aura where the spirit had been able to communicate with the circle. (See *Thirty Years among the Dead,* by Carl A. Wickland, M.D. for detailed accounts of the lost souls rescued through the dedication of the medium Anna Wickland and her husband.)

Another kind of early rescue circle was set up like a séance where the physical medium, sat in a cabinet and a group of dedicated men and women sat facing it. When the curtains of the cabinet were opened, the medium's guides stepped out to address the group. These wise spirits were materialized presences who expressed divine love and gratitude for the group's rescue efforts and their continuing service. The séance members created a strong battery of energy needed to maintain the high vibrations for souls in distress. Often they were encouraged to sing with joy in order to prepare a welcoming atmosphere for a lost soul seeking the light of understanding.

Then a lost soul would appear in a materialized form and members of the group would talk in loving words to draw out the story of the lost soul and eventually, with reassuring guidance from those on the other side, they would help them to the light. Sometimes the soul wasn't ready to go, but the encounter always helped them to move a step closer to finding their way.

Mental Mediumship

In today's rescue circles, mental mediumship is practiced: all members work with their spirit control and bands, to help lost souls who are drawn to the circle by the light, just as I had been drawn in my experience to Elba. Most lost souls who come through are ready to move on from their present state, although some are uncertain and others merely curious. Each member of the circle draws to them, as stated earlier, the person whose life situation seems in some way, to reflect their own.

For example, souls who are lost because they passed suddenly or violently in war, or an accident or suicide, will come to those who have some familiarity with their predicament, and because of this, feel an empathy and understanding for them. Similarly, those who have strong mental and emotional ties to the earth will be drawn to the members in the circle who understand them from their own or their families' experience. They sense that the comfort and empathy that they need will be given them.

A wide variety of people and situations will be drawn to a rescue circle. Families and groups of people who passed together will seek help. Wild and domestic animals, as well as children will be attracted to the vibrational energies of the circle and the selfless intent of its members to serve. Whatever their state, all are welcomed to the healing vibrations of the circle.

A Rescue Circle is Like a Development Circle

Like an unfoldment circle, the rescue circle begins, with a prayer, relaxation and meditation. However, because the circle as a whole wants to attract those in need of rescue, the opening spiritual preparation is longer and more intense. The leader needs to be aware when the group is in an elevated state with the support of spirit guides, teachers and additional spirit workers surrounding it, and ready to make contact with those who seek help. Prayers are sent out to those who are ready to move on, though there will be some curious onlookers who draw near and a few who can't quite take the step right now.

Guided by the leader, and influenced by his or her own spirit band, each member uses their soul senses to become aware of a soul who is 'lost' (or in some cases, a group) and is seeking their help. This is similar to the way in which, in a regular circle, members are drawn to give a message to a specific person. In this case, a particular soul is coming to you for guidance.

The next step is to communicate with the soul you've contacted to help them understand their predicament and awaken them to the truth. Then, like a regular circle, where you identify a spirit loved one for your sitter, in the rescue circle, you identify the spirit loved ones of the lost soul who reach out to them from above. Also you show them the light, and in some cases, angels or spirit workers who all help them to realize their wonderful destiny.

As the soul becomes enlightened and opens to the path ahead, their spirit loved ones and spirit workers are able to draw close and guide their charge towards the light of the higher planes. While the procedure takes place in the unseen world entirely, it follows the same pattern of giving a message in a regular circle. However as we have seen earlier, the medium is also a healer in rescue work.

A Rescue Worker is a Healer and a Medium

When I was lost, Elba, the priest helped me in his mediumship as a *healer*. With his healing vibration expressing to me, I felt more and more of the light within me, more of my spirit when I was in his presence, so that my sense of being in my material body grew weaker. And as he talked with me with loving kindness, I began to wake up to my true condition of the reality of my spirit body. The law of creative responsibility was at work: Through his guidance, I was able to realize my true nature. I was able to *take responsibility* for who I really was – a soul.

He also helped me as a *medium*. Working as a channel, he was able to perceive me, converse and describe my spirit loved one to me so that I could know first-hand, the reality of my brother's existence and realize the continuity of life. With this knowledge of eternal life, I opened to the light of the higher planes and was instantly drawn to it.

Rescue Work and Proof

Many rescue circles were discontinued by mediums because it became clear that they didn't provide proof in the way that it is generally understood. The lost soul has proof of the continued existence of their loved ones, and because of this, they are able to find their way home. But normally, *proof* is understood as evidence that a living person can verify – the sitter in front of you can determine the identity of the person you describe in your evidential messages.

In early séances, proof of the identity of a lost soul was sought through historical records and other means, but it was abandoned because it was impossible in most cases to accurately determine who these souls were. Often, none of the lost souls are known by anyone in the circle. They can come from anywhere in any period of history. However, proof aside, if you are drawn to the rescue of lost souls as a healer and a medium, it is a very worthwhile service. Talk to your spirit guides and teachers about it.

➢ Exercise: Rescue a Lost Soul in a Rescue Circle

Before you come to the rescue circle, sit quietly in your sacred place. Pray and ask that you may serve Spirit to the very best of your ability and help a lost soul to find their way to the light. Ask for compassion and understanding as you listen to their story. And finally, ask that the spirit loved ones and guides of the lost soul draw near to help in the rescue process. Relax and meditate in your preferred way so that you are strong in your soul and optimistic for those seeking help.

Prepare
Sitting in the circle with your eyes closed, pray, relax and meditate. ... Call on your spirit guides, your healer, teachers and other spirit workers who are familiar with this service. ... As you open to God and Spirit, become aware of their uplifting and powerful energy around you and the circle. ... Let their spiritual energies build and strengthen you and everyone in the circle. ... See the fine white vibrations of these higher presences as they gather to help. ...

Contact a Lost Soul:
Now become aware of souls who are attracted to the circle who are seeking help. Trust that they have come because they are ready to progress and that you, working as a channel for Spirit, can help them. Keeping your eyes closed, look up and open with your soul senses to the energies of these souls who are now hovering around the circle. ... As one or more souls draw near, greet them with your inner mind and words. ... Make contact with your soul senses and notice who they are, what they look like, what you sense with them and the sound of their voice – identify them. ...

Send Healing to Your Lost Soul
Call on your healing guide to be with you, and sense the loving light expressing through you to this lost soul. ... Notice how you feel ... and if any changes occur with the spirit before you. ... Ask your spirit healer to continue to use you as a channel of light and love throughout the session. ...

Communicate with Your Lost Soul
Call on your spirit guides and teachers and in particular your spirit control to draw near. Sense yourself uplifted as an instrument of this higher power. ... Continue to open your soul senses and prepare to communicate with your lost soul. ... Ask: Why are you here? ... Listen as they tell their story. ... Why haven't they moved toward the light? ... Reach out with your soul self of compassion, tolerance and understanding. ... Help them to resolve their problem by talking to them and asking questions. ... What do they remember last? ...

Stay strong in your own spirit and your knowledge as you explain the truth – that they are loved; that they are of the spirit for they have died to the earthly world and can now progress to the next. ... Help them to know that they can better help their loved ones on earth from the light as a shining light themselves. ... Teach them that they can let go of earthly things and embrace a wonderful new life – this is their natural destiny, this is their way.

Help Them Awaken to the Light and Loving Spirits
As you are conversing, draw their attention to a bright shimmering light above and at a distance. ... Help them to realize that there are those in the spirit world who can help them; that in all respects, they will find their happiness there. ... Now help them to see loving spirits from the higher planes who draw near – their spirit loved ones, spirit guides and perhaps angels. ... As your charge begins to recognize a spirit loved one (or more), identify this spirit by his or her appearance and relationship to the lost soul if you can. ...

Encourage Them to Go to the Light
Their visiting spirits reach out with their loving hearts, extending their hands to the one so dear to them. ... Encourage your lost soul to take the extended hands, to reach up and go to the light. ... All at once, your charge is no longer lost, but reaches up and opens to their true path. As you watch, bless your charge on their way as they move into the world of light surrounded by their loving family, friends and guardians. Perhaps the one you helped stops at a distance, and turns around in gratitude and then is gone in a flash.

Give Thanks
Give thanks to Spirit for the opportunity to serve and know that the one you helped will remember you and thank you for your loving service. When you are ready, slowly return to your seat in the circle and open your eyes.

▸ *My Experience*

What stands out the most about your experience? _____
_____
_____

How did you feel as you began your rescue work? _____
_____
_____

How did you feel as you ended your rescue work? _____
_____
_____

Who came to you for help? What was their difficulty? Could you identity with their problem? _____
_____
_____
_____

How did you help them? What did they need to know? _____
_____
_____

How were you helped by your spirit guides, and healer. (Perhaps also by teachers and spirit helpers)? _____

_____

_____

_____

_____

At the end of the rescue circle I led, having heard the moving stories by members of the circle of lost souls who found themselves, I ask Hallie about her experience. 'It was interesting. I had a good conversation with a man who shared his life with me. But he wasn't ready to leave.' 'Ah! ' I said 'He didn't want to be rescued? … 'No … ' Hallie laughed softly at herself and the class chuckled with appreciation.

This light humor helped us to release our sorrow at the suffering of others. … And it helped us to embrace our human nature and common humanity. We realized that all of us, on all planes of existence, whatever our conditions, are of eternal life — we are one.

A Journey Beyond

Guided Meditation: Visit the Astral Plane

In this meditation, you will be guided, with the help of your spirit guides and teachers, to the beyond. Here you will meet your spirit loved ones to learn about their journey from earth and their life on the astral plane. Also, you will view your path on earth from there.

Prayer
Let us pray.

Infinite Spirit!

Be with us now as we visit the astral plane and learn from the journey of others. Open our hearts to your loving presence. Open our minds to your divine wisdom. Touch our souls that we may seek in the fullness of our spirit. Release all that is in our way.

We ask that your messengers of light and love draw near to take our hand.

Our soul shines with life. We are truly blessed. We give thanks.

Amen

Prepare
Sit quietly in your sacred place. Relax. … Become aware of the rhythm of your breath as you inhale and exhale. … Relax as you breathe in the loving energy of the etheric plane around you and breathe out the air within. … Let your breath move in and out without effort. … Relax and allow the natural flow of life in and around you. … Now let it flow throughout your entire system … down to the tips of your toes … and back … up to the top of your head … and back. … Relax. … Be at Peace. …

My Spirit Guides and Teachers

Now in this relaxed state, notice how light and free you feel. Call on your spirit guides and teachers to be close, and wait as you open to welcome them. … See who is here to help you on this journey. … A small group of loving and illumined guides appear in uplifting vibrations. How magnificent they are! Your spirit protector and healer are here … and your spirit control … Be aware of their presence. …Who else has come to help you? … Perhaps a teacher joins you. …

My Soul

Let these divine presences clear, cleanse and awaken your soul. They build a golden pyramid around you with their fine uplifting vibrations. Sit in it and a golden wall of burnished gold shines on every side of you. Open your soul senses and look around you. … What is your first impression? … See how high it is at the peak … and notice how you feel sitting in its vibrant energies. … Now sense a wonderful magnetic power that draws out your old thoughts and leaves your mind clear and free. … Next, sense your old feelings drawn away by the amazing force within the pyramid that leaves you feeling full of love and happiness. … Your beliefs and attitudes too, are cleansed and cleared. … You may notice small spirits of light carry away the psychic debris that you no longer need to carry around. … Be aware of how you feel in your soul – full of new life, light and love. …

My Journey to the Beyond

Your spirit guides surround you now and wrapping you in gentle and loving vibrations, they lift you up towards the next sphere of life. … See a shining light above you in the distance. It beckons you to float up as one with your spirit guardians. Notice how easy it is to move towards the light. … Be aware how you feel as you journey here between the worlds, here in the unseen dimension of life, knowing the love and harmony, the perfect peace that awaits you when you arrive on the astral plane. You are going to visit the beyond and to learn from spirit loved ones and others, about their journey from earth, to learn what life is like here. You come to gain insight about your path on earth.

Now the light is so gentle, so loving and absorbing that you almost lose yourself in its encompassing presence. You know you're about to move into the next world. Swept up in the brilliance of the light, you're drawn along what seems like a passage and then suddenly you are aware of a different atmosphere – there is no friction here, the very 'air' is accepting, loving, life giving.

Arrive in the Astral Plane

As you touch into this heavenly realm, what do you perceive with your soul senses? … How do things look? … What do you sense? … And what do you hear? … Look around and take in the beauty of this astral plane. … Become aware now of spirit presences moving towards you to greet you. Your spirit loved ones! Who is here? … Notice how they look. … How do you feel with them? … Embrace them and be aware that your spirit guides and teachers are still with you to help you.

Explore a New World with My Spirit Loved Ones

You walk around this new world with your loved ones. They have been expecting you and are prepared to show you their home and share what they have learned that will help you on your life path. First you talk about your lives together on earth – the happy times, the painful and the things unsaid or misunderstood. As you do, you're amazed to find that in this higher plane, any old friction or suffering is healed in a flash. … And you feel the joy more fully here. …

You marvel at what your spirit loved ones share with you about their purpose and their life here. … You're aware of being very open in your soul, and it's with your soul heart and mind that you are gaining new understanding and feeling a greater closeness to all life. … (I leave you to listen to your spirit loved ones to learn about their life on the astral plane.) …

Learn About the Transition of My Spirit Loved Ones

Imbued by the spiritual glow of this sphere, together you focus on the journey your spirit loved ones took to get here. How did they experience their own passing? ... And what was their transition like? ... What is their glorious learning from their journey? ... (I leave you to receive new understanding about the transition of the soul beyond the earth plane.) ...

Gain Insight about My Earth Journey

Now looking towards your earthly home, and sensitive to the deeper nature of life's divine purpose, your spirit loved ones and guardians show you your life path on earth – how magnificent it looks from heir higher perspective! Through their elevated vision, see your divine self on earth as your journey unfolds. ... Gain the insight you need to make this divine way your reality when you return. ... Listen to the wisdom of your spirit guides and teachers who help you to understand what you have been shown and how to live it. ... (I leave you to do this.) ...

Return

Winding down with your spirit loved ones and spirit guides and teachers, you stay together enjoying each other's silence soul-to-soul. Know that you are always connected in this way, and feel strengthened and comforted by this awareness. Your group of spirits draw near and you embrace your loved ones as you prepare to leave. Thank them and notice how you feel as you are once more surrounded by the loving light of your spirit guides and teachers and move gently away from the light of the beyond to the glow of your earthly home. Thank your spirit guides and teachers as they leave. Slowly, slowly come back ... float down ... and down ... into the earth's atmosphere and gently back to your chair. Feel renewed and awakened to the divine world around you.

▸ *My Experience:*

What spirit guides and teachers were with you and how did you feel with them? _____

_____

_____

How did you feel in the pyramid? _____

_____

_____

What did you experience as you were drawn up to the light? _____

_____

_____

What was your first impression of the astral plane? _____

_____

_____

Who greeted you on that plane? How did you feel with your spirit loved ones? _____

_____

_____

What did you learn about the life of your spirit loved ones here? What changes have they gone through?

What did you experience as you talked with your spirit loved ones?

What was their transition from earth to the astral plane like?

How did your earthly path look as you saw yourself through their eyes? Did you feel strengthened and supported by their higher vision? Or something else?

What wisdom did your spirit guides and teachers offer to help you understand what you have been shown?

Further reflections on my experience:

PART VI   WRITE AND SPEAK INSPIRATIONALLY

Cast aside that which is merely legendary, mythical, or traditional, and dare to walk alone, … unfettered by fear of any conclusion at which you may arrive. Dare to trust God and seek for truth. Dare to think soberly, calmly, about revelation.

To such a seeker shall come a knowledge of which he little dreams … . He will know of things Divine as the traveller knows of a far-off country when he has himself visited it and lived among its people. Round him will centre the ministry of enlightenment, the guidance of the spirits whose mission it is to proclaim truth and progress to mankind.

Imperator, Spirit Teacher of Rev. Stainton Moses,
Spirit Teachings by Rev. Stainton Moses, 199

Seek the Truth Through Inspirational Writing

It's early morning, and I'm sitting in prayer in my sacred place. I begin to relax and open to Spirit. With paper and pen, I focus inwardly and call on my spirit guides and teachers. I know I will gain insight that I never could have anticipated. My need for peace of mind and my desire for inspiration draws me to sit every day and commune with Spirit: I want to be whole, to be rooted in my soul and to be at-one. Then I'm equipped to live in the world and find my way.

I don't know who will come as I reach up and raise my vibrations. I wait for Spirit to draw near and speak to me. Before long, I'm writing 'Shhhhhhh' – the trigger by which I sense the presence of my guide or teacher. With it, I'm transported to a higher state of consciousness and a sense of 'all is well'. I hear the voice of my Yogi teacher as I write his message 'Blessings!'. I see his white clothing and sense his fine vibrations. And as I attune to a yellow gold light that shines behind his head, my whole being is uplifted with joy. His message flows smoothly as I write.

'Rejoice in your work! Rejoice! You are doing what you love. Be at peace. Throw open the doors of your mind and be free – free to receive inspiration, free to grasp the higher truths, free to share your heart and mind. Rejoice! We are with you.'

I had been unaware of the heaviness of my thoughts, but now as I open to my spirit guide soul-mind to soul-mind, I notice the old dark forces dissolve in my new state of light and optimism.

Spirit continues to bring guidance through my pen. The themes reflect the events of my inner and outer life, from the day-to-day to the ethereal. Most startling is their ability to hone in on the central issue I need to resolve – to grasp – in order to progress on my spiritual path. They do this by revealing the unseen nature of things where I gain insight from their higher perspective.

I have been struggling with 'the law of truth'. It has seemed beyond my grasp, something elusive. My mind is a muddle. Today, although I don't ask for insight about the law, Spirit knows my concern. As I sit back and open to whatever comes, My yogi teacher speaks out of the silence through my writing –'Look within. See the law of truth in light of your soul's need and journey'. I do this and with Spirit's sweet words, I feel close to myself; I feel the knowledge close in me, in my soul.

As I connect to my soul with these words, I realize that truth is sought by our soul naturally as our way to move forward on our journey. We seek insight and inspiration from Spirit because, through their compassion and intelligence, the soul discovers more of itself. We own more of our eternal nature.

In grasping a spiritual truth, even the smallest glint of it, one is freed up from some piece of darkness, of separation from our eternal nature, from God and Spirit, from ourselves. In a flash I realize 'Of course! I've been relying on this law all along! The search for truth is my soul's impetus for all my writing, all my seeking!' I give thanks to my teacher, and others who I sense in the background, for the inspiration I have received and the freedom that this revelation has brought to my soul.

The Law of Truth

The *law of truth* states that we naturally seek the truth. It is a force within our soul that guides us through life by our desire to fulfill our divine purpose. As a spiritual law, the law of truth functions in the unseen world. Through insight and inspiration our soul gains the knowledge it needs to grow and find its way – knowledge of the inner workings of things, knowledge that comes from spirit intelligences on the higher planes of life.

Our soul seeks like a small child, without any concern for what we are supposed to believe, but with an open heart and mind, eager to discover whatever might await us no matter where it may lead. The child who saw that the emperor wore no clothes was not influenced by what was considered right or wrong, or what was socially acceptable. Its mind could see the truth because it wasn't entangled in these ways of thinking.

Through inspirational writing we can seek beyond our ordinary understanding and allow the influx of fresh insight into our soul. Our soul's desire to seek the truth from wise and compassionate spirit teachers awakens our mind to higher knowledge. We can release our old constraints and let our mind soar to the heavens and wherever it pleases in its desire for truth.

As you make it part of your daily practice, inspirational writing can free up the old censor in your mind and replace it with loving and wise guides who help you gain the spiritual knowledge you seek. The law guides us as mediums – we are drawn to seek the truth that is available to us from spirit intelligences on the higher planes. And as you become a practicing medium, you will find that people want answers from you, ranging from the afterlife, to the purpose of life and the nature of the spirit. When you ask, Spirit will respond to your honest search for truth and your desire to uplift those who seek understanding.

Inspirational Writing: A Phase of Mental Mediumship

Mental Mediumship

Mental Mediumship refers to communication where Spirit vibrationally affects the mental organization of the medium, in particular, her soul senses, and her mind. This is Spirit's way to convey information from the spirit world to this one. In this phase, spirit presences affect the part of her nervous system that controls conscious or voluntary action; as a result, the medium is in a light trance, conscious and aware of her personality.

Inspirational Writing

Inspirational writing is a phase of mental mediumship where Spirit communicates knowledge, philosophy and spiritual teachings to the medium through the written word. Spirit guides and teachers influence the mind of the medium vibrationally as she opens to them as an instrument. In this close relationship, the soul of the medium awakens to Spirit's loving wisdom that she expresses directly in writing. She receives understanding beyond her normal capacity through insights and inspirations; her writing flows with an unusual clarity and ease. The medium and her spirit inspirer connect soul-mind to soul-mind: her consciousness is elevated by the presence of this divine being with whom she feels at-one, and her mind is lifted to a higher plane that illumines her world view.

Impressional Writing

Impressional writing is also inspired. The medium is impressed by Spirit with what to write – she then puts it into her own words. Impressions are valuable ways to pursue inspirational writing.

Physical Mediumship

Physical mediumship refers to communication where Spirit uses a substance called ectoplasm as the vehicle to work directly on the earth plane. To function in this way, Spirit utilizes the unconscious automatic functions of the medium's body. (You are familiar with *Mental and Physical Mediumship* from Chapter Two.)

Automatic Writing

Automatic writing is a phase of physical mediumship where the mind of the medium is a channel for spirit communication without conscious effort needed to produce the writing. The medium's spirit guides and teachers influence the involuntary nervous system: she is in a semi-conscious state as she writes. The medium may feel compelled to write as she blends vibrationally with a divine power. Spirit can move her arm and hand as the medium carries on a conversation during her writing. Messages, books and lectures have been written this way.

Independent Writing

Independent writing is also a phase of physical mediumship. The medium is in a deep trance, and her energy is used by Spirit to create a 'ectoplasm' to write on a slate or paper independently of the human mind. This form of spirit writing is seldom practiced today.

Spirit Writing

This diagram depicts the different ways in which Spirit brings knowledge from the higher spheres through the written word of the medium who is their instrument. You can see how spirit writing can be viewed as a *continuum* extending from the lightest to the deepest trance, and from mental to physical mediumship. Our focus is on inspirational writing primarily, though we will touch into other kinds of spirit writing.

Spirit Writing

Independent Writing | Automatic Writing | Inspirational Writing | Impressional Writing

deep trance → light trance

Physical Mediumship | Mental Mediumship

Soul Knowledge

All along, we have been seeking the truth from Spirit; now we seek it inspirationally from our spirit inspirers. This kind of knowledge is neither evidential, nor information about a person's life conditions, but it speaks more to that part of our soul that seeks higher understanding about spiritual and philosophical truths.

Inspiration and Insight

Inspiration and insight are the ways in which your soul can gain knowledge of these truths; that is, through revelation rather than intellectual thought, by direct contact with God and the spirit intelligences who live on the higher planes of existence.

These definitions (See Webster's and Oxford Dictionary) clarify the way a medium receives this knowledge:

Inspiration: divine influence, especially that which is thought to prompt poets, artists and musicians, and under which books of Scripture are held to have been written. Stimulus to creative thought or action, motivation by divine influence.

Insight: the ability to see and understand clearly the inner nature of things, especially by intuition. (**Intuition**: the immediate knowing of something without reasoning.)

Can you think of an example when you received knowledge from Spirit through inspiration or insight? What was your experience? _____

_____

_____

_____

Receive Inspiration from Your Spirit Inspirers

Who is Your Spirit Inspirer?

In inspirational writing, Spirit will use your gifts to convey their higher knowledge. Also your spirit inspirer will use your soul mind and thought to bring understanding from the planes beyond. You will receive the information through your pen. Or some of you may prefer the computer. Use whatever method works best for you. Like your messages and readings, your writing will reflect your unique way of working with Spirit as an instrument. These are some of the ways in which Spirit has brought spiritual truths to developing mediums like yourselves through the written word.

Inner or Soul Seeing (Clairvoyance)
Some students see pictures clairvoyantly – scenes and people that unfold like a movie or a story – that they describe in words as an instrument of Spirit. Sometimes the characters have a dialogue or give a running commentary that fills out the narrative. Also, images or visions are brought through from the spirit world that are of an ethereal nature and exude an enlightened message.

Inner or Soul Hearing (Clairaudience)
One of the most common ways to receive insight or inspiration is to hear the words clairaudiently from your spirit inspirer. They may sound very clear like normal hearing, or they come with a softer ethereal vibration, or even as a whisper. Sometimes this is experienced as a soul hearing in one's thought or mind.

Inner or Soul Sensing (Clairsentience)
Knowledge is given to the developing medium through an inner sensing of their inspirer's message. They may write it directly as a channel without their own input or they write it out in their own words (impressional writing).

Inner or Soul Smelling and Tasting (Clairscent and Clairgustance)
At times, you may write with an awareness of smell and taste from your spirit inspirer. Embrace whatever you are given.

Soul-Mind to Soul-Mind
Many students receive their inspiration through their soul thought or mind in an elevated state where they are in direct contact with Spirit's thought or mind that is different from their soul perception.

Just Connecting

Also, insight and inspiration often come to developing mediums through a sense of just connecting through a direct access to the truth from a higher intelligence as the writing flows. You may experience this along with any other of the ways of communicating with Spirit described above.

What, if any, has been your experience of inspirational writing? _____

_____

_____

_____

→ Exercise: Communicate with Your Spirit Inspirer

Have your pen ready to write. As always, read over the meditation. Notice the many places in the script where you are asked to write. In this exercise, like others you have done, stay elevated in your higher soul states as you open your eyes to do this. Then close them again to continue the meditation. Learn to be comfortable moving your awareness between your inner and outer worlds without disturbing your connection to Spirit and the higher planes.

Prepare

Pray. ... Close your eyes and relax: Focus on your breath, and let its soothing life energy flow into your lungs and fill you with peace. Relax. ... Let go of any concerns or tensions as you breathe out. Relax. ... Now sense this energy as a loving light, and let it flow down into your body, legs and feet. Feel its life in every cell and organ, and relax. ... Let it flow back up to your chest and be at peace as you breathe normally and relax. ... See and sense this loving light move up into your shoulders, arms, neck and head. Relax. ... Sense it in every cell and organ. Let it stream gently back to your lungs. Relax. ...

Attune to the Spirit World

Reach up with your heart and mind. Focus into the higher realms. Let go. ... Let yourself move up. Notice how light you feel – free from your earthly body – in your spirit. ... Let yourself float into the finer atmosphere of the spirit world. ... Attune to this divine place with your soul senses. ...

Clairsentience

Open your inner or soul sense to this ethereal place and notice the uplifting vibrations. What do you sense? ... Love? Harmony? Joy? Freedom? ... Let your soul be fed by these soothing vibrations and record what you sense.

*What I sense:*_____

_____

_____

Clairvoyance

Open your inner or soul eye to your surroundings and notice the beauty of this world. What do you see? ... Light? Colors? Images? ... Let your soul be fed by these visual vibrations and record what you see.

What I see: _____

_____

Clairaudience

Open your inner or soul ear to this unseen dimension and notice its sounds. What do you hear? ... Silence? Music? ... Let your soul be fed by these vibrations and record what you hear.

What I hear: _____
_____
_____

Meet Your Spirit Inspirer

Ask Spirit to draw near as you open with your soul senses. ... Look up and become aware of a spirit presence.

What is your first impression of your inspirer? ... Write it down as you receive it. _____
_____
_____

What do you see? ... Sense? ... Hear? ... Write down what you see, sense and hear. _____
_____
_____

Who is Your Spirit Inspirer?

Greet each other. ... Be receptive the thoughts and words of your spirit guide or teacher with your soul mind and ear— and for some, your eye and sense – and write the answers to your questions.

Who are you? _____
_____
_____

Why have you come to me? _____
_____
_____

Where do you come from? _____
_____
_____

Receive Insight from Your Spirit Inspirer

Sense the uplifting vibrations of Spirit and let them infuse your soul mind and senses. Ask for insight and let the message come as you write.

Spirit's insight: _____

Return

Give thanks for all you have received, say goodbye, and return. Float down slowly and gently. … Stay in the elevated state of your soul, shining and bright, as you return to the earth plane. Come back to your chair and open your eyes.

Reflections on My Experience: _____

_____

_____

_____

Receive Daily Guidance Through Inspirational Writing

This exercise will show you how to gain inspiration regularly in your daily practice. It's a great support and source of understanding available right within you. Also it's a way to strengthen your relationship with Spirit and develop an inner power that comes from knowing the truth.

You will have the opportunity to explore three modes of connecting with your spirit inspirer:

- receive insight from Spirit as you write it,
- ask a question and receive an answer through your pen, and
- dialogue with Spirit in writing.

If you have any difficulty receiving insight at the beginning, start writing whatever is on your mind and let it flow as if you were journaling. Don't worry about what you say or how. The difference here is that you are in an elevated state and aware of a spiritual energy so that you are writing with your mind open to a higher vibration and presence. This will start the process of inspirational writing where you can receive insight from your spirit inspirer. Enjoy this time to be able to receive whatever guidance you seek. Keep your mind open to the higher intelligences who come with compassion and a desire to teach you what they know.

Before you begin, light a candle. (An alternative to the candle is to use a gong and let its sound awaken your inner ear. Allow it to resonate within.) Have your pen ready to write.

Prepare

Sit quietly and pray. Relax. … Be aware of your breath and sense its soothing life as you breathe in, and as you breathe out, relax and release any tension or concern. … Relax. … Be at peace. … Focus on the light of the candle, and let it clear and uplift your mind. Now open your inner eye to the light, and let it brighten your soul sight … Relax. …

Be an Instrument of Spirit

Reach up with your heart and mind, and ask your spirit inspirer to draw near to bring inspiration that will help you today. Focus upwards with your soul senses and let yourself become lighter and lighter. … Float up into the ethereal sky. Notice how you feel in your spirit self – Peaceful? Loving? Free? …

Stay open in your inner senses and mind, and wait for Spirit. … Begin to sense the finer vibrations of your spirit who now draws close. Ask your spirit inspirer to give you a trigger that draws you up with a fine vibration and opens your soul to their presence. You may see it (Spirit's light or symbol), sense it (Spirit's peace or joy), hear it (Spirit's voice or words) or write it (Blessings! or Shhhhhh). Describe your trigger and how you feel in the presence of your spirit inspirer.

My trigger and how I feel: _____
_____
_____

Let Spirit Bring Insight

Let Spirit's elevated presence infuse your mind and surround you. Feel yourself as a channel of this loving spirit and notice how right and comfortable you feel, how at home in your soul! As you look up with your soul senses, perceive your spirit inspirer. What do you see … sense … and/or hear? … Different spirits from your spirit group may come to inspire you according to your need. Who has come today? Describe your spirit inspirer in words.

My Spirit Inspirer: _____
_____
_____

Trust in the guidance your inspirer wants to bring to you. Attune with your soul-mind to the soul-mind of your inspirer. Now listen as Spirit speaks to you and write what you receive. Retain your higher state of consciousness as you open your eyes to write, and close them if you need to return within. Let the thoughts flow and the insights come as they will. Allow Spirit's higher mind, thought and voice to express through your pen. You may also receive your insight through images, symbols, sounds and feelings. Enjoy the wisdom of your inspirer!

Spirit's insight: _____
_____
_____
_____
_____

Receive an Answer to Your Question

Now is a good time to ask a question. You are in an elevated state since Spirit's inspiration has drawn you higher in your consciousness, and you can receive with clear insight. Write down your question and wait to receive the answer through your pen.

My Question: _____
_____

Spirit's Answer: _____

_____

_____

Dialogue with Spirit

Here you can express anything that's on your mind, and write as freely as you wish in the presence of your spirit inspirer, stopping to listen to Spirit's insights and pouring out your thoughts and feelings to receive a solution to a problem, insight into a situation in your life or grasping a spiritual concept. You will gain Spirit's higher perspective as you wrestle with old attitudes, feelings and ways of thinking to discover the truth. You can get started here and continue, at length, during your daily practice.

Dialogue: (Me: ... Spirit: ... Me: ... Spirit: ...) _____

_____

_____

_____

_____

End Your Communication

Thank your spirit inspirer. Listen for any last words of wisdom and let Spirit sign off with *Blessings, Love* or your guide's name or symbol. Return to your awareness of your physical presence in your sacred place.

My thanks: _____

_____

Spirit's last words: _____

_____

_____

Spirit's way to sign off: _____

_____

Now that you have begun to communicate with Spirit through the written word, you can enjoy the freedom of writing as much as you can for longer periods of time during your daily practice.

▸ *My Experience*

How did you feel as an instrument of your spirit inspirer? _____
_____
_____

How did you receive your insight or inspiration? _____
_____
_____

What else did you experience that you want to write about? _____
_____
_____

Gain Insight from Spirit through Your Word

This exercise demonstrates the wondrous ways in which Spirit works. I've done this often with a group and the results are always awe inspiring. You can do this on your own and in your circle.

On pieces of paper, write one or two words to identify a spiritual, religious or metaphysical topic that interests you as a developing medium. It may be something that has been discussed in this book. For example, *love, soul, spirit guides, the journey, clairvoyance, spiritual laws, higher planes, truth, service, psychic, medium, goodness, meditation, wisdom and prayer* could be used. Fold each one and put them in a bowl. The aim of this exercise is to gain insight from your spirit inspirer about the topic you pick through inspirational writing.

Before you begin, sit quietly in your sacred place and ask Spirit for a subject that is meaningful for you. Reach into the bowl and select a piece of paper.

What word did you pick? Is it relevant to you as a seeker and medium? How?

My word and its relevance for me: _____
_____
_____

In this exercise, begin to notice how your pen on the paper, or for those who want to use a computer (or typewriter), the touch of your fingers on the keyboard, starts the flow of information from your spirit inspirers from the higher planes. You will become more and more aware of this power as you gain experience of inspirational writing.

Have your pen ready to write when Spirit inspires you.

→ Exercise: Inspiration on My Word

Prepare
Sit in your sacred place and pray. … Relax using a method of your choice. … Be at peace. … Give thanks for this opportunity to commune with higher beings to receive inspiration that is beyond your normal understanding. …

My Spirit Self
With your awareness of your word, leave your sacred place and move up into the higher realms. … Sense yourself becoming lighter and lighter in your spirit. … Look around and see a soft light everywhere. Feel its peace and harmony, and let it flow into you. Listen to the silence as it soothes and relaxes your inner ear. …

My Place of Peace
You are on a path surrounded by infinite beauty. Take in the wonder of this world with all your soul senses. … Walk towards your place of peace – your quiet retreat where your spirit inspirer awaits. See it up ahead. How do you feel as you approach it? … Enter your retreat. This is your special secluded space – just right for you to receive your insight. What is it like? …

In the Presence of Spirit
Your spirit inspirer comes to greet you with love. … Notice how you feel in the presence of this divine being. … What do you see … sense … hear? … You walk around together, and Spirit shows you your place of peace and its meaning for you at this time in your life. …

Receive Insight
You move to a writing area designed just for you. Notice how uplifted you feel, how clear your thought and mind, how free your soul! … Ask for insight into your word to help you on your spiritual path. Open to receive it, and embrace Spirit's higher vibrations that blend with your own. Sense yourself as an instrument. … In your soul-mind to soul-mind connection, write the inspired thoughts, impressions and words as they flow into your higher mind from this wise one who has come to light your way. … I leave you now to do this. …

***My Insight into the Word* _____ :** _____

_____

_____

_____

_____

_____

_____

_____

Return
In a moment, you will prepare to leave your place of peace and return. When you are both ready to close, give thanks for the insight from your spirit inspirer. … You leave your retreat and find your way on your path. … Then slowly … gently … return to your awareness of your sacred place and your physical presence in your chair. Open your eyes and

feel refreshed and revitalized by the inspiration you have received. Give thanks for the blessings of your soul's knowledge of the truth.

▸ *My Experience*

How did you feel in your spirit self? _____
_____
_____

What was your retreat like? Did it help you to write inspirationally? _____
_____
_____

How did your spirit inspirer appear to you? _____
_____
_____

How did you feel in the presence of this higher being? _____
_____
_____

How did your spirit inspirer influence you during your inspirational writing? _____
_____
_____

Are the insights on your word enlightening? In what way? _____
_____
_____

Are there any other experiences or reflections you want to write about? _____
_____
_____

Be Inspired

Spirit Teachers and Their Writings

Spirit teachers will be drawn to you as you seek higher knowledge through inspirational writing. Like your spirit bands who help you in other phases of mental mediumship, here too a team of wise and loving presences gather to help you in your pursuit of truth. This is an opportunity to learn from illumined souls who have journeyed like you and now come from celestial planes with wisdom beyond your present comprehension.

These are some illustrations of spirit writings. While two of them are automatic writing, they are just as relevant to our discussion of inspirational writing.

Spirit Teachings by Rev. W. Stainton Moses

The spirit teacher, Imperator, writes most of this book. Other group members, twenty-two in all, contribute periodic messages. Its theme is Christianity and Spiritualism. Rev. W. Stainton Moses, a bishop in a traditional Anglican church, is presented with Imperator's philosophy of Spiritualism that challenges his core beliefs. He argues against the teachings, in written dialogue with Spirit, but gradually adopts them as his own.

His writing is *automatic* – he would simply hold his hand with his pen on the paper and 'the message is written without the conscious intervention of [my] mind'. (p 1) 'I was in communication with an external intelligence that conveyed thoughts to me other than my own.' (p 6)

He describes his spirit teacher's influence: 'I never could command the writing. It came unsought usually: and when I did seek it, as often as not, I was unable to obtain it. A sudden impulse, coming I knew not how, led me to sit down and prepare to write. Where the messages were in regular course, I was accustomed to devote the first hour of each day to sitting for their reception. I rose early, and the beginning of the day was spent, in a room that is used for no other purpose, in what was to all intents and purposes, a religious service.' (p 6)

Imperator had been a Bible prophet in a former life; his team had lived as philosophers and sages.

Attesting to their ethical and intelligent communications, Stainton says that 'there is no flippant message, no attempt at jest, no vulgarity or incongruity, no false or misleading statement, so far as I know or could discover; nothing incompatible with the avowed object, again and again repeated, of instruction, enlightenment, and guidance by Spirits fitted for the task.' (p 3)

A World Beyond by Ruth Montgomery

The author refers to her guides as 'spirit pen pals'. Her group's spokesperson is Lily, and after his death in 1971, Arthur Ford, the acclaimed medium, joined the guides to communicate many books from the higher spheres.

Ruth was a Washington columnist of world affairs and politics who was introduced to spirit communication through her friendship with Arthur Ford before he passed on. Her writing ability allowed Spirit to use her as a channel capable of clear and rational reportage of unseen worlds beyond.

Each day she is moved by her guides to sit down, poised to write, and let the messages come through her onto the page. Like Stainton Moses, her conscious mind is bypassed by a communicating spirit who writes for fifteen minutes. She later reads the subject matter for the first time and begins to put it in order.

Montgomery's experience is automatic writing which she says 'is as mysterious as the cycle of birth and death, and considerably more difficult to prove. … The source of its intelligence and the propellant which directs the pencil or typing keys is imperceivable by any of our five senses.'

She goes on to say: 'Almost invariably the Source claims to be a discarnate who once lived in the flesh, even as you and I. Some of those who doubt the existence of communication between the living and the dead argue that the thoughts originate within the subconscious. … I can attest that the vivid descriptions imparted were totally unknown to me.'

Montgomery concludes – 'This book I believe to be Arthur Ford's own account of life beyond the portal that man calls death.' (pp xi – xiii)

Testimony of Light by Helen Greaves

This book contains the writings communicated to the author from her former friend, Frances Banks M.A., who passed to spirit and shares her learning experiences and insights as her soul evolves to higher spheres. When on earth together, they founded Group Meditation for World Goodwill for spiritual study and practice. Frances, a former nun and then a convent Sister, described her accounts as 'of an inspirational teaching nature' and 'should be made public, in the hope that a firsthand report of that next phase of living to which we are all graduating, may be of value'. (p 14)

For Helen Greaves, the writings were 'communicated to me by telepathy and inspiration'. The information came like talking on a 'Celestial Telephone' – a soul-mind to soul-mind connection.

She describes her experience: 'I was part of the Light yet the Light issued from beyond me. I felt a One-ness with all that was highest and best and with the eternal self within me. I felt the nearness of spiritual presences. I was swept on into a meditation in which Frances and I had participated some years before. Gently, and with great reverence, it was borne in upon me that I was not only in touch with my own immortal soul, but also with the soul of Frances Banks. This was Communion, silent, still, uplifting; a Communion emptied of all personality challenges, of all limiting human conceptions. This was Communion at soul level. I felt lifted out of myself into wonder and love and light.' (p23)

These two spiritual sojourners had focused their lives on service. This bond created an easy flow of understanding between them from heaven to earth and nothing could shatter it.

The Unique Expression of the Soul

We can examine three elements of these spirit writings to understand how each is a unique expression of the medium's true nature – each expresses the truth in their unique way.

- √   Who is(are) the spirit inspirer(s)?

- √ What are the gifts, interests and abilities of the medium that the inspirer influences? and
- √ What kind of information is communicated in writing and how?

Let's compare these elements in each writer. The spirit band of Stainton Moses was headed by his inspirer, Imperator, who was one of many members of a band of Biblical prophets and sages. One cannot imagine a group of spirit teachers more suited to the task of presenting a radical view of the Christian religion to an Anglican bishop. While Moses also received messages for his personal growth, he removed them. The result is a collection of philosophical discussions on Christianity and Spiritualism.

The guides of Ruth Montgomery – her 'spirit pen pals' headed by Lily and later, Arthur Ford – are exactly right for her, a journalist, to receive information about the nature of the world beyond. Arthur Ford is able to communicate a factual description of the next plane of life through Montgomery's writing. While Moses wrestled and argued in an intellectual debate with his spirit teachers, Montgomery simply recorded what she was given as fact.

In our third example, the spirit inspirer, Frances Banks is able to continue the close relationship with Helen Greaves that was based on their spiritual service on earth. The medium's strong devotion to uplifting others draws them together between the two worlds in an inspiring expression of the soul's experience. Here, we see how the three elements combine to create a piece of writing that captures the medium's true nature.

To Touch The Soul

By now, many of you have experienced a direct connection to your spirit inspirer – as an elevated presence or perhaps a spirit entity – where you sense your soul mind, senses and/or heart in direct contact with the soul mind, sense and/or heart of an enlightened being. You feel the vibrational flow move you deep within. *Your soul is touched* by Spirit and the spark of life in you is rekindled by the inspiration you receive.

You want to nourish this kind of contact with Spirit. And as you continue to seek it, and write whatever you receive, you will produce writings that are expressions of your soul. They will capture the truth that others too can be inspired by, for they convey a universal message from your higher sources of wisdom that haven't been limited by your finite self, but captures your soul's unique expression of a divine message.

Words that Inspire

Let's remind ourselves that, like all phases of mental mediumship, inspirational writing is a way to serve God and Spirit: as instruments of our spirit inspirers, we want to touch the souls of our readers through the written word. The following are inspired passages that move us deeply because they express a higher truth, something inexpressible that connects us to a sense of the transcendent. They liberate our spirit and feed our soul. As you read them, notice how you are affected within.

Meditate.
Live purely.
Be quiet.
Do your work with mastery.
By day the sun shines,
And the warrior in his armor shines.
By night the moon shines,
And the master shines in meditation.
But day and night
The man who is awake

Shines in the radiance of the spirit.
Dhammapada – The Sayings of the Buddha, 104

*For whosoever will save his life shall lose it; but whosoever
shall lose his life for my sake and the gospel's, the same shall save it.
For what should it profit a man, if he shall gain the whole world,
and lose his own soul?*
Holy Bible, St Mark 8, 35 – 36

*In the silence find the glowing pathway of the spirit. …Thy soul shall be blessed with the rich
increase of celestial knowledge, all perplexities shall vanish, all sorrow shall be assuaged.*
NSAC Spiritualist Manual, 131,132

*To see a world in a grain of sand
And heaven in a wild flower,
Hold infinity in the palm of your hand
And eternity in an hour.*
Fragments from Augeries of Innocence by William Blake

*There is a Spirit that is mind and life, light and truth and vast spaces. … He enfolds the whole
universe, and in silence is loving to all.
This is the Spirit that is in my heart, smaller than a grain of rice, or a grain of barley or a
grain of mustard seed.
This is the Spirit that is in my heart, greater than the earth, greater than the sky, greater than
heaven itself.*
The Upanishads from the **Chandogya Upanishad**

➔ Exercise: Inspirational Writings that Touch My Soul

Notice the kinds of inspirational writings that you have in your sacred place. Select several to read as a way to uplift your soul in your daily practice and be aware of the change in your inner states. Talk to Spirit about the kinds of inspiration that suit your spiritual growth as a medium. Perhaps prayers inspire you, or healing thoughts, inspirations or reflections, poetry or the teachings of a particular religion or spiritual group. Does fiction appeal to you? What channeled writings are you drawn to? What kinds of teachings? Explore them. Seek the truth as you are drawn to it by your soul.

What kind of writings inspire you: _____

_____

_____

How do you find inspiration in your life? _____

_____

_____

_____

Many Different Kinds of Inspirers

Explore different kinds of inspirers to broaden your soul mind. Talk to your inspirer about ways to open your mind to different kinds of inspiration. For example, notice if you are drawn to nature and animal spirits, inspirers from ancient cultures, or from different planes of life. Become aware of the inspiration available to you in everyday life. Let your inspirer guide you.

This exercise shows you how deeply you can be moved by the inspiration received from nature.

➔ Exercise: Attune to a Spirit of Nature for Inspiration

The spirit is the essence in all things. When we attune to the spirit in natural things such as rocks, trees, flowers, water, sky, animals, birds, insects or earth, we are lifted up into our soul and receive inspiration.

Prepare
Sit in your sacred place and pray. … Relax and call on your spirit inspirer to be with you on a nature walk. … Wait until you sense your spirit's presence and give thanks. … You may receive a message from your guide before you start.

Message: _____

_____

_____

Go to a Place in Nature
Go to a place in nature that you like and take a pen and notebook or use this book. Walk around a little and adjust to your surroundings. Be aware of Spirit's uplifting presence and notice that you are drawn to a particular area and thing. … Move closer to it. … Sit down and relax. …

Attune to the Spirit of a Natural Thing
With your spirit inspirer beside you, focus on the natural thing you're drawn to. Close your eyes and perceive it within. Attune to it with your inner senses. Reach out to it in the unseen dimension with your soul mind and heart. … Notice what you sense, see and hear as you connect to its unseen aspect – its soul. You may find yourself opening and closing your eyes to make your connection. With a clear mind, open heart and uplifted soul senses, ask this spirit for inspiration. Listen and record what you receive. …

My Message of Inspiration: _____

_____

_____

My Experience of Attuning to a Spirit of Nature: _____

_____

_____

_____

Commune with Your Spirit Teacher in Your Place of Inspiration

Your Place of Inspiration may be a clearing in a woods, crystal palace, garden, structure unlike what you've seen before, white luminous space, place in a desert, monastery or mountain retreat. Whatever it is, it reflects the wisdom you seek at this time – knowledge that inspires you, that awakens you to a higher truth.

A spirit teacher supported by a team of loving intelligences is drawn to you in your pursuit of truth through inspirational writing. This is an opportunity to learn from enlightened spirits who have journeyed like you, and now come from celestial planes with wisdom beyond your present comprehension. Who comes, how they influence your mind and what kind of insight they communicate is just right for your higher learning. Let them illumine your soul.

➤ Exercise: Receive Inspiration from Your Teacher

Have your pen ready to write the inspiration as Spirit moves you. Play your favorite meditation music. Let it absorb you as it transports you to the higher realms on its sound. Float up with it. Let yourself go and enjoy your experience.

Prepare
Pray. … Relax using a relaxation exercise of your own choice. … Listen to the music as it lifts you up in your soul. … Up and up … float gently up into the higher planes of the spirit world. … Reach up from within and notice how light you feel … how free … happy. … Focus upwards with your soul senses, your heart and mind. How easy it all seems. … Feel the love within and around you. Relax. …

Your Place of Inspiration
Desire to be with your teacher, and you find yourself standing at the entrance of a magnificent place. What does it look like? … Sense the quiet and calm here. … Enter and look around your sacred space. Notice how at-home you feel. …

Meet Your Spirit Teacher
Your spirit teacher greets you. How wondrous is this enlightened presence! Who is this wise being? What do you see? … Sense? … Hear? … How do you feel? … I leave you now to be together. …

Receive Inspiration
You sit down and prepare to write. … Sense Spirit's pure vibrations infusing your mind, and open to them as an instrument, soul-to-soul, mind-to-mind, and heart-to-heart with your teacher. Write now as you receive your inspiration from your spirit teacher. …

My Inspiration: _____

_____

Return

Your writing with your spirit teacher is coming to a close. ... Know that you can return for inspiration at any time. ... Say your farewells. ... Give thanks for what you have received and leave your place of inspiration, floating back gently ... down ... down. ... Come back to your physical presence in the room retaining your lucid state of consciousness, and sense of perfect peace.

▸ *My Experience*

What did your place of inspiration look like? How did you feel there? _____

_____

_____

What qualities attracted you to your spirit teacher? _____

_____

_____

How did your spirit teacher influence you during your inspirational writing? _____

_____

_____

Is the inspiration you received beyond your normal capacity? In what way(s)? _____

_____

_____

Do you feel the writing you received is an expression of your true nature? How? _____
_____
_____

How did you feel with your spirit teacher? _____
_____
_____

How would you describe your experience overall? _____
_____
_____

Speak Your Mind

Inspirational Speaking – A Phase of Mental Mediumship

Another way in which we can be a medium is through inspirational speaking. Like inspirational writing, Spirit communicates soul-mind to soul-mind and we receive their thoughts and words of wisdom that surpass our normal understanding. As you open to your spirit teachers as a channel, you will be moved to share the inspiration given to you from the higher planes. You will want to uplift others by speaking inspirationally.

There is a wide range of spirit control here as in spirit writing (and other phases of mediumship): from a state of light trance where you are influenced by Spirit as a channel, but you are also aware of using your own conscious mind to varying degrees, to a deep trance where you are hardly conscious of what is being said. In all cases, the experience is an uplifted state of one's soul mind and an awareness of expressing a higher knowledge beyond one's normal ability.

Two authorities provide insight into the difference between light and deep trance speaking:

Cora L. V. Richmond – an acclaimed inspirational speaker in the history of Spiritualism

> *Inspirational speaking is a form of mediumship in which the medium is not rendered wholly unconscious. It varies from an abstracted consciousness to a partial or intermittent entrancement. In this phase the spirit does not thoroughly control the nerve center through which the organs of speech are manipulated, and therefore, only impinges upon the magnetic aura of the medium and wafts its thoughts upon the brain, which acts as a sort of receiving station.*
>
> *Sometimes inspirational speakers are influenced in the same speech by several spirit intelligences and thus the speech itself will be a combination of the thought of the speaker and the influencing spirits.*
>
> N.S.A.C. Spiritualist Manual, 30,31

Harry Edwards – A renowned Spiritualist healer, speaker and writer

> *Trance speech is simply the giving of form in the shape of words to the thought-flow from Spirit. In 99 per cent of trance speech, the medium is conscious of what is being said. He is, as*

it were, listening to himself speak, without any conscious effort to create the address himself. In this state, the mind of the medium is tensed up, for the thought flow is vigorous and continuous. The mental organization is working freely for the simple reason it is being used by the guide, and the medium does not need to make any conscious effort to construct sentences or provide the substances for them. The guide is doing this.

Life in Spirit, 215

What are You Inspired to Say?

We are focusing on the light trance of inspirational speaking – on mental rather than physical mediumship. Though not completely entranced by Spirit, you will find that your words flow easily without effort and Spirit's infused presence draws your soul up to heights of optimism, clarity and a strong desire to speak the truth to uplift others. Inspirational speaking is natural to everyone, and like other phases of mediumship, it develops as you reach up to Spirit with your soul's longing for the truth. In this way, your spirit guides and teachers can use your unique interests and talents to bring you insight and understanding that move you on your unique spiritual path and ultimately touch the souls of others.

➤ Exercise: A Chat with Friends (3-5 minutes)

This is an opportunity to learn to feel comfortable talking inspirationally with a small group of people in a safe and supportive environment. A spirit teacher will inspire and guide you. Have your pen ready.

Prepare
Sit in circle and pray. … Relax. … Let your soul feel a wonderful peace within. … Know that you are part of a divine world of loving intelligence. You are guided and supported in all you do. … Relax. …

Focus upwards now with your soul mind, open with your inner senses and call on your spirit teacher to draw you up on high. … Allow the universe to carry you upwards and feel your spirit self becoming lighter as you move into the finer vibrations of the etheric realm. … Feel the freedom and joy of your spirit as you are released from the earth. …

Your Spirit Teacher
You are here to seek inspiration for your talk from your teacher. Be aware of the approach of your teacher as you experience a supreme silence and deep quietude within. …

Greet your teacher as you attune with your soul-mind. … Experience Spirit's soul-mind infusing yours, and feel the love, clarity and higher understanding that is beyond your normal state. … Open your soul and be inspired by the truth.

Ask for Inspiration
Ask for specific inspiration that will enlighten you and uplift your circle friends. Let the thought-flow of your spirit teacher's wisdom pour down into your mind. As these communications come from your teacher, write the inspiration you receive. I leave you now to do this. …

My Inspiration: _____

_____

_____

When you are ready, return to the circle. Your teacher accompanies you. Keep your consciousness in a heightened state as you slowly come back to your chair.

Prepare Your Chat

Maintain your contact with your spirit teacher as you prepare your chat. Reread your inspiration; clarify and expand any ideas that will fill out your subject. Ask your spirit teacher for help with a title that captures your theme.

My Inspirational Chat: _____

Speak to the Group

Speak to the group using the material you've prepared. You may want to read some of it and intersperse it with your own words. Stay open to your spirit influence as you speak. You can speak to the group in three different formats depending on your comfort level:

- sitting,
- standing at the front of the circle that has been opened a little to form a horseshoe, or
- standing in front of the group that is seated theater style facing you. Also you may want to use a podium.

Some of you may feel moved to speak as a channel for Spirit without notes. Let the inspiration flow out through your words.

Feedback Received from My Circle: _____

▸ *My Experience:*

Create A Talk

As a practicing medium, you will be asked to speak inspirationally to groups. You are expected to have insights that uplift others because you have access to spirit intelligences. Here is a guideline to help you with a full-fledged talk if you choose to speak for audiences outside your circle.

Like your chat to your friends, some of you may end up speaking quite spontaneously, influenced by Spirit without an outline or notes. But I recommend the following three step process as a way to seek the truth and gain higher knowledge from your spirit teachers. As you do this, or something similar, you will be given insight from your spirit guides and teachers to develop your own philosophy. Then you can speak confidently from that inspired understanding that is also true to your own soul's higher nature.

→ Exercise: Create a Talk for a Public Audience

This process can be done in one sitting or over a period of days or weeks, as you are drawn to it. Have paper and pen ready.

Prepare
Sit in your sacred place and pray, relax and meditate according to your needs. Call on your spirit teachers and inspirers as you have done in the exercises above. Each of the following steps assumes that you have made contact with Spirit and are open to their inspiration. Record what you receive while maintaining your higher level of consciousness.

A Theme That Inspires You
Let a *theme* come to you though Spirit's inspirational influence. Trust in your soul's hunches about what you want to explore no matter how different or unorthodox it may seem. Have the courage to follow your own heart. Converse with your spirit inspirer through writing and ask for help, even for example, direction to a book or song. Trust the subtle insights that come to you both during your sessions with Spirit and when away from them. Often the source of an inspirational theme is a creative, religious or spiritual one, such as:

- Inspiration from your spirit teacher: 'Seek higher ground.'

- A well-known saying: 'Let go and let God.'

- Words of wisdom: 'We do not want riches. We want peace and love.' Red Cloud, Sioux *Native American Wisdom. 13* (Compiled by Kent Nerburn, Ph.D. and Louise Mengelkoch, M.A.)

- Words of a hymn: 'Sweet hour of prayer! sweet hour of prayer! that calls me from a world of care,' …

- An insight: 'Even a simple kindness can have such a powerful and positive effect!'

- A quote from a religious text: 'The seer's duty is to be tranquil in mind and in spirit.' *Bhagavad – Gita*.

- A Spiritualist principle: 'We have the divine right to seek the truth within our own hearts.'

- A realization: 'How blessed we are!'

Inspirational messages are also available in daily life. Ask Spirit to heighten your awareness of the spiritual significance of ordinary things to get your inspiration. For example, stories and events, interactions with friends and family, the ways of animals, or your personal experiences, can be the subject of your talk. Select a topic that excites you, that rings true to you at this time in your soul's search for the truth. Then, when you speak from this source of truth, Spirit entrances you more harmoniously and your inspiration is contagious for your audience.

Enlarge Your Theme
Once you have selected a theme, ask Spirit to help you *expand it,* to open your mind to other insights related to it, and to information that is needed to make sense of your topic. Jot down these ideas as you let them flow freely. Play with them. Stretch your imagination and enjoy this time in communication with your spirit inspirers as you ask questions and explore new ideas. Let stories and illustrations that help to make your points come to mind. Throughout this process, don't impose ideas on your mind, but let the inspirations and insights be your dominant mode of thought.

Write Your Talk
Once you have five to seven points, more or less, that relate to your theme, reflect on what you want to say. In particular, notice your point of view that emerges from your creative process. Reassess your points in light of your unique slant on the subject. This gives your talk your own voice, and your audience readily responds because you are sharing your genuine heart and soul. It helps them to follow what you're saying too.

Still in your heightened state of awareness with spirit contact, *write* your talk from your points and notes. Some of you may want to write an outline and speak from that. Reflect on your audience as Spirit advises you and helps to fine tune your talk to suit the group.

My Talk Or Outline
(You will want to use a lot of blank paper to write your talk, but you can get started here in the space provided.)

_____
_____
_____
_____
_____
_____
_____
_____
_____
_____
_____
_____
_____
_____

The Presentation

Once you take on the challenge of inspirational speaking, entrust your spirit inspirers and teachers with your soul's longing for the truth and you will be sustained and given the strength you need. No doubt, you will also gain a deeper understanding of your talk that you initially realized. And the service you give to help others along their path returns to you – you are helped along your own way and brought closer to Spirit.

Checklist – Do I …

… make it easy on myself and more enjoyable by being prepared?

I've prepared spiritually through prayer, meditation and communication with Spirit. I'm in an enhanced state of consciousness. I arrive on time and I'm dressed comfortably, but professionally. My materials are in order and include a short biography for the chairperson to introduce me.

… use good platform decorum?

I graciously recognize the chair and other workers. I speak within the time frame allotted and I observe the protocol of the church, group or institution.

… begin my talk in a relaxed yet alert state?

After the introduction, I take my time and approach the podium. I take a deep breath, call on Spirit and trust that I am here for a purpose and that my talk will touch and uplift at least one soul. I open my mouth and let the words flow.

… engage my audience and establish a rapport at the beginning?

I begin with warm words directed to the audience in a friendly way. At the same time I stand strong in my truth and my desire to share the truth. I may begin with something light hearted that puts everyone at ease. Or I may begin with something that touches them deeply right away and presents my theme. I keep my heart center open and pour my love out to the group. I open my soul-mind and thought to my inspirers and allow the words to flow.

… remain confident and connected to Spirit during my talk?

I keep my words flowing, my thoughts uplifted and I trust in Spirit as I stay open to the inspiration I receive. I also glance at my written talk or outline to keep on track as I continue. I stay focused despite any disruption. I speak to the audience, looking either towards the back of the room or at people's faces

…keep my audience interested?

With my gestures, tone of voice, and pitch, and especially with my vitality and passion for my subject, I enlist the attention of the group.

… close with grace and gratitude?

I end on an uplifting note and express my thanks for the opportunity to share my insights with the group. I acknowledge the chairperson and other workers, and sit down.

> *My Experience:*

What did I learn from my inspirational talk? _____

_____

_____

What will I do differently the next time I speak? _____

_____

_____

_____

Guided Meditation: Receive Inspiration in Your Temple of Wisdom

You can use the inspiration you receive in this meditation as writings to share or as the basis for a talk. Some of you may not want to write the inspiration you receive; rather you retain it in your mind and use it to speak spontaneously.

In This Meditation
You are guided to your Temple of Wisdom in the spirit world to meet your master teacher who communicates inspirationally as you write the higher knowledge you receive.

Have your pen ready. Light a candle.

Prayer
Let us pray.

Infinite Spirit!

We come with open hearts and minds to receive inspiration to uplift us on our way.

Help us to embrace the truth. Teach us to seek your wisdom with our soul.

We ask that your messengers of light and love draw near to guide us as we journey to the Temple of Wisdom to receive the word.

Amen

Prepare
Sit in your sacred place and pray in your own words. … Look into the candlelight and relax. … Let the external light open the inner light in your third eye. … Close your eyes. See and sense the light in your mind and relax. … Let it soothe you and relax your mind. … Now let the light spread throughout your body and feel it releasing any tension within. … Be at peace. … Let the light flow into your heart and feel the love that pours into every part of your being. … Be at one with your loving self. Relax. … Let the light calm you as it clears your mind and thought. Relax. … Feel the harmony within. Feel the peace. … Be at home in the light. Relax. Be at peace. …

In this inner state of peace, notice how quiet you are within. How still! Sense a stillness in your mind and enjoy your complete peace of mind. … Be aware of the silence in your mind and all around you, now as you open your soul senses and mind to the etheric sky. …

The Higher Realms
Focus up and reach into the higher planes with your soul's desire for knowledge. Feel yourself releasing from the pull of the earth and let yourself float up … and up … into the beyond. Notice how light you feel in your spirit self. … How free you are. … Be aware of the state of your spirit. … What else do you feel? … Joy? … Love? … A desire to dance and move? … A sense of wholeness? … Let yourself open to this world where the vibrations are fine and your soul is free. … And notice your surroundings … What do you see? … Sense? … Hear? … Be aware of the soothing peace that spreads throughout this realm. …

My Spirit Guide
Looking ahead, see a spirit guide coming towards you shining in a loving light. How do you feel with this spirit? … Open your soul senses and notice what you see … and sense. Listen as your guide greets you with an opening message. … How good you feel with such a welcoming presence! … As you continue to talk, you realize you are being taken to the Temple of Wisdom without any effort and purely by the power of your spirit guide's thought. …

My Temple of Wisdom
You stand outside your temple. … How magnificent! You could not have imagined anything quite like it. … Notice your uplifted states within as you prepare to enter. … The door opens and you step into your temple. What is your first impression of this place of wisdom? … Look around and take it all in with your soul senses. … Notice how you feel here … at home … with a sense of being at-one with yourself and your world. … Your mind is uplifted and at peace in a way you haven't known before. … Walk around your temple with your spirit guide and embrace your higher states of your soul. …

My Master Teacher
Still looking around in awe, you see your master teacher approaching. You know this because of the fine luminous light that surrounds this spirit and the compassion that expresses from its presence. Your guide introduces you and leaves you both. Who is this presence? … How do you feel as your teacher greets you and begins to communicate? … Notice your teacher's features and appearance … How do you feel in the presence of your master teacher? … Why has this spirit presence come to you today? … You realize that your soul-mind, and soul senses are completely open to the opening messages conveyed through your spirit's soul-mind. … You feel close to your teacher; you are comfortable with this learned presence and grateful to receive the inspired teachings.

Soul Knowledge in the Temple
You walk together and you realize that all understanding is available to you here. Whatever you want to learn is accessible. You only need to want it and make yourself ready to receive it. Different areas of the temple offer teachings of all kinds that touch every aspect of human life. The atmosphere is hushed and teachers are working quietly. They are bathed in different kinds of luminosity that reflects the kind of knowledge they're immersed in. You know this; you know things here that you need not be told. That is the nature of this temple and the way knowledge is grasped – directly by the soul – without effort; with insight and inspiration.

Communication with My Master Teacher
Your master teacher tells you what you have come to learn. Listen now and write down the teachings you receive as you open your eyes without altering your higher state of awareness. Your teacher seems to know your dreams as a medium and the insight you receive is beyond your expectations. …

Listen and record the wisdom given to you. Enjoy your interaction and close your eyes to make contact when you wish. Ask questions and discuss whatever is on your mind. Feel free to pour out your heart to this enlightened soul who comes to uplift and teach. Stay in communication as long as the power remains strong.

My Inspiration from My Master Teacher: _____

Your teacher signals to you that it is time to close your first session together. Know that there will be many more, and each time, your relationship deepens and your soul-mind is more attuned to the wisdom of your master teacher.

Return

Your spirit guide who brought you here returns to lead you back. Before you leave your temple, you turn to look around this divine place. … Your master teacher bids you farewell with a few parting words. … Giving thanks, you leave the temple.

In a flash, you are in the etheric sky, and still immersed in the fine vibration of the higher realms, you come slowly down … down … and gently return to your chair in your sacred place. Your spirit guide stays with you until you are fully back in your world. You thank him for his help and he's gone.

> *My Experience*

*Preparation*_____

The Higher Realms _____

My Spirit Guide _____

_____

_____

_____

My Temple of Wisdom _____

_____

_____

_____

My Master Teacher _____

_____

_____

_____

Soul Knowledge in My Temple _____

_____

_____

_____

Communication with My Master Teacher _____

_____

_____

_____

Further Reflections on My Experience _____

_____

_____

_____

PART VII EXPLORE YOUR GIFT OF PROPHECY

It is a truth that spirits commune with one another while one is in the body and the other in the higher Spheres – and this, too, when the person in the body is unconscious of the influx, and hence cannot be convinced of the fact; and this truth will ere long present itself in the form of a living demonstration. And the world will hail with delight the ushering in of that era when the interiors of men will be opened, and the spiritual communion will be established.

Andre Jackson Davis' prediction of the coming of modern Spiritualism,
Principles of Nature, 675.

What is Prophecy?

It's a hot day and I'm stuck in traffic without air conditioning. My cat, Cali, is beginning to pant with the heat. She isn't a good passenger even in the best of conditions. I'm in a line of cars waiting to cross the border and I'm at a standstill midway across the bridge over the Niagara River. Although I can't see the water below, I know the steep cliffs on either side that cut into it, and I can feel myself suspended above it with a sense of not being rooted to anything. We aren't moving. I feel irritated. Why can't the officials in charge move us along? I'm getting more and more impatient. I look back at Cali and for the first time, I feel fear – almost a panic – for her and me. I'm afraid of what might happen.

As the heat becomes more ominous, I begin to pray, especially for Cali suffering in her fur coat. I look up into the sky. It goes on forever; its clear blue is soothing, cooling. Sea gulls are everywhere and their presence is a comfort.

Suddenly I am transported into a whole new world. The gulls float effortlessly in slow motion, pure white beauties soaring in an ethereal world. The sky is infinitely deep, its bright blue is alive with a loving harmony that I'm immersed in so that I feel a complete ease with where I am, with my situation. I and my cat and my car all seem to be in a perfect world, a place of infinite peace and wholeness. I am still in the same situation yet it is completely altered. I know we're going to be fine.

I return from that heightened state to an awareness of myself sitting in my car yet I feel completely calm, no longer anxious. I look back at Cali and she too is changed. She is no longer panting. She is more at ease. I know that 'all is well'; that no matter what my circumstances, that ultimately, the world is in perfect order. What elation! What a new sense of stability and security! All is well no matter what I face, no matter what the struggle!

In a few minutes the traffic starts to move slowly and we're on our way, Cali and me.

Prophecy: A Phase of Mental Mediumship
(Prophecy can also be practiced as a form of *physical* mediumship.)

A *prophecy* is a message that foretells the future for a group – a family, community, nation or world – that could have a significant impact on humanity. A prophecy can be given to an individual who has influence over a group such as a president, or a pope. Though it may seem to be the domain of a select few, it is available to everyone, like all forms of mediumship.

An additional meaning of prophecy includes inspired teachings and interpretations of spiritual and religious thought. You will see how this kind of insight goes hand in hand with your awakening awareness of an expansive sense of life that includes the future. You will also realize how prophetic messages are a continuation of your search for the truth through inspirational writing and speaking, and all forms of mediumship.

A medium can receive information of future events through communication with an enlightened guide – a spirit prophet – whose mission is to guide humanity in its progression. The knowledge is often received in a vision that reaches into the hearts and souls of those who listen, and helps them to move forward on their path to fulfillment. The spirit prophet is an intelligence from the higher planes who speaks with the authority of a teacher or seer through a medium who is a pure channel for these communications. The medium is in an elevated state of consciousness and receives the message that is bathed in the fine vibrations of the beyond so that the soul knows it directly, recognizes its truth and is influenced towards achieving a higher good.

Prediction

A *prediction* is the foretelling of any kind of future event. When it involves the fate of nations or large units, it is termed *prophecy*. (See *A Popular Dictionary of Spiritualism* by Norman Blunsdon.)

A prediction can be experienced in different ways (such as a premonition), and come from a variety of sources (for example, in a dream). However, we will focus on its use in messages and readings. Here a *prediction* is information from the spirit world that foretells the future for an individual that affects his or her life. It is a blessing and a comfort to be able to gain insight from a higher source about the future for oneself and others.

Many of you have already discovered this kind of guidance by attuning to Spirit in your daily practice. Also, as a medium, you can give and receive this knowledge about the future that is accurate, uplifting and empowering. It will come from your sitter's spirit loved ones following your evidence that identifies them, or from your own spirit guides and teachers. We will focus on predictions in the next chapter.

The Law Of Progression

Like all phases of mediumship, the medium is supported in his ability to prophesy by a law that operates in the unseen and is built into our soul – *the law of progression*. This law states that the soul naturally seeks its own fulfillment; we progress by the movement forward of our soul, our desire for wholeness. We don't simply seek the light, we seek it to be more complete, to be at-one.

In my story, as the traffic moved steadily ahead, I realized that my soul knew perfection. That state of 'all is well with the world' is what supports us in our progression, no matter what the circumstances. When we are in touch with our soul, we don't move forward in life fearful of what tomorrow will bring. Our soul seeks full flower, we seek to fulfill our soul's divine purpose. We do this by living in our soul's divine state of awareness – aware of the perfection within our world – and we embrace the future. In this context, the foretelling of the future makes good sense.

Prophecy is not about fear and limitation; it's about helping our souls to awaken to our path, to unfold, to progress. A group too has a natural progression and unfoldment that it strives to fulfill. Prophecy is guidance from a higher plane that touches the soul consciousness of the group and shows it the way.

Prophecy is a Fact

Prophets have accurately predicted significant events that affected nations and large groups of people throughout history. It seems that every culture in every age was familiar with prophecy. Many prophets were highly respected in their time, such as St. Hildegarde, a female saint whose predictions were held to be the 'Voice of God'. Others, like Nostradamus, were treated with mistrust so that he had to disguise his predictions to protect himself from the powerful.

Despite the truth that prophecy provided, it was often ridiculed and sometimes its messenger was attacked or ostracized. Consider Joan of Arc who was burned at the stake for her predictions, and the modern prophet, Edgar Cayce who faced the scrutiny of the law and the public. Jean Dixon's voice was ignored despite the good her messages would have achieved.

Today prophecy is still mistrusted. Why is this? The truth of prophecy is hard to grasp by our normal minds. While it's understood by our soul mind and heart, it often seems preposterous to our conscious minds. No clear conceptual understanding helps us to move from the familiar reality of today to the unusual inner and outer conditions of the future. At one end of the spectrum, it may seem too unsettling to contemplate, at the other, too magnificent to believe. This is important for us as mediums to understand because as we begin to explore prophecy, we need to reach into the higher planes and allow ourselves to be 'inspired by the prophetic vision' as Nostradamus called it without any awareness of our own thought about our reality, and let an entirely new vision of it be given us. We also need to put aside our deep seated thoughts about how the world ought to be and what people ought to do, and let the compassionate, wise teachers and prophets reveal their higher understanding to us.

We can accomplish this as we trust in spirit presences beyond our present awareness and refrain from our own interpretation. Recall, when you began, how you hesitated because some messages seems too odd to share. Yet with courage, you gave them out and were surprised at the sense they made. Seek the same kind of trust and allowing, and the same kind of releasing of your preconceptions of what is possible, true and accurate. Know too that the insight will be given to your soul in the same kind of non-linear language Spirit already communicates to you. Let's reinforce our belief in the truth of prophecy; that it is possible for us to foretell future events that affect large numbers of people; and that the impetus behind it is to help awaken the soul to its higher purpose and progression.

These are some facts about prophecy.

Tibetan Prophecy: Wheeled vehicles were forbidden because of an ancient warning 'When wheels come into the country, peace goes out.' One day, the wheels of the Chinese military came in and the prediction proved true.

Christ's Birth Foretold: A Hermetic Egyptian priest predicted Jesus' life, teachings, last supper and death – in the year 1000 BC! His birth was prophesied by the Druids and East Indian sages. A Roman priestess looked at a meteor and knew that a child had just been born who would be a good king of the world.

Buddha's Calling Foreseen: In a dream, Buddha's father saw his son leave his kingdom and all his riches, and walk away barefoot to fulfill his spiritual mission – to relieve the suffering of the world.

Oracles of Ancient Greece: The philosophers, Socrates, Plato and Pythagoras, all sought the advice of the oracle at Delphi who was renowned for her prophetic words.

Prophets of Europe: Nostradamus, who lived in the 1500's, accurately foresaw events affecting Europe, including details of the French Revolution and the succession of kings, queens and popes. His prophecies are relevant to our present world.

Emanuel Swedenborg offered prophetic wisdom in his revealed interpretation of the Bible and his visions of the conditions and activities of spirits and angels on the higher planes. He predicted the assassination of the csar of Russia, Peter III.

Modern Predictions: Edgar Cayce, 'the sleeping prophet', saw the coming of earth changes – changing land masses, polar melting and a shift in the earth's axis. Even more importantly, according to his biographers, are the many predictions about the soul's increasing awareness of itself and an unprecedented search for spiritual development that we are witnessing now.

Jean Dixon accurately foresaw political events including J.F. Kennedy's assassination and Robert Kennedy's death.

Religious Prophets: The founders of many of the religions practiced today were prophets, and their followers throughout the ages have received prophetic communications from higher spiritual powers. Also, well known in the west, are the predictions of the prophets of the Old Testament in the Bible.

Spiritualist Prophet: In 1856, the medium Andrew Jackson Davis predicted the coming of cars and trains that could travel from the east 'through to California in four days', and 'aerial cars … which move through the sky from country to country'. He foresaw modern materials like concrete and even portable houses. In his prevision, the future was a material heaven that would free the soul to 'post – mundane climes' and elevated spiritual growth. (see *Penetralia: Being Harmonial Answers* by Andrew Jackson Davis)

For further brief accounts of prophets and prophetic facts, see *The World's Greatest Psychics*, by Francine Hornberger and *The Story of Prophecy* by Henry James Forman.

The View of Facts from the Spirit World

When we read these facts, we understand them with our normal thought and perceive many of them as negative and frightening. But the medium receives the prophetic vision soul-to-soul from the spirit world. The experience is of light, love and infinite life. At the same time, the prophecy embraces the truth and addresses the facts. The facts are shown to us by God and Spirit through the elevated states of higher understanding, compassion and oneness. My story demonstrates this. In my normal state of mind, I experienced my situation as dark and threatening. In my higher soul state of oneness with the Infinite, I knew the truth about my condition. I experienced the facts in their true state.

I imagine that if we were to step into the hearts and minds of the seers and prophets such as Jackson, Dixon, and Cayce, who were devoted to God (and Spirit), our visions would reflect the presence of the Divine, and we would understand the facts with the enlightened view of our soul.

Let us remember, as we move ahead in our grasp of prophecy, that the prophet *doesn't create* the future conditions of the world, but seeks to help others understand them.

Meet Your Spirit Prophet

How is it possible to know the future? The unseen world, the source of prophetic messages, is not bounded in space and time. Your spirit communicators are free of these restraints and can know of events far into what we would call the future and past. How much of this knowledge is available to us on this plane depends on the path we've chosen, our need for it and our capacity to grasp it.

➤ Exercise: Insight from Your Spirit Prophet

Have your pen ready to record your experience.

Your aim is to

- meet your spirit prophet, and
- gain insight into the nature of prophecy.

Prepare

Sit quietly in your sacred place. Pray. ... Close your eyes and relax. ... Focus on your breath, and let its soothing life energy flow into your lungs and fill you with peace. Relax. ... As you breathe out, let go of any concerns or tensions ... Continue to breathe normally. Relax. ... Now sense this energy as a loving light, and let it flow down into your body, legs and feet. Feel its life in every cell and organ, and relax. ... Let it flow back up to your chest and be at peace as you breathe and relax. ... See and sense this loving light move up into your shoulders, arms, neck and head. Relax. ... Sense it in every organ. Let it stream gently back to your lungs. Relax. ...

Open to the Light

Look up to a loving light above your head and open your mind to its soothing vibration. Sense its purity and let it clear your mind and thought of old concerns and attitudes that you no longer need. Notice how pure your mind feels. ... Perhaps you sense your goodness. ... Stay open to this divine light. ...

Attune to the Spirit World: Reach up with your heart and mind and let the light draw you up into the higher realms. ... Let go. ... Let yourself move up. Notice how free you are as you float up in your spirit self. ... Now, be aware of the finer atmosphere of the spirit world. ...

Attune to this heavenly place with your soul senses. Notice what you sense. ... Love? Harmony? Joy? Freedom? ... What do you see? ... Light? Colors? Space? ... Do you hear anything? ... Silence? Music? Voices? ...

How I perceive the spirit world. _____

_____

_____

Meet Your Spirit Prophet

See a winding path before you. Step onto it and notice how you float along it without effort. Everything seems just right as you realize you're moving up on an ethereal trail that winds around a mountain. Sense the finer uplifting vibrations as you go higher. ...

Looking ahead, see the figure of a spirit guide – a prophet – coming towards you. You are filled with excitement and optimism as you greet. How at home you feel with this presence! How uplifted and free from any anxiety about anything in your life!

Take a few moments and notice everything about your spirit prophet. What is your first impression? ... What do you see? ... Sense? ... Hear? ...

My first impression: _____

_____

What I sense: _____

_____

What I see: _____

_____

What I hear: _____

Who is Your Spirit Prophet?:

Now notice, as you open your soul heart and mind to your spirit prophet, that you are attuned to a higher intelligence – a visionary – of a fine uplifting vibration. You have a new sense of your own mind – a sense of expansiveness, of seeing into a vast distance all around you. You look out from this mountain and are surprised how far up you have come. ... The height adds to the sense of being awakened to a higher understanding as you open to the divine light of the unseen world. You feel the peace and love that your spirit prophet expresses, and you bask in the warmth that pours into your heart and surrounds you. ... Sense your guide's compassion for all living things and desire for the progression of humanity. ...

Now sit down together, and prepare to receive information about your spirit prophet. Listen as you receive answers to the following questions.

Who are you? _____

_____

Why have you come to me in particular? _____

_____

Where do you come from? _____

_____

What can I call you and by what trigger will I know you are present? _____

_____

Receive Higher Understanding from Your Spirit Prophet

Stay in your elevated state and attune to you spirit prophet's heart and mind. Listen to your guide's teachings about knowledge of the future and gain insight from this visionary to help you develop this gift of your soul.

What is prophecy? _____

_____

_____

How is it possible? _____

_____

_____

Does prophecy imply that I have no free will? _____

_____

_____

How can I learn to prophesy? _____

_____

_____

Take a few more minutes with your spirit prophet before you prepare to return. Perhaps you want a final message or a question answered.

Message: _____

_____

_____

_____

Return

Prepare to return. Give thanks for all you have received. Say goodbye and know that your spirit prophet will be with you to teach and uplift you as you explore your gift of prophecy. Return now, coming down slowly and gently… down… and down. … Stay in your elevated state of your soul – shining and bright in your mind, peaceful and loving in your heart-- as you come back to the earth plane. … Return to your chair and open your eyes.

*Reflections on My Experience*_____

_____

_____

_____

Strengthen Your Gift of Prediction

Predictions and Their Soul Benefits

Here are some definitions of the different kinds of foreknowledge (knowledge of the future) that you may experience. (See *A Popular Dictionary of Spiritualism* by Norman Blunsdon)

Presentiment: The prediction of vague future events of a personal nature only.

Prevision: Presentiment in a visual form.

Premonition: The prediction of non-personal events where details are not precisely outlined. They may be received in normal, trance, hypnotic or dream states.

Precognition: Prediction in which the percipient is correctly positive that a particular event is going to happen. This is in contrast to *retrocognition* which is knowledge of the past, supernormally acquired.

Review: Predictions You Have Received

You have received messages from your spirit guides and teachers about future events in your life as you learned to attune to Spirit for guidance in your daily practice beginning in Part I, Chapter Four. Many of you have also received information about your future in a message or reading from a medium. And you have probably given information as a developing medium in a message or a reading.

These are two predictions that I have received from Spirit for myself. The third is one that I received from a medium. As you read over my illustrations, reflect on those predictions you have received or given.

My Future Home

As I was looking for a place to live on my own following a turbulent separation, I became discouraged by the places available to me – they looked drab and ugly. One evening, I prayed and asked my spirit guides and teachers to show me my future home. The next morning in meditation, I received an answer: I saw a section of a wooden fence with soft sunlight on it, and the corner of a patio door. I felt elated. I didn't know exactly what it depicted, but I felt a sense of

Spirit's presence in it and was comforted. A week later, I was shown a place, and on the second floor, I saw a door onto a balcony with a section of brown fence in dappling sunlight. I knew I had found my new home.

My Red Dot Holiday

Since I have had to travel in winter conditions to teach and present workshops over the years, I have relied on my spirit guides and teachers to guide me safely to my destination. They have shown me such things as detours, heavy traffic conditions, windows of opportunity between storms, problems with black ice and even large numbers of traffic police on the highway! While I check with the weather experts, I find that Spirit can bring us an individualized guide for our specific needs.

Near the end of November, I checked as usual with my spirit guides and teachers to get an overview of the winter ahead. I wasn't thinking so much about travel as about my daily life and how the cold would impact it. The message: I saw a little red dot on a calendar near the end of December. I checked it again and again and saw the same thing. I wasn't sure what condition it referred to and it didn't seem to be a big thing, so I ignored it.

In the meantime, I was planning a trip to the west coast to visit my children for the Christmas holiday. I was excited about it and in the rush to get off, I didn't reflect on the red dot – until I was on the interstate highway in the middle of the worst blizzard I have ever encountered, with a half dozen other cars in treacherous conditions with vehicles strewn in ditches on both sides. By the time I made it to the airport, I thought I was free. But half way across the country, I learned that airports everywhere were closing. After canceled flights and a night at an airport hotel, I finally arrived two days late, bedraggled and exhausted.

My Flowered Jacket

The first medium I consulted gave me this message about the future: I see you standing before a group of people in a flowered jacket with your hands in its big front pockets. You are in the northern part of the country and there are large trees around you. You're writing a book that will be successful.

I went away questioning its accuracy. I had a cotton top with embroidered flowers on its front pockets that weren't big enough for my hands. I thought she might be referring to a trip I was taking to the northern part of another country. And I was writing a series of articles about mental self-help that I thought of collecting in a book,. Still, it didn't seem to ring true.

About fifteen years later, my daughter sent me a colorful flowered jacket. I thought it looked too big and decided to give it back for her to return. When I gave it to her, I tried it on and she pointed out that it was just the right fit and I ended up keeping it. I began to like it; the flowers were colorful and uplifting. And when I wore it, I received many compliments.

Five years later, I wore the flowered jacket to an outdoor service in which mediums gave public demonstrations of the continuity of life to large numbers of visitors. I got up to give messages and as I stood in front of the group, I became aware that my hands were in my big front pockets and I was looking up at tall magnificent trees all around me. The prediction! This was the northern part of the country and I was writing this book.

I offer this prediction because it occurred twenty years later, and, it seemed, it could have so easily not been fulfilled. And I would add that my book is already successful if only for all the learning that I have gained during its writing.

Your Predictions

Describe several predictions you have received for yourself or others (that you have verified). Give each a title. Notice what soul senses you used to receive this message. Be aware, too, of how you felt with it.

*(The Title of My Prediction)*_____

_____

_____

_____

_____

*(The Title of My Prediction)*_____

_____

_____

_____

_____

The Benefits

Let's examine the benefit of each of the predictions we received. Become aware of the benefit to your soul. For example, notice how the knowledge helps you to feel more connected to your soul, your world or path. Even guidance about your travel can help you to feel more in tune with life, less stressed and therefore less alienated. Or you may feel confirmation in your deepest self that you are being given support from a higher source, or that you are being taught how to live more simply or how to let go of old emotions. In other words, notice how you are touched in your soul by the prediction.

These are the benefits of my predictions that I experienced in my soul.

My Prediction	Its Benefit to My Soul
My Future Home	I felt supported in my soul by the higher powers, and reassured that there was a place available for me where I felt at home.

My Red Dot Holiday	I realized the importance of listening to my soul and not forcing my will on any situation no matter how much I may want it, and I was grateful to God and Spirit that I was kept safe in such a threatening circumstance.
My Flowered Jacket	I was filled with awe at the unfathomable workings of Spirit and I felt confirmed in my service as a medium.

Identify the benefits of your predictions that you experienced in your soul.

My Prediction	Its Benefit to My Soul

We Create Our Own Destiny

Overcome Fear of the Future

Someone comes to you for a reading and says 'Please don't tell me anything negative about the future.' They express our basic feeling about predicting the future – fear. We're not sure we want to know what's in store for us. Yet the essential teaching of mediumship – and of most religions and spiritual practices – is the truth of eternal life: We are spirit beings, the world is of the spirit and our purpose here is to realize our divine heritage.

In my experience on the bridge on that hot day, I realized that truth: When I opened to the infinite unseen world, I lost all fear of what might happen. I was in touch with my soul and the infinite. I experienced the truth of eternal life first hand.

In light of my experience, one can understand that from God and Spirits' perspective, there is nothing to fear. And from our soul's point of view also, no message is 'negative'. As mediums, we help our sitter when we help them to realize this truth also.

Foretelling

(Please note that we are talking of *foretelling* the future—not *fortune telling*. The latter is a derogatory term for predictions that reinforce fear through a belief in the power of harmful forces to control an individual's life.)

To grow in our soul can be challenging, and to understand the unseen workings of the laws can be difficult. But we have an inborn power that moves us forward towards our higher good. And the unseen world always supports us in the law of progression. We may have done things that have harmed others. We have made mistakes. But this doesn't alter our essence, our goodness.

We need to be strong in our awareness of our inner life force that shines in the face of difficulty and optimistic in the face of doubt to overcome our mistakes and false ways. Our spirit guides and teachers support this divine way, and it finds expression in our messages and readings as we serve as an instrument of Spirit.

Destiny and Free Will

We create our own destiny by embracing our soul's progression. The law of progression (like all the spiritual laws) relies on the fact that our soul's growth arises from within. Nothing can harm us from the outside. Predictions are intended to touch us in our soul where we can be helped to move ahead on our chosen path. The more we become aware of our soul and listen to our inner guidance, our heart and higher insights, the more we are in sync with our world and supported by it. As we grow, our feet are more firmly rooted in the truth and we are able to be more attuned to our unfolding path and future and feel aligned with it.

We have chosen our earthly journey in accordance with our soul's desire to learn and progress in this lifetime. To accomplish our divine purpose, we will face difficulties along the way. To help us realize how to do this with a positive attitude and trust in the support of the higher powers, let us remember the lives of spiritual leaders of all ages who embraced impossible challenges with an enlightened understanding and gentle compassion for humanity. They seemed to know that impossible challenges were part of their divine purpose; that even their suffering could be a comfort and inspiration for others.

How Can We Understand Our Future In This Way And Help Others To Do So?

When we are devoted to God and Spirit and want to serve as instruments to uplift others, then we are grounded in our soul, and future difficulties are simply part of our unfolding path. We can embrace them with a strength and power that comes from being true to our higher purpose. And in that state, anything is surmountable.

Can We Change a Prediction?

Some things are more fixed because we have chosen them for our life's progression, our soul's learning. Yet some we can change. It isn't always easy to know which is changeable but Spirit can help us. Since you will be working with others giving them insight into their future, it's important for you to develop your own understanding, your philosophy, guided by your spirit prophet's insight and understanding.

Gain Your Own Understanding

To work closely with our spirit prophet, we need to raise our vibrations higher and open our soul mind to the celestial planes of the unseen world. From here, the understanding we seek is given to us. In order for you to delve deeper into these subjects and gain your own understanding, let's ask your spirit prophet for more enlightened insights.

➔ Exercise: Insight from Your Spirit Prophet on Predictions

To gain insight from Spirit about predictions that seem to be 'negative' and those we want to change, think of an example of each before you contact your spirit prophet. Think of a prediction you have received that you feel is 'negative' because it appears to have no soul benefits.

A 'negative' prediction I have received: _____

_____

_____

Think of a prediction you have received that you would like to change with the help of your spirit prophet.

A prediction I would like to change: _____

_____

_____

Prepare

Sit quietly in your sacred place. Pray. … Close your eyes and relax. Focus on your breath, and let its soothing life energy flow into your lungs and fill you with peace. Relax. … As you exhale, let go of any concerns or tensions. … Continue to breathe normally. Relax. … Now sense this energy as a loving light, and let it flow down into your body, legs and feet. Feel its life in every cell and organ, and relax. … Let it flow back up to your chest and be at peace, as you breathe and relax.… See this loving light move up into your shoulders, arms, neck and head. Relax. … Sense it in every organ. Let it stream gently back to your lungs. Relax. …

Open to the Light
Look up to a loving light above your head and open your mind to its soothing vibration. Now sense its purity and let it clear your mind and thought of old concerns and attitudes that you no longer need. Notice how pure your mind feels. … Perhaps you sense your goodness. … Stay open to this divine light. …

Attune to the Spirit World
Reach up with your heart and mind and let the light draw you up into the higher realms. Let go. … Let yourself move up. Notice how free you are as you float up in your spirit self. … Now, be aware of the finer atmosphere of the spirit world. …

Communicate with Your Spirit Prophet
Sense the harmony here. Now notice that your spirit prophet is coming towards you bathed in a divine light. It may be your familiar guide or someone different. What is your first impression? … Greet each other and open your soul senses to this presence. Notice what you see … sense … and hear. …

Feel the peace and love from your spirit prophet. … As you sit down together, open your higher understanding to Spirit's guidance. Listen to your guide's teachings about knowledge of the future and in particular, about predictions for yourself and others. Open your soul heart and mind to receive answers to these questions.

What are the benefits of predictions? _____
_____
_____

Why are we afraid to know the future? How can we overcome this fear? _____
_____
_____

Teach me to understand a 'negative' prediction from your view point. (See my example above.) Please show me its benefit, if any. _____
_____
_____

How can I make sure I don't reinforce fear in my work as a medium? _____
_____
_____

Help me to clarify the role of destiny and free will in foretelling the future. Are some things destined (unchangeable) in our lives? Are others malleable to our free will (changeable)? _____
_____
_____

Teach me to understand how to change a prediction. (See my above example.) Why did I receive it? _____
_____

Do you have any other guidance for me at this time? _____

_____

_____

Return
Give thanks to your spirit prophet for the understanding and inspiration you have received. Say your goodbyes and slowly return to your sacred place. Let yourself come back … and when you are ready, gently open your eyes.

Sharpen Your Predictions for Yourself

➔ Exercise: Determine the Time and Place of Predictions

You learned how to perceive the particulars of space and time in messages received from Spirit in Part II, Chapter Eight. In this exercise, you will sharpen your gifts of prediction as you use some of the same time and place co-ordinates. Here you want to focus on future events.

Prepare
Sit quietly in your sacred place. Pray, relax and meditate in a way that's comfortable. Call on your spirit guides and teachers. Allow Spirit to take you up into your spirit body and relax. … Be at peace. … Enjoy your sense of your spirit as you feel light in weight. … Your mind is clear and open to the infinite, and you feel the freedom of your higher self. … Let a spirit guide or teacher draw near and notice who is here. Great each other. … Now with this presence in and around you, open to a these simple methods to know the time and place of predictions. Enjoy your exploration!

Past, Present and Future
Suppose you see your sitter looking very happy and waving a piece of paper in his hand, and above him the word 'Congratulations!' You want to be able to identify the time frame for this event – was it in the recent past? The present? or the future?

Spirit shows me the past on my left or the sitter's right side, the present is around, below and above the sitter, and the future is on my right or the sitter's left. Ask Spirit now to indicate how to perceive them.

How Spirit shows me the past, present and future: _____

_____

_____

Near and Far
You want to know if a message is for the distant or more recent past. Is it in the distant future or is it near? Spirit shows these to me by indicating the space close to or far away from the sitter.

How Spirit shows me near and far: _____

_____

_____

Date
You may want to know the year, month and day for a message in the past or future. Spirit shows me a calendar with the year and flips through to a month and day on it. Or for a quick rough future date, I sense a season, such as spring with birds singing and a new green countryside, or I feel the crunch of the dead leaves of autumn under my feet. With them, I see a number such as 1 or 2 to indicate how many years ahead.

How Spirit shows me the date for a message: _____

_____

_____

Time
Knowledge of the time can also be very helpful in placing a message. I see a clock: It may be digital or the hands may go round to settle at a specific time. You can practice this during the day and learn to rely less on a watch.

How Spirit shows me time: _____

_____

_____

Day and Night, Weather Conditions, Geographic Locations
Earthly conditions can help to identify a message or help to understand it both through its literal and symbolic meaning. For example, a bright sun can indicate good results with a project or it can mean that something will take place where it's sunny or in summer.

How Spirit helps me to identify the earthly conditions

Day and night: _____

_____

_____

Weather conditions: _____

_____

_____

Geographic locations: _____

_____

_____

Additional earthly conditions: _____

_____

_____

Other Kinds of Information
There may be other kinds of information you want to know to pin point a message in a time and place. Ask Spirit:

How Spirit helps me with *other methods:* _____

_____

_____

Return
When you are ready, thank your spirit guide or teacher for what you received and slowly return to your awareness of your sacred place.

Predict and Prophesy

Predict the Future

With your new grasp of foretelling the future and your contact with your spirit prophet, you can now gain greater clarity and access to higher understanding, and even visions regarding your soul self, your mediumship and your path.

→ Exercise: To Predict the Future for Myself

Before we begin this exercise, think of the conditions in your life for which you may seek future guidance from your spirit prophet such as, family, house, work, finances, health, self-concept, relationships, spiritual growth, mediumship, travel, celebration, or new project.

Read over the exercise and fill in the blanks with two conditions and one event for which you would like your guide's predictions. For example for the first condition, I may put *finances* because I want information about my financial situation as I make changes in my life. For the event, I write in *travel* because I am looking for reassurance that my holiday will go well. And for the last condition, I insert *house* because I like the comfort of knowing my house will sell—hopefully in the near future. In each of these cases, the guidance that I receive from Spirit will help me move ahead in my life in a way that is beneficial to my soul.

Next, let's see if you can prepare and attune to the spirit world to meet your spirit prophet on your own with the following guidelines. Your spirit prophet may be a guide or teacher such a as a spirit control, familiar teacher, spirit loved one, or someone entirely new. Whoever it is, trust that this presence is just right for you to learn to predict the future at this time. Have a pen ready to record what you receive from your spirit prophet.

Prepare
Sit in your sacred space and close your eyes. Pray. … Relax by focusing on your breath. … …

Attune to the Spirit World
Call on your spirit prophet or guide. … Reach up … Feel your spirit self … Open your soul senses …

Meet Your Spirit Prophet
See your guide approaching … What do you see … sense … hear? … Greet …

Communicate with Your Spirit Prophet

Now attune to your prophet's soul mind and sense the vibrations of higher knowledge infusing in your mind. Sense your soul heart filled with your guide's pure gentle compassion, and listen to the guidance regarding the predictions for you. As you receive the message, feel the security and support that your guide expresses through such an elevated spirit presence. Know that all is well. Rest secure in the stability of being rooted in a good world to which you belong and in which your soul feels at home. Experience this; rest in this awareness. …

When you are ready, open to guidance from your spirit prophet. Know that it may come in symbolic messages, in conversation or both.

Guidance about predictions for myself from my spirit prophet: _____
_____
_____

Attune closely to your spirit prophet's presence so you can perceive your soul's progression from Spirit's view. Soar above your circumstances to see your future in the light of your soul's progression. With your spirit guide at your side, let there be a clearing or a space before you where your messages can be clearly perceived and ask:

Please give me an uplifting and helpful prediction for the following condition. (Describe my condition.) _____
_____

Tomorrow _____
_____
_____

Next month _____
_____
_____

Next year _____
_____
_____

Guidance about my future condition _____
_____
_____

Please bring information that is beneficial to my soul regarding an upcoming event. (Describe the event.) _____
_____

Prediction of an upcoming event: _____
_____

Guidance about the future event: _____

_____

_____

Please bring me information about the future for the following condition: _____
(Identify my condition.) Include a time and place if applicable.

Prediction for my condition: _____

_____

_____

Guidance about my future condition. _____

_____

_____

Notice that when your predictions are viewed in the unseen dimension, they offer a combination of inspiration, encouragement about your ability to create your path, and symbolic or literal information about your life. You're shown your power to bring about the path you've chosen. With the support of Spirit urging your soul forward, feel a new strength to accomplish what is in your heart.

Discuss any concerns you have about your predictions with your spirit prophet. _____

_____

_____

Predict the Future for Another

Enlighten Your Sitter about Predictions

When you predict the future for a sitter in a message or a reading, you may want to preempt it with a brief explanation of your own view. Share with them the guidance you have received from your spirit prophet that has helped enlighten you about knowledge of the future.

Often I say something like 'I believe that destiny and free will operate together and it's not always easy to determine what is fixed and what is open to change.' Following a prediction suggest that get their own intuitive sense of their situation. I urge them to seek their own inner counsel. 'Pray, ask for your own insight and wait for your answer. It may come the next day or week, but persist and you will receive what you're seeking, often when you least expect it.' You want them to know that they are choosing their life path through their soul's progression and help them to listen to this life force within so they can embrace their journey. You also want them to know they are always supported by God and Spirit.

Keep in mind that you are *the messenger* of news of the future, not *the creator* of the future event. Still you want to help your sitter to understand and grow as you share what you receive as a channel of Spirit. As we've discussed above, the way Spirit presents the information is positive. Do your best to leave the sitter with a sense of empowerment and optimism about their life and that good news always comes from the spirit world. It is the truth of eternal life, the truth about ourselves.

Predicting Death

Most mediums don't predict death. Even when a sitter asks about it for a chronically ill relative, it is not advisable. It's a very sensitive issue, because it's a private matter between the person who is dying and their God or Universal Power. When a dying person wants someone to know, they can send the message from their soul mind or thought. This is a common way for families to get a premonition of death. Also, spirit loved ones will communicate this message to the family and the dying person in order to bring comfort and reassurance to all concerned. (I recommend that you revisit our discussion of death in Part IV Chapter Fifteen, *Sensitive Issues and How to Handle Them*.)

What is Right for You

Some well-known psychics of the past like Jean Dixon, predicted death. Sometimes it helped loved ones to spend quality time together that they otherwise wouldn't have done. Often her message was intended to warn of a death. This was the way she was guided to help people progress in their lives.

Like so many choices, seek your answers from within from your spirit prophet or control. They know what is suitable for you, given your path and values. Follow their guidance and help others as you have been helped by them.

Predictions in Messages and Readings

You have by now been moved by your spirit control to give messages for your sitter which include predictions. After you have brought evidence to identify a spirit loved one, and in the course of offering guidance from the spirit world, you may receive a prediction about a condition to help your sitter move forward in their daily life.

Let's focus now on just this part of the message (or reading) from Spirit. Your spirit guides and teachers may want to help your sitter embrace her path and progress with her soul's creative force by opening to the foreknowledge of an event that your spirit prophet can bring. They may want to reinforce her capacity to create her way according to her soul's desire and to also help her realize that she isn't alone on her future path – that her soul is part of a higher order that sustains and helps her through her ups and downs. The information that comes through to you from the spirit world may bring the opportunity to help your sitter own her future and realize that she participates in her own progression as a soul who is becoming more and more complete.

↠ Exercise: Predict the Future for a Partner

Decide who will be the medium and sitter. At the end of the exercise, change roles. Both of you need to have a pen ready to record what you receive.

Medium

Sit facing your partner and follow the same procedure as the previous exercise; that is, see if you can again prepare and attune to the spirit world to meet your spirit prophet on your own with the following guidelines. Let your partner read the instructions to you.

Sitter

Reflect on the conditions and future events in your life. Note the ones for which you would like to understand their future progression. Release all concerns you may have for the future.

As you read these guidelines for your partner, do your best to relax, call on Spirit and raise your consciousness so that you too experience your elevated soul state. As the medium proceeds, record the information you receive in the space provided under *Predictions for the Sitter*.

Prepare
Close your eyes and pray. ... Relax by focusing on your breath. ... ...

Attune to the Spirit World
Call on your spirit prophet. ... Reach up ... Feel your spirit self ... Open your soul senses ...

Meet Your Spirit Prophet
See your guide approaching ... What do you see ... sense ... hear? ... Greet ...

Communicate with Your Spirit Prophet
Now attune to your prophet's soul-mind and sense the vibrations of higher knowledge infusing in your mind. Sense your soul heart filled with your guide's pure gentle compassion, and listen to the guidance regarding the predictions for you. As your spirit prophet speaks with you, feel the security and support that your guide expresses through an elevated spirit presence. Know that all is well. Rest secure in the stability of being rooted in a good world to which you belong and in which your soul feels at home. Experience this; rest in this awareness. ...

Now open to the prophet's teachings about your attitude towards your partner's future. Listen to the inspiration and insight you receive about giving information that predicts the future for another. Let Spirit open your soul heart and mind as you receive this comforting message. As you do this, your partner is silently praying, relaxing and meditating in his chair facing you, and giving over to Spirit all his concerns about the future. He has ready his sheet to record the predictions he receives from you.

Next, be aware of yourself as a medium and prepare to convey information from the spirit world as an instrument for your spirit prophet. Let your spirit's presence infuse your heart, mind and soul senses as you open to receive predictions for your partner. With your spirit at your side, let there be a clearing or a space before you where your messages can be clearly perceived.

Ask Spirit to show you a condition in your sitter's life at the present time. What do you see ... sense ... hear ... and perhaps smell or taste? ... What condition or situation do you perceive? ... When you are ready, share what you have received ...

Ask Spirit to reveal the condition at a future time. Open your soul senses to receive the prediction. ... Notice all the details. ... Can you pick up a date and/or place for it (if they are applicable)? ... When you are ready share what you have received. ...

Ask your spirit prophet to bring you guidance for your sitter, concerning this situation. Share what you receive keeping in mind your desire to empower and uplift your sitter as he moves forward in his life. ...

Next, ask Spirit to bring you a prediction of an upcoming event in your sitter's life. Open your soul senses. ... Can you pick up a date and/or place for it (if they are applicable?) ... When you are ready, give out what you have received....

Finally, ask for guidance for your sitter regarding this event. ... Share what you receive. ...

Teachings from Your Spirit Prophet

Since this is a learning situation, open to receive any further teachings from your spirit prophet to help you and your partner understand these predictions. Listen as you receive higher understanding to help your partner's soul progression. …

Open to questions from your partner and receive the answers from your spirit prophet who provides a wisdom that is beyond your normal understanding. Are some predictions those that your sitter has already set by the path she has chosen as a soul? Learn from Spirit and grow through it just as your sitter does. …

Return

When you are ready, give thanks to your spirit prophet and close your session with a prayer. Come back slowly to your awareness of your self sitting in your chair.

Medium's Reflection

What I liked about my messages: _____

_____

_____

_____

What I would like to improve: _____

_____

_____

_____

Predictions for the Sitter

My Condition

My condition in the present: _____

_____

_____

_____

My condition in the future: _____

_____

_____

_____

Guidance about this situation: _____

_____

_____

My Event
Prediction of my upcoming event: _____

_____

_____

_____

Guidance about the event: _____

_____

_____

_____

Sitter and Medium
Feedback and discussion: _____

_____

_____

_____

Prophesy as an Instrument of Your Spirit Prophet

Here in Part VII, we are explaining our gifts of prophecy. To prophesy requires the attunement of a subtle aspect of our soul that most of us haven't used in our lives. Know that to fully enfold these gifts takes time, experience and practice. The exercises provided will help you begin this wondrous journey of discovery. And with a persistent desire to learn, you can serve God and Spirit with this divine faculty as their instrument.

The Soul of a Group

Just as we have a soul, so does a group. It is its essence, its life. The soul expresses the true nature of the group.

To prophesy as a medium in communion with your spirit prophet, you want to attune to the soul of a group in order to envision its future unfoldment. Let's begin to do this.

➔ Exercise: The Soul of a Group

Sit in your sacred place and pray to be able to perceive the soul of a group to which you belong, and understand how it can grow and progress as it moves forward. Relax. … Notice your breath and relax. … Ask Spirit to draw near … reach up into your higher states … and sense the presence of your spirit prophet in and around you. … Now, become aware of a clear space in front of you and open your soul senses to receive answers. … You may see, sense, hear, smell or taste the information, or it may come in symbols, thoughts or sensations. … Stay uplifted in Spirit's presence as you continue. …

1. Think of a group that you belong to and care deeply about. Describe it. _____
_____
_____

2. Can you identify its essence or its soul? Describe what you are receiving. Notice all the details. How do you feel with it? Discuss the meaning of the message with your spirit prophet. _____
_____
_____

3. What uplifts the soul of the group and helps it to progress? Describe what you are receiving. Notice all the details. How do you feel with it? Discuss its meaning with your spirit prophet. _____
_____
_____

4. Let your spirit prophet show you a future event bathed in the light and love of Spirit involving the group and notice how the group could be helped in its soul by foreknowledge of it. Use your soul senses, thought and insight to discern the message. Discuss it with your spirit prophet. _____
_____
_____

Reflections on the messages about my group: _____
_____
_____

Explore your Gift of Prophecy

In the following exercise, you will work with your spirit prophet to perceive a future situation that is *beneficial* to a group. In prophecy, the more you care for a group and the more you desire the happiness of humanity, the more accurate are your predictions, for this identification with the group draws you close to its life and soul.

Here you want to perceive the future of these groups through Spirit's mind, heart and senses. You want to be able to clearly discern the future as you perceive it in the unseen world infused with Spirit's higher perspective. Free your mind from any predisposition to perceive a group in a particular way.

➔ Exercise: To Prophesy

In this exercise for the first group, your family, I will guide you using the same four steps above, only in the last step; your prophet will show you a prophetic vision instead of the future event you perceived. Remember that these visions are beneficial for your group, so relax your mind and allow Spirit's messages to unfold. For the remaining groups, your community, country, and world you will use a symbol to receive your messages from your spirit prophet. For example,

HOW TO BECOME A MEDIUM

the symbol of a flower will be used to perceive your community's soul and its progression. In this way, your preconceptions of the group and its future won't color your message. You can explore your gift of prophecy freely.

As you have done in the last section, prepare and attune to the spirit world to meet your spirit prophet on your own with these few guidelines.

Prepare
Close your eyes and pray. ... Relax by focusing on your breath. ... ...

Attune to the Spirit World
Call on your spirit prophet or guide. ... Reach up. ...   Feel your spirit self. ... Open your soul senses. ... ...

Meet Your Spirit Prophet
See your guide approaching. ... What do you see? ... Sense?... Hear? ... Greet... ...

Communicate with your Spirit Prophet
As you walk together, be aware of the divine light expressing from your spirit prophet that is purer and finer than you have experienced before. In the presence of your guide, you are transported to a higher state. Your soul mind is lucid; in your soul heart you feel the same compassion your spirit prophet has for the wellbeing of others; and your soul senses are translucent – open to the deeper meaning of things.

Sitting down, a space clears before you as you open your soul senses to receive your answers. You may see, sense, hear, smell or taste the information, or it may come in symbols, thoughts or sensations. ...

My Family
Think of your family and reflect on what you love about it. Describe what you think and feel. _____
_____
_____

Can you identify its essence or its soul? Describe what you are receiving. Notice all the details. How do you feel with it? Discuss the meaning of the message with your spirit prophet. _____
_____
_____

What uplifts the group and helps it to progress? Describe what you are receiving. Again notice all the details. How do you feel with it? Discuss its meaning with your spirit prophet. _____
_____
_____

Let your spirit prophet show you a vision of a future event affecting your family and notice how the group could be helped in its soul by foreknowledge of it. Use your soul senses, thought and insight to discern the message. Discuss it with your spirit prophet. _____
_____
_____

Reflection on the messages about my family: _____
_____
_____

As you close, see a loving and uplifting light around your family. Feel their happiness. Sense the presence of Spirit supporting them on their path. When you think of them, keep this awareness of them present in your mind.

My Community (Or Other Group)

Ask for a *flower* in the space before you by which to perceive the essence or soul of your community. Stay up in your inner senses and notice what you see, sense and hear with your flower. ... Notice all the details. ... As a member of the group, how do you feel with it? Discuss the meaning of it with your spirit prophet. ... When you are ready, record what you received.

Messages: (What you perceived and how you felt with it.) _____
_____
_____

Higher Understanding from Spirit (The meaning of what you received.): _____
_____
_____

Now, go ahead in time and ask your spirit prophet for another flower with which to perceive the group at that time. What kind of flower is it and what is it doing? ... What do you see, sense, hear and smell? ... How do you feel with this flower? When is this? Notice the details given to you. ... Discuss it with your spirit prophet. ... When you are ready, record what you received.

Messages: _____
_____
_____

Higher Understanding from Spirit: _____
_____
_____

As we leave your community, see a loving and uplifting light around it. Sense the presence of Spirit with your community, happy and uplifted in its divine unfoldment. See and sense the members of your group bathed in light, love and life.

My Country

Ask your spirit prophet for a tree by which you can perceive the soul of your country. What do you see, sense, hear and perhaps smell? ... What is your first impression with this tree? ... How do you feel with it? ... Do you perceive anything else with your tree? Listen to its message. ... Discuss it with your spirit prophet. ... When you are ready, record what you received.

Messages: _____
_____
_____

Higher Understanding from Spirit: _____
_____
_____

Now move ahead in time and notice the date that your spirit prophet gives you. Ask Spirit to show you an animal by which to understand a prophecy for your country, and let the animal interact with the tree. What kind of animal is it? ... What is it doing? ... How do you feel with it? ... What do you see, sense, smell and hear with it? ... How do the animal and tree relate? ... Discuss the meaning of this message with your spirit prophet. ... When you are ready, record what you have received.

Messages: _____
_____
_____

Higher Understanding from Spirit: _____
_____
_____

Perceive Spirit shining a light to the soul consciousness of your country and surrounding it with love to support its progress and divine unfoldment. Keep this awareness of your country, its leaders and members, in your heart and mind to nurture their progression.

My World

Ask your spirit prophet to give you a message that shows you your world's essence or soul in the form of a bird. As you open your inner senses to the space before and above you, what do you see? ... Sense? ... Hear? ... What do you feel with it? ... Notice all the details. Discuss its meaning with your spirit prophet. ... When you are ready, record what you received.

Messages: _____
_____
_____

Higher Understanding from Spirit: _____
_____
_____

Move ahead in time and ask Spirit to show you a future date. When is it? Look up, open to the space before you and let your spirit prophet show you the same bird at this time. What do you see? ... Sense? ... Hear? ... What is your first impression with this bird? What do you feel? ... Notice all the details. ... Discuss it with your prophet. ... When you are ready record what you have received.

Messages: _____

_____

_____

Higher Understanding from Spirit: _____

_____

_____

Perceive Spirit pouring a shining light into the soul of the world and surrounding it with love to support its progress and divine unfoldment. Keep this awareness of the world in your heart and mind to nurture its progression.

Explore Your Gift of Prophecy in a Cave of Crystal

Here you will rely on your spirit prophet to use your gift of prophecy to bring you insight into a future event that is just right for you. The kind of group that Spirit will focus on and the nature of the message will be something within your range of interest and capability.

Consider the prophecies of Nostradamus, Jean Dixon, Edgar Cayce and Andrew Jackson Davis, and their suitability to the life situation of each person. For example, Nostradamus was a physician for the royal family and a well-known member of the court. It is fitting, then, that his prophecies involved the monarchy and people in influential positions. So too with Jean Dixon: Her family belonged to the upper echelons of society and her life was closely linked to the concerns of Washington. Edgar Cayce was especially interested in helping those who sought readings from him to realize the importance of the growth of their soul. And his most important prophecies reflect this. His interest in the welfare of humanity also included predictions about the earth's changes. Andrew Jackson Davis' prophecies were about the future opportunity for humankind to communicate with Spirit and understand the truth of eternal life.

In each case, the prophet was able to receive a prophecy that could help a group of people in a significant way because the medium had compassion for a group that was close to their soul, heart and mind. As I discussed above, this compassion was needed in conjunction with their gift of prophecy in order for their spirit prophet to bring the message through.

In light of this understanding, first, reflect on your own soul interests. Your spirit prophet uses them to bring you a prophetic message. Where is your soul heart and mind when it comes to the future of a group? What group of people is closest to your heart? What does your soul desire for the souls of this group of people?

Secondly, consider your gifts. Notice the kind of information you receive from Spirit through your gifts. As you use your gift of prophecy more and more, you may discover that you pick up information about the earth's changes, or your gifts may be more about inventions and knowledge of a particular kind. You may perceive the inner states of people and be interested in their psychological and/ or spiritual growth, or your focus may be on social, political and religious trends or events around the world. Your interest may be with certain kinds of people and their values, beliefs or behaviors, or your heart may resonate more with animals, plants and their future. Spirit will help you begin to decipher these things for yourself in this meditation.

→ Exercise: Explore Your Gift of Prophecy

Have your pen ready to describe the visions and insights you receive from your spirit prophet.

Prepare
Light a candle and before you close your eyes to prepare with prayer, sit quietly and look into the flame. Let its light enter your mind and clear away your thoughts. Embrace the light within your mind and sense the inner quiet this brings to your inner world. …

Close your eyes and pray
Relax. … Open to your inner silence and be at peace. … Pay attention to your breath and relax. … Become aware of the inner light in your mind. … See it shining into your entire body with its life energy and notice how you feel. … Sense this pure light in every cell from the top of your head to the tips of your toes. Sense the new life that flows in you and be at peace. …Now let this light flow out from you into the space that surrounds you and fill your aura with new life. … Notice how your heart opens with this shining light and your love pours out into your world. …

Journey to the Cave of Crystal
Look up and let your inner light reveal a star in the distant sky. Your heart is drawn to it and as you reach up with your shining soul, you find yourself transported from the earth to a higher plane of life. Notice the immense quiet … how calm you feel … Attune to the fine vibration here and to your spirit self. …

Now the star is closer and it seems to shine right into your inner heart and mind. … In a flash, a veil is lifted and you are standing in front of a cave. Its door, that is usually part of the rock formation, opens to an inner dwelling that is bathed in divine light. What do you see? … Sense? … Hear? … Smell? … Taste? … How do you feel? …

Meet Your Spirit Prophet
A figure emerges in the light – your spirit prophet. … Notice your first impression. … Open your inner senses and your shining soul heart and mind to this wondrous spirit. Notice what you see … and sense in the presence of this wise and loving soul. … Is your guide familiar or is this another member of your spirit group of prophets? …

Your prophet greets you and you feel the fine vibrations uplifting yours beyond your present experience. … Listen to your prophet's opening message.

Opening Message _____

_____

_____

_____

The Cave of Crystal
You walk with your guide into the cave and notice how the light draws you deep within. How do you feel? … You enter into a large dome of crystal. … What does it look like? … What do you sense? … Notice how silent and still it is here. … You feel you have come into a deep place in your soul where you feel more rooted in yourself than ever before.

Gain Insight from my Spirit Prophet
You sit down together as your spirit begins to teach you about prophetic vision and how to receive it. Sitting here, you notice that the light emanating from the crystal awakens a new vision in you that combines prophetic vision and higher understanding. Let your prophet enlighten you now about the gift of prophecy and what it means for you.

The Gift of Prophecy and Its Meaning for Me _____

_____

Receive a Prophetic Vision Through My Spirit Prophet

You are guided to sit beside your spirit prophet and face a crystal wall that looks like a mirror. Feel the influence of your guide's presence on your soul senses, mind and heart … Notice your higher state … and prepare to receive a vision before you. …

Your spirit prophet waves with his hand and reveals a vision of the future as it unfolds on the mirror wall of the cave of crystal. See it in the light of the crystal that shines everywhere. You may not yet link it to any earthly condition as you notice the images and sense its vibrations. It may be a symbolic or literal message. Let it come alive as it expresses its life to you. See a dynamic living scene play out before you. …

Let your spirit prophet help you as you perceive the details of your vision. You may see sense, hear, smell or taste it; you may pick it up through sensations, thoughts or insights. Don't try to understand its meaning yet. When you are ready, describe it.

My Vision of the Future: _____

_____

_____

_____

_____

_____

_____

Your prophet helps you to understand the meaning of your vision as you sit looking at it. You are reminded that all is seen through the light of the infinite when you live on the higher planes, and your guide comes to teach you how to understand the world this way. Listen and understand the meaning of your vision.

The Meaning of My Vision: _____

_____

_____

_____

Receive a Closing Message of Guidance

With a wave of your spirit prophet's arm, once more, your vision fades away. Before you return, open to receive guidance to take back with you to help you in your soul progress as a medium. Listen.

A Closing Message of Guidance: _____

_____

_____

Return

Your visit is coming to a close. Know that you can return at any time to learn from your spirit prophet. Give thanks for what you have received. Your guide leads you back out of the crystal cave and you say your farewells. ... The star shines above and you come back slowly as it recedes into the inner sky. ... Come back to your physical presence and retain your clear visionary mind.

▸ *My Experience:*

My Preparation _____
_____
_____

My Journey to the Cave of Crystal _____
_____
_____

My Spirit Prophet _____
_____
_____

The Crystal Cave _____
_____
_____

Insight from My Spirit Prophet _____
_____
_____

My Prophetic Vision _____
_____
_____

The Meaning of My Vision _____
_____
_____

My Closing Guidance _____
_____
_____

28

Receive A Vision of Humanity from the Ancient Ones

A Guided Meditation: The Ancient Ones

I will guide you to your spirit prophet who takes you on a mountain path on the celestial planes of life to its summit where you receive a prophetic vision of humanity from the ancient ones.

Prepare questions about your mediumship and your future path to put to your spirit prophet.

Questions for My Spirit Prophet: _____

_____

_____

Have your pen ready to record your experience at the end of your meditation while it is still fresh. You may want to light a candle, and before you close your eyes, look into its flame and let it clear your mind and warm your heart.

Prayer
Let us pray to the God of our own understanding. This prayer may suit you or you may want to pray in your own way.

Divine Spirit!

Thank you for your loving support on my journey to become a medium. Please draw near and touch my soul. Help me to grow, to leave my old ways and embrace my future.

I reach up and open to your divine presence. I open my mind to your light. I open my heart to your love. I open my body to your life. Touch my soul that I may be at-one with you! I feel your spiritual manna, your purity and goodness, your gentle kindness. Keep me with you. Guide and protect me. With you I know that all is well. With you I embrace my future and the opportunity to help others embrace theirs. Thank you!

Thank you for all my blessings. I step forward on my path of mediumship and you illumine my way.

Thank you!

Amen.

Prepare

Sit quietly in your sacred place. ... Pray in your own words. ... Relax. Breathe in the air of the etheric plane that surrounds you in the unseen world. ... Breathe out any tension or concerns of the day. ... Let them go and relax. ... Continue to breathe in ... and out. ... Be at peace. Sense the air you take in as a loving light within you. ... Let it fill your lungs with new life. ... See it spreading into your heart and your lower body to the tips of your toes. ... Relax. Feel your lower body bathed in peace as the loving light flows back up into your lungs. ... As you breathe in and out, see the loving light flow into your upper body to the top of your head. ... Relax. ... Sense it moving back to your chest and be at peace. ... Notice how you feel within.

The Higher Realms

Focus up and reach into the higher realms with your desire to be with your spirit prophet and ancient ones to learn from them. ... As you do, you see a star above that shines with a divine light. ... Open to it and feel its clear crystal light pour down into your soul mind and heart. ... Let yourself be drawn up by it, free from the pull of the earth. Let go ... float up ... and up ... into the etheric sky.

Notice how you feel in your spirit self. ... Free?... Happy? ... Loving? ... Let the crystal light of the star draw you further up ... and up ... into the atmosphere of the celestial plane. ... Attune to its pure vibrations ... embrace its goodness. ...

Your Spirit Prophet

Guided by the crystal light, you arrive at the edge of a clear turquoise lake where your spirit prophet stands framed by a mountain behind him. Here everything glistens with a celestial light. You may have already met or perhaps this is a new spirit guide. ... Now greet each other. ... You feel you belong in this ethereal world with your wise and compassionate teacher. Your soul senses are clear as you perceive your spirit prophet. What is your first impression? What do you see? ... Sense? ... Hear? ...

Sitting together, listen as you learn who your prophet is, why this spirit is helping you and the importance of the prophetic vision for your mediumship. ...

A Vision of Your Future Path from Your Spirit Prophet

Ask your questions about your progression as a medium. As your spirit prophet speaks, you grasp the truth: Your soul's longings unfold as you seek your natural progression to higher ground through service to God and Spirit. You are shown how this can come about. You notice that the surface of the lake is like a mirror that reflects the clear sky so that the entire space before you from earth to sky is an infinite space. Your spirit prophet waves a hand into the vast expanse before you, and sensing this spirit's soul mind and vision enveloping yours, you perceive a prophetic vision of your future path. ... Let it unfold before you in the crystal light of the celestial plane and notice what you see ... sense ... hear. ... How do you feel? ... Be aware of how you are supported by the law of progression in your path of service. ... Discuss your vision with your spirit prophet. ...

The Mountain on the Celestial Plane
The scene before you returns to its former state. Your spirit prophet prepares to take you to the mountain top to the ancient ones. With a thought about them, you are swept up to the home of the ancient ones. You step into a place where everything is bathed in celestial light. It seems finer and purer than before. In its vibration, notice how your thoughts and feelings are pure and weightless. ... Sense the air that exudes goodness, harmony and love. ... and your own pristine goodness. How does this feel? ...

Your spirit prophet shows you around and explains that this is a summit refuge where the presence of the ancient ones illumines the world. From here, their compassion can touch the soul of humanity and their wisdom can enlighten its progression. You are told there are many such places on the higher planes where evolved spirits care for humanity in their own ways. You listen and look out into a vast expanse on all sides, and are filled with wonder. How grateful you are to be here. ...

The Ancient Ones
In this state of wonder and gratitude, you are aware of maze of rooms and spaces, and many ancient ones inhabit them. They go about their business seamlessly with their quiet gentle ways of harmony. ... As you become aware of them, notice what this is like for you. ... Let your soul self attune to the divine order here and sense how natural and effortless life can be. ...

Now, an ancient one approaches and greets you. What is your first impression of this prophetic seer? ... What do you see? ... Sense? ... Hear? ... How do you feel and what are your thoughts in the presence of this being? ...

Higher Understanding of Prophecy from the Ancient One
Listen as you learn why the ancient one is drawn to teach you. ... Your spirit begins to explain prophecy by reminding you that in your soul, you chose to come into this world at this time and in these circumstances to learn and fulfill your soul's purpose. Reach into your higher mind and attune to the soul mind and heart of the ancient one to gain insight into the path you chose in this lifetime. Understand prophecy from this perspective. ...

Now open your inner senses and receive the teachings. They may come as words, images, thoughts or sensings. ... Keep reaching for higher understanding. ...

A Prophetic Vision of Humanity from the Ancient One
Prepare to receive a prophetic vision. As you do, you receive this insight from the ancient one. Know that prophecy involves your own soul's interest according to your path. Your prophetic vision comes to your soul from the higher planes where your deepest desire for the welfare of humanity is touched. In a sense, all people know the future of humanity – how its soul is progressing – and each individual contributes to its unfoldment as they follow their own chosen path. Since your soul is of the group soul of humanity, deep within, you're intimately attuned to it and sense its pain, joy and its striving. ...

The ancient one comes to help you sense the real nature of humanity – its strength and beauty, its wisdom and selflessness. Embrace your divine humanity and the wonder of the human race. Come to prophecy with the attitude of your joyous soul. Come to it with a tender and loving heart for the life of all. Come with a deep desire to do your part as an instrument of service to the higher powers of goodness and enlightenment.

Your prophetic vision may be an angelic presence with a light, a green hillside full of rejoicing creatures of all kinds, a sense of immense peace like a huge ocean that is still, planets revolving in quiet serenity, or a streaming of souls bathed in divine love moving upwards and forward singing together softly, moving in an endless stream of glorious life. ... Whatever way your vision comes, see its light and love streaming down from the celestial plane to assuage the suffering of humanity, with awareness of the spirit within that sustains life though all eternity. ...

Now open your soul senses and attune to your ancient one. ... Sense your mind infused with this spirit's soul mind and your vision is filled with the light of divine inspiration. ... You are uplifted to your higher state of pure light and understanding. ... Feel the love pouring into your heart ... Then in a flash, you are given a prophetic vision directly from the ancient one. It's a vision of the future progression of the soul of humanity. ...

What is your prophetic vision that your ancient prophet brings to you? ... You may see, sense or hear it. ... You may understand it in thought or words. ... You may receive an insight or experience yourself in it. ... Stay attuned to the ancient one to receive your vision. ... Open to this vision and let it speak to you in silence, in words or feelings. Be with this vision. ... Stay awhile with it and let it sink into your consciousness. ...

Let the ancient one help you understand it. ...

Final Teaching from the Ancient One

When you are ready, come back gently from your absorption in your vision. ... Listen to a final teaching from the ancient one. ...

As you take your leave from the ancient one, you are aware of a new clear understanding of prophecy, and you feel a freedom and lightness in your spirit. Your heart is filled with a love that you pour out to the universe and to all its creatures. You thank the ancient one as you both depart.

Return

Prepare to leave with your spirit prophet. As you both think it, you descend to the turquoise lake with the crystal star light shining. Give thanks to your spirit prophet with whom you feel close. You leave with gratitude for all you have learned. Come back slowly ... slowly ... and as the star fades away, you return to your sacred place. As you look around, notice that you see it now through the uplifted vision of your spirit prophet and the ancient one. You pray that you may always retain this higher awareness of the truth of all life – of its eternal nature and progression.

▸ *My Experience*

The Higher Realms _____

_____

_____

_____

_____

Your Spirit Prophet _____

_____

_____

_____

A Vision of Your Future Path from Your Spirit Prophet _____

_____

The Mountain on the Celestial Plane

The Ancient Ones

Higher Understanding of Prophecy from the Ancient One

A Prophetic Vision of Humanity from the Ancient One

Final Teaching from the Ancient One

In Closing

Your Unfolding Path

We have come to the end of our journey together. Congratulations for your devotion to God and Spirit and your commitment to loving service. I have shared the guidance and teachings from Spirit with you that have shown you the way to become a medium. You are now ready to move forward—bathed in the loving light of your spirit guides and teachers—a medium in your own right.

You can continue to benefit from the teachings in this book. You will gain something new each time you revisit them. Remember that we are all students and that you will learn from the precious souls who come to you seeking the help of Spirit.

Stay humble. Trust in God and Spirit. Know that with loving service and your soul's connection to the higher planes of existence, you bring solace to others and to the world that you may never fully realize.

Trust in your daily practice. Trust in the goodness of people everywhere no matter how things may seem. Trust in the truth of eternal life. Keep seeking and know that you are never alone.

Blessings on your way!

Bibliography

Andrews, Ted. *Animal-Speak: The Spiritual and Magical Powers of Creatures Great and Small.* St. Paul, Minnesota: Llewellyn Publications, 2001.
_____. *How to Use and Develop Psychic Touch.* 1999.

Austen, A.W., ed. *The Teachings of Silver Birch.* London: Psychic Press Ltd., 1993.

Awtry, Marilyn J. *River of Life: How to Live in the Flow.* Bloomington, Indiana: Author House, 2007.

Berkowitz, Rita and Deborah S. Romaine. *The Complete Idiot's Guide to Communicating with Spirits.* New York: Alpha Books, 2003.

Blake, William and Ostriker, Alicia. *The Complete Poems.* New York: Penguin Putnam, Inc., 1978.

Blunsdon, Norman. *A Popular Dictionary of Spiritualism.* New York: Citadel Press, 1963.

Brennan, Barbara. *Hands of Light: A Guide to Healing Through the Human Energy Field.* New York: Bantam Books, 1988.

Butler, W.E. *How to Read the Aura, Practice Psychometry, Telepathy and Clairvoyance.* New York: Warner Destiny Books, Inc., 1978.

Byron Thomas, trans. *Dhammapada: The Sayings of the Buddha.* Boston: Shambhala Publishing, 1993.

Conan-Doyle, Sir Arthur. *The Wanderings of a Spiritualist.* Berkeley, California: Ronin Publishing, Inc., 1988.

Cooke, Ivan ed. *Arthur Conan Doyle's Book of the Beyond: With Two White Eagle Teachings.* Cambridge University Press, Great Britain: The White Eagle Publishing Trust, 1994.

Davis, Andrew Jackson. *Death and The After-Life: Eight Evening Lectures on the Summer-Land.* Pomeroy, W.A.: Health Research Books, 2010.
_____. *The Principles of Nature.*

Edwards, Harry. *A Guide to Spirit Healing.* London: Psychic Press Ltd., 1989.
_____. *Life in Spirit.* Surrey, England: The Healer Publishing Co. Ltd., 1985.

Eynden, Rose Vanden. *So You Want to Be a Medium? A Down-to-Earth Guide.* Woodbury, Minnesota: Llewellyn Publications, 2013.

Fodor, Nandor. *An Encyclopedia of Psychic Science.* Secaucus, New Jersey: The Citadel Press, 1966.

Fontana, David. *The Secret Language of Symbols: A Visual Key to Symbols and Their Meanings.* San Francisco: Chronicle Books, 1994.

Forman, Henry James. *The Story of Prophecy: In the Life of Mankind from Early Times to the Present Day.* New York: Tudor Publishing Co., 1940.

Greaves, Helen. *Testimony of Light.* Essex, England: Neville Spearman Publisher, 1993.

Health Research Books, 2014.

Hornberger, Francine. *The World's Greatest Psychics.* New York: Citadel Press, 2004.

Juan Mascaro, trans. *The Upanishads.* New York: Penguin Putnam, Inc., 1965.

Leadbeater, C.W. *Chakras.* Wheaton, Illinois: The Theosophical Publishing House,1987.
_____. *Man Visible and Invisible.* 2000.

Montgomery, Ruth. *A World Beyond.* Coward, New York: McCann & Geoghegan, Inc., 1971.

Moses, Rev W. Stainton. *Spirit Teachings.* London: Psychic Press Ltd., 1992.

Nerbum, Kent ed. *Native American Wisdom.* Novato, California: New World Library, 1991.

Nohavec, Janet. *Where Two Worlds Meet: How to Develop Evidential Mediumship.* San Diego: Aventine Press, 2010.

N.S.A.C. Spiritualist Manual. Lily Dale, N.Y.: National Spiritualist Association of Churches, 2004.

Ouseley, S.G.J. *Colour Meditations: With Guide to Colour-Healing.* Pomeroy, WA : Health Research Books, 2011.

Richmond, Cora L.V. "Definition". *N.S.A.C. Spiritualist Manual,* Lily Dale, N.Y: National Spiritualist Association of Churches, 2004.
_____. *Presentation of Spiritualism,* A Paper for the World's Parliament of Religions. Washington, D.C.: National Spiritualists Association, 1893.

Storm, Stella ed. *The Philosophy of Silver Birch.* London: Psychic Press Ltd., 1989.

Tuttle, Hudson. *Mediumship and Its Laws: Its Conditions and Cultivation.* Elm Grove, Wisconsin: The Sycamore Press, 1974.

Wallis, E.W. and M.H. Wallis. *A Guide to Mediumship and Psychical Unfoldment.* Pomeroy, W.A.:

White, Stewart Edward. *The Betty Book: Excursions into the World of Other-Consciousness.* New York: E.P. Dutton & Co. Inc., 1949.

Wickland, Carl A., M.D. *Thirty Years Among the Dead.* Pomeroy, Wisconsin: Health Research Books, 2014.

All the books listed in the bibliography are available. Many can be ordered from the National Spiritualist Association of Churches, PO Box 217, 13 Cottage Row, Lily Dale, New York 14752, email: nsacbookstore@nsac.org.

CPSIA information can be obtained
at www.ICGtesting.com
Printed in the USA
BVOW07s0458020816
457477BV00003B/1/P